STEPPING LIGHTLY
ON AUSTRALIA

A TRAVELLER'S GUIDE
TO ECOTOURISM

TEXT AND PHOTOGRAPHY BY
SHIRLEY LAPLANCHE

The
Globe
Pequot
Press
Old Saybrook, Connecticut

To all those who helped in the preparation of this book: our domestic airlines, state and territory tourism offices, national parks' staff, ecotour operators and the numerous lovers of nature who responded so willingly to my requests for help — a big thank you. And a special thank you to my husband for his patience and support.

The publisher and author would also like to acknowledge Rankin Publishers for permission to reproduce the quote from *Classic Wild Walks of Australia* by Robert Rankin, which appears on page 96.

PRINTED ON RECYCLED PAPER

Published by:

Angus&Robertson
An imprint of HarperCollins*Publishers,* Australia
(ACN 009 913 517)
25 Ryde Road, Pymble, Sydney, NSW 2073,
Australia

The Globe Pequot Press, Inc.
6 Business Park Road
P O Box 833
Old Saybrook, Connecticut
06475-0833

by arrangement with HarperCollins*Publishers* Pty Limited, Australia

Library of Congress Cataloging-in-Publication Data

LaPlanche, Shirley.
Stepping lightly on Australia: a traveller's guide to ecotourism/ text and photography by Shirley LaPlanche.
p. cm.
Includes index.
ISBN 1-56440-904-X
1. Natural areas—Australia—Guidebooks. 2. National parks and reserves—Australia—Guidebooks. 3. Ecotourism—Australia.
4. Australia—Guidebooks. I. Title.
QH77.A8L375 1996
919.40463—dc20 95-43033
CIP

Map on page 8 and 9 by Merv Godfrey
All other maps by Dianne Bradley

Printed in Hong Kong

First edition/First printing

CONTENTS

INTRODUCTION

Every Sunday my parents would take my brothers and I to the river. My father would pack the car with blankets and bandages, towels and toilet paper, matches and the weekend newspaper. My mother would make a pile of sandwiches and big bottles of orange cordial.

The place we went to was our secret place. A quiet bend in the river that no-one else knew about. I would swim in the cool, crisp pools letting the sparkling rapids tumble me over the rocks like a fallen leaf. Then I would lie on the smooth river rocks, warmed by the sun, and listen to the sounds around me — the breeze rustling the leaves, the river tinkling its way to the ocean, the songs of the birds, the bleat of a lamb in the distance, the hum of bees on the wild broom and the soft snore of my father under the newspaper.

If I opened my eyes, I would see the clay-coloured banks eroded by floods, the dark, silent holes where furry rabbits lived, and the moulded, green hills nibbled to a mossy carpet by the sheep.

As our parents dozed in the shade, my brothers and I would build little ponds to fill with cockabullies, small fish which lived in the river, and we would pick sweet wild blackberries which would stain our fingers red. Sometimes I would pull slivers of grass out from their cocoon-like base and nibble the tender white end, or suck the sweet nectar from flowers whose names I never learnt.

At the end of the day we would pile back into the car, towels soggy, skins glowing, souls at rest, and we'd sing or sleep all the way home.

Nature is the tonic of the soul. Wherever I have lived in the world, no matter how many people or problems have surrounded me, I have been able to close my eyes and return to the tranquillity of that river in New Zealand.

This book is written for those who want to touch nature but do not know where to start. It gives

ideas and directions. Each chapter is a signpost presenting an idea, expanding on the idea then telling you how to go about it. If that idea does not suit then move on to the next chapter, it may offer more what you are looking for.

You do not have to be an expert on wildflowers or birds or coral reefs to enjoy their beauty. Nor do you need to be a poet to feel your soul sing when you stand atop a mountain or a precipitous escarpment. Everyone has their own idea of what their 'secret place' should be like and this book presents hundreds of places in the hope that one or more will meet that ideal. It has been written for the person who wants to experience nature. It is not for those who like to travel in a large coach and photograph 12 famous places in one day.

To enjoy nature you need time.

Time to sit and look, time to smell the air before rain, time to hear the different birdsongs, time to touch the softness of a petal and to let the earth run through your fingers. Experiencing nature is a personal matter. You cannot touch nature when you are with a huge group which spills out of a tourist coach like puppies from a basket, cameras flashing and feet trammelling. You need to be alone or with a small group of likeminded people.

The places mentioned in this book are not limited to one price range because people from all walks of life seek enjoyment from nature, and each chapter focuses on different interests. The chapters National Parks, World Heritage Areas and Bushwalking are for people and families who want to camp and explore deep into the bush.

In the chapters Birdwatching,

A tranquil moment on the Mossman River, Far North Queensland

and Coast Watching I explain where to find wildlife in the wild; while the chapter entitled Wildlife Parks and Sanctuaries tells where you can see native wildlife in enclosures as near to their natural environment as possible. Wildflowers have rated a special chapter because Australia is so rich botanically: Wordsworth's daffodils have stiff competition from the sandplains of Western Australia in spring. The chapters Cycling and Diving suggest exciting ways to enjoy nature without harming it and will help the experienced as well as the novice.

Accommodation lists some splendid lodges and cabins, built with consideration for the survival of the natural beauty around them. And Tour Operators is for people who like to travel in a small group, or want to explore a remote area with the security of an experienced and knowledgeable guide. I have slipped Photography in here because it is my hobby and the means by which I can relive the beauty of my Australian travels.

What I emphasise in this book is that nature is explained so you, the visitor, leave with a greater understanding of the ecosystems you have passed through and of the need to preserve the delicate balance of nature. Nowadays this is called ecotourism, which the Ecotourism Association of Australia describes as: 'Ecologically sustainable tourism that fosters environmental and cultural understanding, appreciation and conservation'.

Australia is a large island continent with a small population and vast areas of open space where you can travel for days without seeing another person. It is the world's last great frontier where you can quickly leave cities and towns behind to walk awhile through rainforests, wooded hills, coastal heathlands, desert plains and sandy beaches.

But before you jump into your car and head off towards a distant horizon, be aware that the isolation you seek can be dangerous. The vast plains that have made the Outback such a favourite with painters and photographers are hot and mostly waterless. Before you start your big trek ensure you have a reliable four-wheel-drive vehicle, good maps, plenty of water, a medical kit and a two-way radio. I find the silence and distant horizons of the Outback restore my spirits and I am fascinated by the way kangaroos rise to their full height to watch me pass, nervous but not necessarily frightened, and the way predatory kites float on air currents like black crosses against a blue backdrop.

But not everyone loves the Outback. There are people who are terrified by so much open space with such meagre vegetation and intense heat. For these people there are forests of trees and lush valleys all along the Great Dividing Range, magnificent karri and jarrah forests in Western Australia, old forests in Tasmania and ancient tropical rainforests in northern Queensland. Most of Australia's wooded areas have parks and reserves which provide good picnic areas and walking trails.

And Australia's beaches are legendary. The oceans that lap its shores are cool in the south and warm in the north, and provide an astonishing variety of seascapes — sandy beaches with waves rolling sweetly onto the shore, pretty coves, bluffs with fearful drops, and rocky cliffs where the raging waters crash and tear in unexplained fury.

There are beaches for everyone. You can swim, dive, surf, fossick or merely sit watching the waves tumble in and smelling the fresh ocean air. The Great Barrier Reef on the east coast and Ningaloo Reef on the west coast are among the most pristine in the world, and you will find dolphins all around the coast, sea lions at Kangaroo Island and little penguins along most southern shores.

Nature provides us with many opportunities to find beauty and discover peace. But the spaciousness of the Outback is very different to the enveloping richness of a rainforest, so take a moment to sit quietly and think about the type of countryside that suits you best. For me it is a riverbank with dappled shade, tinkling water and sun-warmed rocks. I hope this book will lead you to a few places where you too can touch nature and enjoy its timeless beauty.

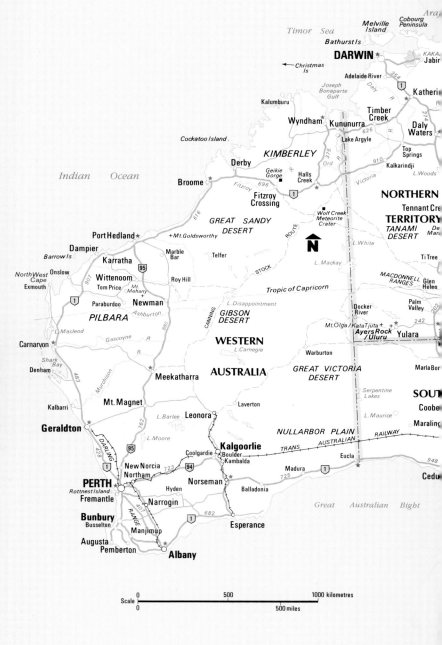

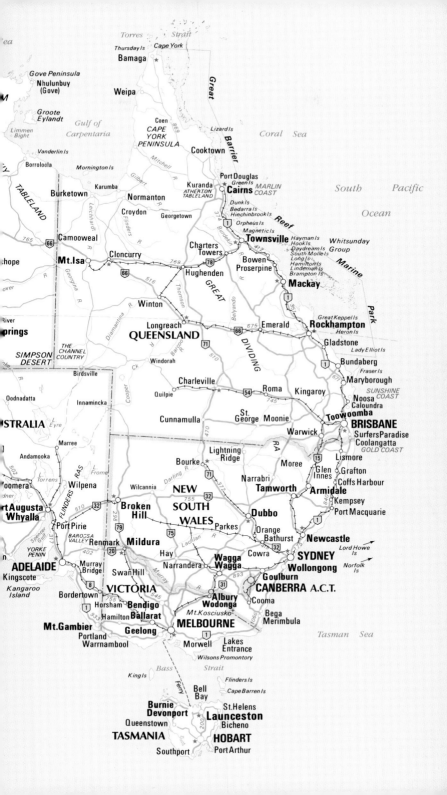

USEFUL INFORMATION

Australia is an island continent of 7 682 300 km² (2 966 152 m), which is about 25 times the size of Britain and Ireland and about the same size as mainland United States, excluding Alaska. It is almost square, being 4025 km (2501 m) east–west and 3220 km (2000 m) north–south. Its coastline sweeps for 36 735 km (22 826 m) (47 000 km (29 204 m) including its islands) of lovely bays, long sandy beaches, rocky outcrops and tortured cliffs. The Great Barrier Reef extends for 2300 km (1429 m) down the northern half of the east coast, making it the largest system of corals and associated plants and animals in the world. Less well known, but also important for its coral and marine life, is Ningaloo Reef on the west coast.

The population of less than 18 million people is one of the most urbanised in the world. Seventy per cent of the population lives in large urban areas concentrated on the east, southeast and southwest coasts. The reason for this irregular distribution is that a large proportion of the centre of Australia is arid and semi-arid desert, with little rainfall and a climate too harsh for crops and most livestock.

The Aboriginal people have lived in Australia for an estimated 50 000 years. They were hunter–gathers who

JOURNEY DISTANCES

The figure in the box where the horizontal and vertical columns meet is the road distance in kilometres between two towns.

*Road distances to Hobart exclude the Melbourne-Davenport ferry journey.

Adelaide	Albany	Alice Springs	Ayers Rock	Brisbane	Broken Hill	Cairns	Canberra	Darwin	Hobart*	Kununurra	Mackay	Melbourne	Mount Isa	Perth	Port Headland	Surfers Paradise	Sydney
2673																	
1533	3588																
1578	3633	443															
2045	4349	3038	3254														
506	2810	1670	1715	1539													
3352	5656	2457	2900	1716	2846												
1196	3846	2706	2751	1261	1101	2568											
3022	4614	1489	1932	3463	3159	2882	4195										
1001	3674	2534	2579	1944	1123	3251	918	4023									
3219	3787	1686	2129	3660	3356	3079	4392	827	4220								
2783	5087	2505	2948	976	2277	740	1999	2930	2682	3127							
731	3404	2264	2309	1674	853	2981	648	3753	270	3950	2412						
2742	5106	1209	1652	1829	2406	1248	2561	1634	3075	1831	1296	2805					
2781	409	3696	3741	4457	2918	5764	3954	4205	3782	3378	5195	3512	4905				
3783	2057	3416	3859	5390	3920	4809	4956	2557	4784	1730	4857	4514	3561	1648			
2125	4429	3118	3334	80	1619	1796	1341	3543	2024	3740	1056	1754	1909	4537	5470		
1412	3970	2830	2875	1001	1160	2495	286	4034	1142	4516	1926	872	2400	4078	5080	921	

JOURNEY TIMES (Hours.Minutes)							
ROUTE	AIR	COACH	RAIL	ROUTE	AIR	COACH	RAIL
Sydney-Adelaide	1.40	24	26	Adelaide-Brisbane	2.15	33.30	36.45
Sydney-Canberra	0.35	4.15	5.25	Darwin-Alice Springs	1.50	19	-
Sydney-Melbourne (inland)	1.10	14.30	13	Darwin-Kakadu	-	4.30	-
Canberra-Melbourne	0.55	9.30	9.15	Alice Springs-Ayers Rock	0.45	6	-
Melbourne-Adelaide	1.05	9.30	10.15	Cairns-Brisbane	2.05	25	33.25
Melbourne-Broken Hill	1.50	19	24.45	Brisbane-Sydney (inland)	1.15	17	16
Adelaide-Alice Springs	2.00	20	21.10	Brisbane-Sydney (coastal)	-	17	-
Adelaide-Perth	3.05	35	38	Brisbane-Melbourne	1.55	25	26.55*

Melbourne-Hobart 1.05 (Air)	Melbourne-Devonport 14.5 (Sea)	Melbourne-GeorgeTown 7.5 (Coach)

* Overnight stay in Sydney

lived in harmony with the land, the seasons and the animals. Europeans arrived a little more than 200 years ago and the first British colony was established in 1788 on the shores of Sydney's harbour. On 1 January, 1901, with a population of nearly four million people, Australia became a federal Commonwealth.

The Commonwealth of Australia consists of the six states of New South Wales, Victoria, Queensland, Western Australia, South Australia and Tasmania, as well as the two mainland territories — the Northern Territory and the Australian Capital Territory — and several external territories. The main language is English, but Australia is a multicultural society and you will hear many languages spoken here. Travellers should have no difficulty in finding staff who speak foreign languages at major hotels and large department stores.

Australia is the world's driest inhabited continent with a rainfall that varies extremely in both the geographic and seasonal senses. The centre receives less than 150 mm (6 in), but western Tasmania and parts of the tropics receive more than 2 m (6½ ft). The climate is pleasant most of the year. More than one-third of the country is north of the Tropic of Capricorn and is tropical with typically hot, wet summers. South of this it is temperate, with snow only in the high regions of the southeast and Tasmania. The seasons are: summer: December–February, autumn: March–May, winter: June–August and spring: September–November.

The currency is decimal with the dollar as the basic unit (100 cents equal one dollar. The electric current is 240/250 volts, AC 50hz, and a 3-pin power outlet is used. The metric system of weights and measures is used.

Driving in Australia is relatively easy and is on the left-hand side of the road. Good highways link all main cities and towns and the country roads are generally well maintained. In the Outback most major roads are sealed, but all others are unsealed and poorly served with

Early morning, Mary River, Northern Territory

fuel and water stops. If venturing into the Outback, you should check where the fuel and water stops are before you set off; you may need to carry your own supplies.

Public transport is excellent with an extensive network by road, rail and air. Comfortable air-conditioned coaches link all cities and main towns. The railways cover vast distances with modern, air-conditioned trains with sleepers and dining cars on most of the long routes between major cities. The Ghan, which travels from Adelaide to Alice Springs in the central desert, is a popular tourist train with superb amenities.

Air services have an outstanding safety record, are regular between all main centres, and have spread their tentacles into some of the most remote areas of the country. The main international gateways are Sydney, Melbourne, Brisbane, Perth, Adelaide, Cairns and Darwin and connecting flights to other destinations can be taken from these ports.

WORLD HERITAGE AREAS

A World Heritage listing is a life raft for areas of natural and cultural heritage that may be at risk. Increasingly, conservation-minded Australians are becoming more aware of the benefits of a World Heritage listing and are reaching for it with enthusiasm.

Once an area has been listed as a World Heritage Area, that country commits to protect and conserve it for future generations, however this does not mean locking it away. It should still be a part of the life of the community. Thus you find the Great Barrier Reef supports a commercial fishing industry, scientific research and tourism, while at Willandra Lakes in southwest New South Wales pastoral activities continue as they have for several generations. However, more attention is paid to these activities, and any that could damage the natural or cultural heritage of the listed area are ceased, or limited to prevent further damage.

Rock art, Kakadu National Park, Northern Territory

A World Heritage listing also has other benefits. It makes an area much more attractive to tourists, and increased tourism stimulates employment and brings more income into the local community. As well, listed areas receive additional government resources for planning and visitor facilities. World Heritage listing also promotes local and national pride, developing a feeling of responsibility to preserve the area for future generations. Australia was one of the first countries in the world to ratify the World Heritage Convention, nominating three sites within five years of it coming into force in 1975. Eleven sites are now listed.

To be accepted by the World Heritage Committee, nominated areas must meet specific criteria of outstanding universal value from either a 'cultural' or 'natural' point of view. Among the nearly 400 areas listed worldwide are: the pyramids of Egypt; the Grand Canyon in the United States of America; the Taj Mahal, India; Westminster Abbey, England; the Great Wall of China and Sagarmartha National Park (containing Mount Everest) in Nepal. Few properties in the world qualify under both cultural and natural criteria, although Australia has four: Kakadu National Park, Willandra Lakes, the Tasmanian Wilderness, and Uluru–Kata Tjuta National Park. It also has four properties that qualify under all four criteria for natural heritage: the Great Barrier Reef, the Tasmanian Wilderness, the Wet Tropics of Queensland and Shark Bay in Western Australia.

The following is a list of Australia's eleven listed areas, with relevant information on access and facilities for visitors.

Kakadu National Park

NORTHERN TERRITORY

This 20 000 km^2 (7722 m^2) park in the tropical north extends from the 500 km (311 m) long sandstone escarpment of Arnhem Land in the east, to the mangrove-rich tidal flats of Van Diemen Gulf in the north and nearly as far south as the Katherine Gorge. It encompasses almost the entire drainage basin of the South Alligator River system.

This rich and varied environment supports an estimated 900 Australian plant species, almost one-third of all bird species, a quarter of freshwater fish species, countless insects, many reptiles, mammals and amphibians. In the wet season the rivers and creeks flood and spread out over the broad floodplains, forming immense wetlands that attract thousands of ducks, geese and wading birds. The myriad birds that gather here, and the dense beds of lilies reflected in still waters are spectacularly beautiful. The best time to see large concentrations of birds is during the dry season (May–September) when the wetlands are reduced to a few creeks and waterholes. Brolgas, jabirus and magpie geese, once widespread in Australia, have a refuge here. The dry season population of magpie geese is estimated at an amazing 1.5 million. Crocodiles also live in the waterways and are fascinating to see, although you must keep clear of the saltwater variety which is fast and dangerous.

Wetland areas can be seen from the road or you can take a boat cruise on Yellow Water. Most wetland areas have picnic spots and marked walking tracks which are flat and easy to follow.

The spectacular Jim Jim Falls plunges down the Arnhem Land escarpment into a deep pool where you can swim in the dry season. Another lovely swimming pool is Maguk, known as the Barramundie Gorge.

Kakadu is listed for cultural as well as natural reasons because of its wealth of Aboriginal archaeological and art sites. The Aborigines have lived here for at least 25 000 years and possibly for 50 000 years. Some art sites date back to the Ice Age and archaeologists have found the world's oldest evidence of the technology of edge-ground stone axes here. Art styles highlight the progress of time, starting with early naturalistic paintings of animals, then contact with the Macassan people during the 17th century and the Europeans in the 19th century. Well-maintained walking trails lead to the major art sites at the base of Nourlangie Rock and Ubirr.

You should choose your time to visit the park with care. The 'green' period from November to March is rich and bountiful but the humidity is high and many tracks are flooded and impassable. The main visitor season is from May to September when the weather is warm and dry.

This huge park starts 120 km (74½ m) east of Darwin, and is about 120 km (74½ m) from east to west and 210 km (130 m) north to south. The main entrance is along the Arnhem Highway from Darwin or you can take the Kakadu Highway from Pine Creek, but this may be closed in the wet season.

All the major attractions are quite a distance apart and, although there are one-day tours from Darwin, you cannot possibly enjoy Kakadu in such a short time. As all of the main roads are sealed you can use a standard car to reach most attractions, but you will need a four-wheel drive to negotiate the side roads. If you do not have a car, ask at any tour desk in Darwin and you will be presented with a pile of tour options.

The only town is Jabiru and the visitors' centre nearby has displays, audiovisuals, maps and other useful information. You can pay your park entry fee at the entrance stations, the visitors' centre, or at your place of accommodation if you arrive after hours.

Accommodation in the park includes the Gagudju Crocodile Hotel, several holiday complexes with motel, lodge and camping facilities, designated camping areas and a youth hostel (dry season only). You may camp elsewhere but you will need a permit from the visitors' centre (allow two days for processing).

Willandra Lakes Region

NEW SOUTH WALES

When the Willandra Lakes in the semi-arid country of southwest New South Wales dried up 15 000 years ago, the Aboriginal people lost a favourite fishing spot. However, they stayed on, drawing water from soaks along the old river channel and quarrying stone from rock outcrops on the lake floor. Their amazing resilience to changing climates is recorded in a trail of skeletal remains, stone tools, ancient hearths and middens. This is one of the earliest known sites of humankind in the world, dating back an estimated 40 000 years.

The World Heritage listed area covers 3700 km² (1428 m²) of ancient environments and landscapes. Most of this contains pastoral stations but 10% has been set aside as the Mungo National Park, which is open to visitors. Of particular interest to archaeologists are the cremation sites found at Mungo. A cremated female uncovered in 1968 is estimated to

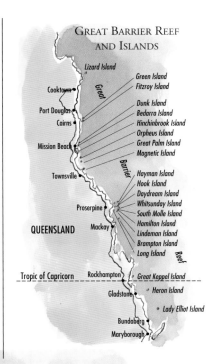

GREAT BARRIER REEF AND ISLANDS

Lizard Island

Green Island
Fitzroy Island

Cooktown

Dunk Island
Port Douglas
Bedarra Island
Cairns
Hinchinbrook Island
Orpheus Island
Mission Beach
Great Palm Island
Magnetic Island

Townsville

Hayman Island
Hook Island
Daydream Island
Proserpine
Whitsunday Island
South Molle Island
QUEENSLAND
Mackay
Hamilton Island
Lindeman Island
Brampton Island
Long Island

Tropic of Capricorn
Rockhampton
Great Keppel Island

Gladstone
Heron Island

Lady Elliot Island

Bundaberg
Maryborough

Great Barrier Reef

AUSTRALIA'S WORLD HERITAGE AREAS

Kakadu National Park

Riversleigh Fossil Site •
Wet Tropics of Queensland

Great Barrier Reef

NORTHERN TERRITORY

QUEENSLAND

WESTERN AUSTRALIA
Uluru – Kata Tjuta National Park

Fraser Island

Shark Bay

SOUTH AUSTRALIA
East Coast Temperate and Subtropical Rainforest Parks

NEW SOUTH WALES

Lord Howe Island •

Willandra Lakes Region

Victoria Fossil Cave •
VICTORIA

TASMANIA
Tasmanian Wilderness

be 26 000 years old — the pyramids of Egypt are only about 5000 years old — and the ochred burial of a male Aborigine was dated at 30 000 years of age, about the same time when ochre burials were common in Europe.

To take a Foreshore Walk around a lake that has been dry for 15 000 years allows you time to dream a little and imagine what it must have been like when the Aboriginal people's campfires glowed in the dark, and the now extinct super roos and large emus came in to drink.

Although the vegetation is sparse, the park supports a good variety of wildlife with big red kangaroos, western grey kangaroos, echidnas, native mice, bats, 40 species of reptile and numerous inland birds including parrots, cockatoos, finches, emus and pretty galahs which arrive after rain. The feral rabbit is also evident here and is of particular concern.

Mungo National Park is 110 km (68 m) northeast of Mildura and 150 km (93 m) from Balranald. The drive from Sydney takes about 13 hours or you can fly to Mildura and hire a car there. You need a car to drive through the park and you really need to stay a few days to soak up the atmosphere.

The visitors' centre can provide you with information on walks and drives in the Park. Walking trails have signs explaining the natural and cultural features of the area and the Drive Tour Loop circles through mallee country and the Walls of

China, a dramatic lunette, or crescent-shaped dune. This is the most spectacular of the lunettes, especially when seen at dawn or dusk when shadows darken the sandy gullies.

Accommodation is available at two camping areas, in shearers' quarters and at Mungo Lodge, which has motel rooms, cottages, a licensed restaurant and an airstrip for small aircraft.

The Tasmanian Wilderness

The southwest of Tasmania is one of the last truly wild places left in the world. Its mighty rivers, rugged peaks, buttongrass plains, temperate rainforests, tall eucalypts and stands of ancient huon pine cover an area of 13 836 square kilometres (5342 square miles).

This wonderful wilderness, protected by its difficult terrain, a harsh climate and now a World Heritage listing, is unpeopled and unpolluted. It is the domain of bushwalkers who follow its many marked trails or make their own route, camping and enjoying the views and the solitude. Among the best known walks are: the Overland Track (80 km (50 m)) with spectacular alpine scenery; the South Coast Track (85 km (53 m)) for coastal scenery; Frenchmans Cap (4–5 days return) an arduous walk with steep climbs and large sections of mud; and the one- to two-day Walls of Jerusalem walk which is renowned for its lovely lakes and ancient pencil pines.

Its flora includes the tallest flowering plant species in the world, *Eucalyptus regnans*, and the world's smallest eucalypt, *Eucalyptus vemicosa*. A feature of the region is its alpine heathland with dwarf shrubs, crystal-clear pools and clear, green cushion plants, which create their own dams to ensure a captive water supply. Magnificent alpine moors with 1000-year-old pencil pines, can be reached easily on a day trip by car up the Western Tiers from Deloraine.

The wildlife includes the Tasmanian devil, spotted-tailed quoll, eastern quoll, wallabies, possums, pademelons, glow-worms in limestone chambers and hundreds of species of birds, including the endangered orange-bellied parrot.

Archaeological sites of outstanding value show evidence of human occupation during the last Ice Age and earlier, with stone tools from Beginners Luck Cave in the Florentine Valley having been dated to 20 000 years ago.

The glaciers of the Ice Age left jagged ridges and carved spectacular gorges down which many rivers flow. Nowadays cruise boats offer a gentle ride up the Gordon River, famous for its dark, tannic water which produces superb reflections. The Franklin River provides the more adventurous with sensational whitewater rafting along rapids with names such as the Trojans, the Pig Trough and Rock Island Bend.

There are only a few areas where you can drive into the World Heritage listed area and, with the exception of the highway through the northern section, these do not penetrate very far. Generally you drive to a border area and walk or take a boat cruise from there. Charter flights offer an excellent introduction to the wilderness character of the area, and some land for lunch in remote and beautiful spots.

Tasmanian devil

Winter at Dove Lake, Cradle Mountain, Tasmania

Although there are a few mountain huts for walkers within the World Heritage Area, these are often full, so accommodation is usually a tent carried on your back. Accommodation outside the Park is available at Strahan on the western border, at Cradle Mountain Lodge (cabins, bunkhouses and camping) on the northern border, and on the eastern border there are rooms and cabins at Derwent Bridge and a motel in the township of Strathgordon.

The Great Barrier Reef

QUEENSLAND

The Great Barrier Reef extends from the tip of Cape York Peninsula down the Queensland coast for 2300 km (1429 m) to almost reach Fraser Island. It covers an area of about 348 700 km^2 (134 634 m^2) (nearly the size of Japan) and is undoubtedly the largest system of corals and associated life forms in the world. It consists of 619 continental islands which were once part of the mainland, and 300 coral cays most of which are unvegetated. Anyone who has ever donned a snorkel and sunk slowly into the warm, tropical waters knows what a wonderland lies below. More than 300 species of hard, reef-building corals have created amazingly colourful castles and valleys which support myriad fish as well as anemones, crustaceans, marine worms and echinoderms.

As well as the vast number of colourful tropical fish which live on the Reef, it is also a major feeding ground for large populations of dugong (a large, docile, herbivorous marine animal), a nursery for the humpback whale, which comes here in winter to give birth, and is the nesting ground for the endangered green and loggerhead turtles. And naturally, with all this food about, the skies are teeming with sea birds.

Visiting the Reef is one of the biggest tourist attractions in the country, so you will have no difficulty finding a boat charter to suit your needs. You can choose from a large catamaran to a small cruiser and dive, snorkel or just sit in a glass-bottomed boat and view the Reef from there. The best known 'jump-off' points are Cairns and Port Douglas in Far North Queensland, but cruise boats leave from most towns along the Queensland coast as well as from island resorts. The best charters are those that have marine biologists on board to explain the Reef and its many intricacies. Understanding what you are seeing makes it so much more interesting and will help you understand how important it is to protect the Reef from possible harm. People unwittingly damage the Reef by touching and standing on living coral. If diving, be careful not to knock the coral with your tank or flippers and do not stand on it when you feel tired — get out and rest in the boat. And if you go for a reef walk, stay on the dead coral or on the sandy patches.

The Reef is managed by the Great Barrier Reef Marine Park Authority (GBRMPA) whose role it is to monitor and protect the environment, while at the same time allow people to enjoy its unique commercial and recreational qualities. Like a guiding parent, it restricts activities in any area that

starts to show signs of stress and it keeps a register of all commercial boat operators.

There are many towns along the coast where you can stay and about 20 of the islands have resorts. Some of the island resorts are large and crowded (especially the Whitsunday group), some allow day-trippers which makes them busy during the daytime, some are exclusive and expensive, and some fit between all these categories. Islands offering good accommodation, educational experiences and excellent coral and fish viewing are Lady Elliot (reached from Bundaberg) and Heron (reached from Gladstone).

The Wet Tropics of Queensland

The Wet Tropics of Queensland cover an area of about 8900 km^2 (3436 m^2), extending in patches from Townsville in the south to Cooktown in the north. The listed area has many rare and threatened plants and is home to the highest concentration of primitive flowering plants in the world. It also has the largest number of ferns in Australia and vast mangrove forests which cover an estimated 400 km^2 (154 m^2). Within all this richness lives the greatest diversity of wildlife in the country.

It is an area of breathtaking beauty. Tropical plants tumble over each other and crowd along the banks of fast-flowing rivers, deep gorges and waterfalls. Flitting about through all this greenery are butterflies so big and dazzling they compete with the beautiful tropical birds for attention. Frogs, bats, snakes and many other creatures live here and on warm evenings you may see the glow of fungi, and fireflies flashing their mating signals. Culturally, the area contains the only recognised records of the existence of Australian Aboriginal rainforest inhabitants. The oral pre-history of this surviving Aboriginal rainforest culture is the oldest known for any non-literate indigenous people.

One of the largest rainforest wilderness areas in the country surrounds the Daintree River and numerous tours by four-wheel drive, foot and boat are available. The wildlife that lives in the tropical rainforests of the low coastal areas includes cassowaries, buff-breasted paradise kingfishers, giant white-lipped tree frogs, striped possums and green tree ants, which build their distinctive nests of leaves. The rivers are home to jungle perch, freshwater prawns and the saltwater crocodile.

At Cape Tribulation the rainforest spills down to meet the sea and the coral wonderland of the Great Barrier Reef — long sweeps of sand, fringed by the many greens of the ancient rainforest on one side and lapped by the azure water of the Coral Sea on the other. There are very few places in the world where this happens and the effect is pure enchantment. A sealed road goes all the way from the Daintree River crossing to Cape Tribulation and limited accommodation is available in resorts, backpacker lodges and camping areas.

South of Cairns lies Mount Bartle Frere, the highest mountain in northern Australia. The area around Mount Bartle Frere comprises ancient rainforests, spectacular crater lakes, moist paths, waterfalls and crystal-clear rivers which often have dangerous undercurrents. The walking and climate on the mountain are difficult and only recommended for experienced bushwalkers, although the lower areas are quite safe.

The Tully River in the Tully Gorge National Park is good for swimming and canoeing and is a major whitewater rafting area. The lower rainforest areas have less extremes of climate and are easily reached from towns all along the coast.

The best time to visit is during winter as the summers are usually wet and uncomfortably hot, although the lower rainforest areas have less extremes of climate. The rainforest can be accessed from the Bruce Highway which runs down the coast, or the inland roads passing through the Atherton Tableland. There is a wide range of accommodation in the local towns, and camping areas in many of the national parks and state forests.

Shark Bay

Western Australia

Located at the most westerly point of the Australian continent, Shark Bay is home to a population of 10 000 dugong which feed on the largest seagrass banks in the world, and bottlenose dolphins that voluntarily

Early morning calm, Daintree River tributary, Far North Queensland

come into the shallow waters at Monkey Mia to swim among humans. It is an area of infinite peace and beauty, comprising peninsulas, islands, ocean cliffs, quiet bays, inlets and sweeping beaches of sand or shells. People come here to walk a little, swim a little, meet the dolphins, fish, go boating, and to see the stromatolites (sedimentary rock consisting of layers of fossilised algae representative of life forms present some 3500 million years ago) at Hamelin Pool.

The listed area covers 22 000 km^2 (8494 m^2), of which about 66% is marine. The seagrass beds cover an amazing 400 km^2 (154 m^2) of the bay and are the reason so many dugongs live here. Other marine creatures include manta rays, several species of sharks, green and loggerhead turtles and humpback whales which stop to rest on their migration along the coast.

The Bay is the meeting point of three major climatic regions, with many species of flora and fauna reaching the limits of their range here. For example, it is the northern limit for birds such as the regent parrot, the western yellow robin and the blue-breasted fairy wren, and the southern limit for mangrove herons, brahminy kites and dusty fly-eaters. The isolation of the region's peninsulas and islands has allowed them to become a haven for wildlife and five of Australia's endangered mammals live here: the burrowing bettong, the rufous hare wallaby, the banded hare wallaby, the Shark Bay mouse and the western barred bandicoot. There is also a great diversity of amphibians and reptiles with nearly 100 species adapted to the semi-arid conditions. The endemic sandhill frog is believed to live without needing surface water.

Shark Bay is 700 km (435 m) north of Perth and can be reached by air from Denham.

Accommodation is available at Denham, the Monkey Mia Dolphin Resort and the Nanga sheep station.

Uluru–Kata Tjuta National Park

Northern Territory

Uluru (Ayers Rock) is one of the most recognised of Australia's landmarks. Rising some 340 m (1115 ft) from the flat, red expanse of the centre of Australia, its strangely moulded shape has been the focus of cultural and traditional significance for Aboriginal people for thousands of years.

Uluru was listed for its natural features in 1987 and for its cultural landscape values in 1994.

Kata Tjuta (the Olgas), about 42 km (26 m) west of Uluru, has not one, but 36 bare domes, the tallest rising to a height of 500 m (1640 ft). There are some interesting walks through these domes, the most popular being the Valley of the Winds (a return trip takes about three hours). There is something mystical about the Olgas and many people come away with a lasting impression of its strangeness.

Both Uluru and Kata Tjuta are contained within the 132 566 ha (327 578 a) World Heritage area, which is owned by the Aboriginal people and managed jointly by the Federal Government and the Anangu people. This is the arid heartland of Australia, with sparse, low vegetation and occasional eucalypts where there is an adequate supply of water to sustain them. However, it is not as barren as it may seem. Quite a population of animals and birds live here, including 22 species of native

Rainforest meets the sea at Cape Tribulation, Far North Queensland

mammals, more than 150 species of birds, reptiles, frogs, an astonishing number of lizards including Australia's largest, the perentie, and several venomous snakes.

The roads to both attractions are sealed and suitable for standard cars.

Most visitors make the steep walk to the top of the Rock but it is an arduous climb and should only be attempted in the relative cool of the very early morning. Although this walk is allowed and is very popular, most Aboriginal people would like to see it stopped in respect of its traditional religious and cultural significance. An excellent guided walk is available around the 9 km (5½ m) base of the Rock where caves containing Aboriginal paintings record the history of the area. An easier tour of the base can be made by coach or on the back of a Harley Davidson motorbike, however, these follow the circular road and you do not see the caves very well.

Nights are a special time in the desert. As evening approaches, the flaming orb of the sun casts long shadows across the red desert sands, elongating the straggle of trees. It disappears amazingly quickly over the horizon and in the total darkness that follows, the stars emerge, crisp and clear with no street lights or pollution to dull their shine. There is a very good Night Sky Show at Ayers Rock Resort which explains the southern skies in an interesting way.

Accommodation and camping are not allowed within the Park but the large Ayers Rock Resort, 5 km (3 m) from the entrance, provides

everything from camping facilities to a five-star hotel to the services of a small town. The visitors' centre has a comprehensive supply of information (in several languages) on tours, walking tracks, flora and fauna, as well as displays, photographs and videos. The Resort is 446 km (277 m) southwest of Alice Springs and can be reached by air.

Fraser Island

QUEENSLAND

As you move through this island and marvel at its outstanding natural beauty, you have to keep reminding yourself that it is made of sand; it is the largest sand island in the world being about 120 km (74½ m) long and 15 km (9 m) wide.

Fraser Island is the only place in the world where tall rainforests grow on sand dunes at elevations of more than 200 m (656 ft). The most spectacular tree on the island is the satinay, or Fraser Island turpentine, which has a straight trunk and grows to a height of approximately 60 m (197 ft). Its resistance to marine borer has made it a favourite for marine developments and it has been used in the construction of the Suez Canal and London's Tilbury Docks.

Fraser Island has half the world's total of perched dune lakes (40), which are formed when organic matter builds up and hardens in depressions created by the wind. These lakes support only a few fish and frog species because of the purity, acidity and low nutrient levels of the water. However, they are lovely for a cooling dip on a summer's day.

What can live here — and does in large numbers — are birds. The abundant fresh water and rich vegetation supports some 240 species of coastal and forest varieties. It is also an important resting stop for migratory wading birds travelling from southern Australia to Siberia. You will also see handsome dingos hanging around the camping areas looking for hand-outs, however, they should not be fed. These dingos are the purest strain remaining in eastern Australia because of the island's isolation from the mainland.

Many walking tracks and drives have been constructed for visitors and four-wheel-driving is allowed on the beaches. This is extremely popular and you can either bring your own vehicle across on the ferry or hire one on the island. Drive carefully though and do not disturb the sand dunes, which form and reform as part of the natural evolution of the island. Fraser is renowned for its coloured sands and magnificent dunes, which often reach up to 240 m (787 ft) above sea level.

Access to the island is by vehicular barge, private aircraft, passenger launches, commercial tours or private boat from Hervey Bay. Limited resort accommodation is available and camping is allowed.

East Coast Temperate and Subtropical Rainforest Parks

NEW SOUTH WALES

This is not one area, but more than 40 protected areas covering about 366 358 ha (905 290 a) — all that is left of the extensive New South Wales/southeastern Queensland rainforests after 200 years of European occupation. The sites extend south from south and west of Brisbane almost to Newcastle, north of Sydney, and encompass numerous national parks and reserves including Mount Warning, Border Ranges, Washpool, Dorrigo, New England, Barrington Tops, Springbrook, Lamington, Mount Barney and Main Range national parks.

It contains four major types of rainforest: subtropical, dry, warm–temperate and cool–temperate, with many plant species evolved directly from the ancient southern landmass, Gondwana. It is home to many rare and endemic animal species, including the Parma wallaby, (previously considered extinct), rufous scrub-bird, pouched and sphagnum frogs and the Hastings River mouse.

A popular park with dense rain-forest, an impressive escarpment, panoramic views, waterfalls and crystal-clear rivers is Dorrigo National Park, 60 km (37 m) inland from Coffs Harbour. Easy walks range from a 15-minute stroll to the two-and-a-half hour Wonga Walk that goes past massive stinging trees (avoid touching these) via the Crystal Shower and Tristania falls. It also has a skywalk, which takes you into the rainforest canopy, and a visitors' centre.

For stunning scenery there is little to compare with Mount Warning National Park, one of the largest calderas (the crater formed by a collapsed volcano cone) in the world. It has numerous rainforest walks, waterfalls, picnic and camping areas

Uluru (Ayers Rock) after rain, Northern Territory

and spectacular views over the Tweed Valley. Energetic visitors can climb Mount Warning (a round trip of about five hours) for a 360-degree view of the enormous caldera. It is located 12 km (7½ m) west of Murwillumbah, off Murwillumbah–Kyogle Road.

The Washpool National Park protects the largest undisturbed area of warm–temperate rainforest in New South Wales and contains the largest remaining expanse of coachwood forest in the world. The Washpool–Gibraltar Range group has a great diversity of wildlife and excellent walks leading through rainforest, woodland and up onto high granite stacks for expansive wilderness views. Both parks are on the Gwydir Highway, about 70 km (43½ m) northeast of Glen Innes.

Kata Tjuta (the Olgas), Northern Territory

Pristine perfection, Lake McKenzie, Fraser Island

East of Armidale, is the New England National Park, which falls from a high plateau and has fabulous walks and views. The vegetation varies from cold-tolerant, snow gum woodland and cool–temperate rainforest on the higher areas, to subtropical rainforest and tall sclerophyll forest at lower levels. Wildlife is abundant, with numerous birds such as lyrebirds, scrub turkeys and one or more species of cockatoo. Lamington and Springbrook national parks are described in the chapter National Parks (see page 29).

Lord Howe Island Group

NEW SOUTH WALES

The group covers an area of 145 000 ha (358 303 a), encompassing Lord Howe Island, the Admiralty Islands, Mutton Bird Island, Ball's Pyramid, and associated coral reefs and marine environments. It was formed nearly eight million years ago by a large volcano and has been eroded by sea and wind ever since. It is an area of dramatic natural beauty with Mount Gower (875 m (2870 ft)) and Mount Lidgbird rising from the sea and dominating the low-lying tail of the island. Misty forests on the summits change to wooded hills, palm groves, swamps and grassy areas as you descend. Around the shoreline, dark blue ocean waters wash over rocky outcrops and sweeping beaches, and the Lagoon contains the most southerly coral reef in the world.

The island is renowned for its many rare and endemic animals, plants and invertebrates and is a major nesting area for seabirds. The flightless Lord Howe Island woodhen is one of the world's rarest birds and has only been saved from extinction by a captive breeding program.

Bushwalking, cycling, bird-watching and diving are the main attractions, although the population of less than 300 people is appealing to city folk who need to escape crowds and traffic for a few days.

Tourism is well established with accommodation in small family-run motels and apartments. There are six restaurants, boat cruises, bowls, golf and tennis facilities, horse and buggy rides and hovercraft rides. Hire shops cater for fishing, scuba diving, snorkelling and cycling. All this may sound commercial, but the island will never be overrun by visitors as the number of tourist beds is limited to 400 at any one time and camping is not allowed. The best time to visit is during summer as June, July and August can be cool and wet.

Located 700 km (435 m) northeast of Sydney, 700 km (435 m) southeast of Brisbane and 550 km (342 m) east of Port Macquarie. The only way to reach it (unless you have your own boat) is by air. There is a good selection of flights and holiday packages from towns along the New South Wales coast, as well as from Brisbane, Sydney and Melbourne.

Australian Fossil Mammal Sites

QUEENSLAND AND SOUTH AUSTRALIA

This listing covers Riversleigh in north western Queensland and Naracoorte in southeastern South Australia. Fossils represent two of the key stages since Australia separated from other major landmasses, and tell much of the evolution of Australian marsupials.

The fossil deposits at Riversleigh span a record of mammal evolution over at least 20 million years. More than 20 000 specimens representing 150 faunal assemblages have been identified. This variety has led to an understanding of how the environment changed over time from rich rainforest to semi-arid grassland, and how the animals changed too. Riversleigh has attracted extensive attention, including a visit by Sir David Attenborough who described it as one of the rare treasure houses of palaeontology.

The site is within the Lawn Hill National Park about five hours' drive north of Mount Isa along a mostly dirt road. There is a camping area at Lawn Hill Gorge and the fossil site is another 65 km (40 m) along a rough road, best suited to four-wheel drive vehicles.

The cool caves at Naracoorte provide a quite different view of evolution. Here on the southern edge of a drying continent, a natural pit-fall trap into the caves caught a vast array of creatures, ranging in size from tiny frogs to buffalo-sized marsupials. The Victoria Fossil Cave comprises an underground gallery decorated with interesting formations and a rich collection of fossil bones. This is one of the richest deposits of Pleistocene marsupial fossils in the world containing the preserved remains of some 93 vertebrate species. The bone bearing sediments accumulated between 170 000 and 18 000 years before the present. The natural beauty of the chambers and the large volume of skeletal material has been attracting visitors since 1885.

The caves are 100 km (62 m) north of Mount Gambier and 10 minutes from Naracoorte. There is plenty of accommodation in Naracoorte and Coonawarra and a camping area with a kiosk. Tours to the fossil caves are run regularly throughout the day and bat tours are held on summer evenings.

NATIONAL PARKS

There are approximately 800 national parks across the country and many are close to cities and towns, making them very accessible. No single definition of a national park exists, but generally they are large areas where one or several ecosystems survive without undue damage by human contact, or where there are aspects of scientific, educational or recreational value, or the natural landscape is of exceptional beauty.

Australia's national parks are surprisingly diverse. Parks along the eastern seaboard embrace rainforests, mangroves, woodlands, deeply carved gorges, high plateaus, heathlands, beaches, coastal cliffs and alpine areas. In the centre they encompass thousands of square kilometres of semi-arid regions which explode into a vast garden of wildflowers and birdlife after rain. Across the top of the Northern Territory sparsely vegetated plains are slashed by wondrous escarpments, richly vegetated chasms with long waterfalls and immense wetlands. On the west coast the parks change from awesome gorges in the north to dazzling wildflowers and skyscraping karri and jarrah forests in the south.

Most parks have limited vehicular access but provide good parking areas and well-marked walking trails from the carparks. The more popular parks usually have a visitors' centre with a comprehensive range of informative brochures, displays, videos, maps and souvenirs. Park rangers conduct walks and talks in the popular parks during school holidays.

Increasingly, park authorities are building viewing platforms and raised boardwalks to protect the flora. However, this does not mean you lose the feeling of communing with nature because the more nature is protected, the better chance it has to propagate and the more you will eventually see.

Camping in the parks is very popular and most have designated camping areas which provide toilets, barbecues, showers and water. For the more adventurous, bush camping (no amenities) is usually allowed but you should check first as some areas are declared off-limits to protect endangered flora or fauna. When walking deep into parks always advise someone of your program — it is quicker, easier and cheaper to find a lost bushwalker who has left a schedule behind.

All flora and fauna is protected in national parks and it is illegal to remove *anything*. It is also unwise to feed the wildlife as this produces a dependence on humans for food and can cause digestive disorders which may lead to death.

Many parks do not allow fires and in some dry regions total fire ban days are proclaimed, making it advisable to carry a fuel stove. It is vitally important that fire bans are

Dawn highlights the volcanic plugs of the Warrumbungle National Park, New South Wales

observed as the Australian environment is susceptible to uncontrollable wild fires which destroy vast areas of bushland and kill thousands of native animals and reptiles. In any case, branches should *never* be pulled from trees and remember that any dead wood on the ground is a habitat for many small creatures. When bush camping always follow the minimal impact rules as outlined in the chapter on bushwalking (page 87).

Australia has no really dangerous wild animals, other than the saltwater crocodile, which lives in the rivers and estuaries across the northern regions. It is territorial and looks upon humans as food, so you should never swim in areas it inhabits. Treat all waterways in the northern regions with great caution as crocodile warning signs are not always posted. Australia does, however, have some very venomous snakes and spiders although, of the 150 snake species which are venomous, only about 15 have been known to kill humans. The two poisonous spiders are the funnel-web which is found around Sydney, and the redback which is found all over Australia. Snakes or spiders normally do not attack without provocation; unless you stand on one or enter its territory during breeding

season, you are unlikely to be bitten.

The weather in some parts of Australia is more of a threat to travellers than wildlife. The Outback is exceedingly dry and hot — dehydration and sunburn occur very quickly. Always wear protective clothing and sunscreen and carry twice as much water as you think you need. In the mountainous regions, especially in Tasmania, bad weather can close in with little warning. What looks like pleasant weather at breakfast can become rain — even snow — by lunch time, so be prepared.

The rock art of the Aboriginal people, much of which is within national parks, is among the oldest in the world. In some parks, especially in the northern desert regions, Aboriginal people work as rangers and guides and give interesting and informative talks on their traditions and way of life.

Entry fees into national parks vary considerably. Some are free but, increasingly, a small fee is being levied to fund maintenance and provide better facilities. There is almost always a fee for camping. If you are travelling through a state or territory and plan to visit several national parks, ask if there is an annual or multi-use pass because these are good cost savers.

Australian Capital Territory

The mountainous **Namadgi National Park** covers nearly half of the Australian Capital Territory and is less than an hour's drive south of Canberra. It comprises the most northerly section of the Australian Alps, which stretch from Victoria through New South Wales to finish here. Only 0.15% of Australia is alpine country, which makes these alps and their wildlife habitats a significant part of Australia's diversity.

The park has an extensive range of habitats starting with broad open grassland, dry woodland and tall wet forests on the lower levels, and rising to snow gums, heath and alpine wildflowers in higher areas. Snow falls on much of the park during winter and the area beyond the Mount Franklin Road is popular for cross-country skiing. The best parts of the park are beyond its roads and picnic areas, so collect a map from the visitors' centre showing the 150 km (93 m) of marked walking trails and set forth. The trails lead to some beautiful nature areas and high points where the views are spectacular. Some of the walks, such as the Yerrabi Track, start along grassy flats and rise up through subalpine forest to good lookouts. These are particularly pleasant during summer when the wildflowers are out.

As you walk you will see signs of human occupation. The Aboriginal people have been here for an estimated 20 000 years and European pastoralists arrived in the 1830s. There is a shelter with rock paintings along the Yankee Hat walking track and evidence of European occupation can be seen along the Naas Valley where you pass old cattle yards and a settler's hut built in 1879.

Bush camping, fishing and horse riding are allowed in the park with some restrictions. No facilities are provided for caravans, but there are tent camping areas at Mount Clear and Orroral and many lovely picnic spots with toilets and barbecues. For more information call in at the visitors' centre on the Naas Road, 2 km (1.2 m) south of Tharwa. Also, check the fire restrictions as this area becomes very dry and total fire bans are often in force.

New South Wales

Name your preference and New South Wales can deliver. This state has 4 million ha (9.8 million a) (nearly 5%) of its total area protected by 76 national parks and many reserves. Its 1900 km (1180 m) of coastline has stunning cliff drops, rocky outcrops, surf beaches and quiet inlets of sand and soft waves. Running parallel with the coast is the Great Dividing Range where the panoramic views, eucalypt forests, richly vegetated valleys, crystal-clear rivers and spring wildflowers provide a year-round playground for picnicking, snow skiing, whitewater rafting, bushwalking and cycling. About two-thirds of the state lies west of these ranges and comprises vast, flat pastoral lands and deserts. This is where the red soil meets the blue sky on a distant horizon and the sands

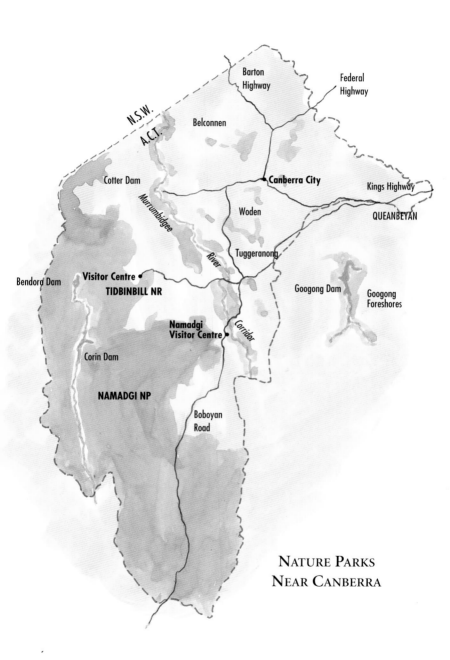

Barton Highway

Federal Highway

N.S.W.

A.C.T.

Belconnen

Cotter Dam

Murrumbidgee

Canberra City

Kings Highway

Woden

QUEANBEYAN

River

Tuggeranong

Bendora Dam

Visitor Centre

TIDBINBILL NR

Googong Dam

Googong Foreshores

Corridor

Corin Dam

Namadgi Visitor Centre

NAMADGI NP

Boboyan Road

NATURE PARKS
NEAR CANBERRA

create a surreal beauty. It is a countryside loved by artists and photographers and some of Australia's best-known artists have homes at Broken Hill in the far west.

The state's wildlife is as varied as its countryside. Thousands of birds share the skies and many species are found in the cities and suburbs. Kangaroos, wallabies, possums, lizards and snakes are widespread, with an estimated 10 000 magnificent red kangaroos to be found grazing on the Mitchell grass plains of the Sturt National Park in the far northwest.

Sydney, the state's capital and the largest city in the country, is arguably one of the most beautiful cities in the world. It has a large, sheltered harbour with beautiful walks and bays and a long coastline of famous headlands and surfing beaches, all within easy access of the city. There are numerous reserves within the city which can be reached by public transport — try the Manly Scenic Walkway which takes about half a day, or the Gap Bluff Track at Watsons Bay which has dramatic cliffs and stunning views.

Large animals have mostly deserted this city of red-roofed houses and skyscrapers, but you will see plenty of colourful birds, lizards, possums and maybe even a fox in the forested reserves along the waterways.

To add to its charms, Sydney is bordered on three sides by large national parks and on the fourth by the ocean. All three parks — Ku-ring-gai Chase, the Royal and the Blue Mountains — are no more than an hour's drive from the centre of the city.

Ku-ring-gai Chase National Park has the rugged beauty of wooded hills falling into calm, blue fjords and secluded bays. This is a popular boating area but not so popular that you cannot find a quiet bay to yourself. If you do not have a boat you can hire one from Bobbin Head or Akuna Bay. More than 180 species of bird and 40 species of fish have been recorded in the area and if you are very quiet you will see swamp wallabies, koalas, possums, echidnas, leaf-tailed geckos, bats, rats and snakes. Aboriginal people lived here long before the arrival of Europeans and their rock engravings, cave art, axe-grinding groves and middens can be found throughout the park.

The park is 26 km (16 m) north of Sydney and good roads lead to pretty picnic spots and numerous walking trails. Maps are available at entry stations, the Wildlife Shop at Bobbin Head and the Kalkari visitors' centre on Ku-ring-gai Chase Road. There is only one camping area, located at the Basin on the western foreshores of Pittwater, and it is reached by ferry from Palm Beach. It is popular so you would be wise to book ahead. A Youth Hostel at Towlers Bay can be reached by foot from West Head Road or by ferry from Church Point.

On Sydney's southern border lies the 15 014-ha (37 100-a) **Royal National Park**. When this park was gazetted in 1879, the philosophy of national parks was very different to that of today. It was established to provide land to which the poor could escape the overcrowding in Sydney and experience the healthy outdoors. The early settlers, still yearning for their homeland, chopped down the native vegetation to cultivate formal gardens and European trees. They introduced deer, exotic birds and fish, and built roads, guest houses, camps and the Audley tourist village. Fortunately, later generations have taken a more conservative approach and have allowed the park to return to its former state.

The scenery is dynamic. Along its 30 km (18½ m) coastline the cliffs have been eroded by winds and rain to expose the beautiful soft colours of the sandstone. Sandy bays provide good swimming and surfing. A lovely spot for a picnic is Wattamolla Creek where the water tumbles over a steep cliff into a deep pool then meanders across a sandy stretch to slide silently into the ocean. Along the plateau the soil is poor but is covered with low scrub that explodes into a blaze of wildflowers in spring and attracts large numbers of birds. In all, there are 700 species of flowering plants in the park and more than 200 species of birds. Where the Hacking River and other watercourses have cut deep gorges into the plateau the vegetation is taller with forests of turpentine, blackbutt, bluegum and Sydney red-gums, which are lovely to picnic under.

There are many ways to enjoy this park and it caters for all fitness levels. You can drive to a picnic area or hire a boat from Audley and paddle to one. There are 150 km (93 m) of walking trails ranging from an exhilarating stride along the wind-swept ocean cliffs, to the easy 1 km (½ m) marked walk to Bungoona Lookout, with views over the park and the Hacking River. (This walk is suitable for wheelchairs.)

Bush camping is allowed but a permit is required. The only established camping area is at Bonnie Vale in the north. Maps and permits can be obtained from the visitors' centre at Audley. The park is 30 km (18½ m) south of Sydney by road, or you can take the train to Loftus, Engadine, Heathcote, Waterfall or Otford and join a walking track from the station.

The **Blue Mountains National Park** is one of Australia's best-known and most photographed parks. Its panoramic views, waterfalls, sheer cliffs of gold and red, densely clad gorges and the famous Three Sisters peaks are widely recognised. It is also easily accessible, being one-and-a-half hours' drive west of Sydney and on a main rail line. As you drive up from Sydney, stop to look back at the fabulous views over the coastal plains and the sprawl of Sydney.

The Blue Mountains are not really mountains but a series of sandstone plateaus, cliffs and chasms. The vegetation changes from low heaths on the infertile plateaus, to ferns draping from damp cliff ledges to rainforest and tall eucalypts in the valleys. The bluish haze you see is the result of eucalypt oils evaporating from the leaves.

The 218 000 ha (538 690 a) park is crisscrossed with well-maintained walking trails ranging from easy to moderately difficult. The Three Sisters at Katoomba is reached by a short walk and, if you do not suffer from vertigo, across a little foot bridge. The popular Grand Canyon Walk (3 to 4 hours) descends from Evans Lookout Road at Blackheath, to a gully, 150 m (492 ft) below, of lush rainforest, coachwood, giant ferns and thick mosses, weaves past a variety of habitats and waterfalls and eventually climbs back to where you began. There are numerous trails but experienced bushwalkers may prefer to make their own path through the wild valleys, and bush camping is allowed, with some restrictions.

The mountains have four distinct seasons, each with its own beauty. Spring is my favourite because this is when the mountains are waking from their winter sleep and the wildflowers are in bloom. The Blue Mountains are a haven for arts and crafts people and they sell their wares in numerous galleries, boutiques and antique stores. Little coffee shops sell homemade goodies and there is plenty of accommodation in the various villages. Visitors' centres are located at Blackheath, Echo Point, Wentworth Falls and Glenbrook.

The **Warrumbungle National Park** rises in dusty green peaks and jagged rocky spires on the eastern edge of the vast, flat, western plains, 490 km (304 m) northwest of Sydney. Some 13 to 17 million years ago a low volcano shook the area and

the main cone rose 1000 m (3281 ft) above the plains. Over the years, erosion has exposed the hard trachyte plugs which blocked the volcano's vents and they remain like sentinels guarding the dense bush and abundant wildlife of the hills and valleys surrounding them. The effect is dramatic and the park is a favourite with bushwalkers, photographers, artists, and rock climbers — the Breadknife has a 90 m (295 ft) sheer rock face.

The park has an unusual climate,

BORDER RANGES NP

• Byron Bay

Moree •
GIBRALTAR RANGE NP

GUY FAWKES RIVER NP

NEW ENGLAND NP
• Coffs Harbour
DORIGO NP

WARRUMBUNGLE NP
• Coonabarabran • Tamworth
OXLEY WILD RIVERS NP

← Nyngan

WOKO NP
• Port Macquarie
BARRINGTON TOPS NP

• Dubbo

WOLLEMI NP
MYALL LAKES NP

Parkes •
• Newcastle

BLUE MOUNTAINS NP
KU-RING-GAI CHASE NP
Cowra •
Sydney
ROYAL NP

rrandera
• Cootamundra

Canberra

MORTON NP

• Batemans Bay

Albury
DEUA NP
KOSCIUSKO NP
• Jindabyne
WADBILLIGA NP

NEW SOUTH WALES
NATIONAL PARKS

which enables it to support plant and animal species from the moist east coast as well as those from the dry western plains. It has 620 semi-arid and temperate plant species, 180 bird species, 15 species of snake and the abundant spring wildflowers are brilliant. This is one place you are sure to see a koala perched up in a tree, and hordes of kangaroos — especially in the early morning and evening — in the grassy valley near the visitors' centre. Emus stride through the grasslands, feeding and arrogantly ignoring curious spectators.

There are 30 km (18½ m) of walking trails weaving through the park, ranging from the White Gum Lookout which is suitable for wheelchairs, to the Breadknife–Grand High Tops walk. This walk takes up to five hours return, passing dense forest and volcanic plugs and scenic lookouts. Fans Horizon is a great sunset lookout, but be prepared to climb an arduous 600 steps.

There are ample camping areas in the park but do take a fuel stove with you as the collection of wood is not permitted. There is a fee to enter the park and also for camping. If you are planning to bush camp or rock climb you must get a permit from the rangers at the visitors' centre. Basic accommodation is available at Balor Hut below the Breadknife (holds up to six people), and the Woolshed which accommodates groups.

For accommodation outside the park, there are camping areas and motels along the eastern road to Coonabarabran and self-contained accommodation at Gumin-Gumin, one of the original homesteads in the area on the west.

The **Myall Lakes National Park** provides a total contrast to the craggy beauty and isolation of the Warrumbungles. This is one of the state's largest coastal lake systems and is an important waterbird habitat and fish breeding ground. Here life floats along on a hired houseboat with nothing more to do than sip wine and take photographs. Bush walks can be taken along level ground on the lake side, or to the wind-sculptured sand dunes along the ocean beach. On the Mungo Brush Rainforest Walk, an easy 30-minute stroll through coastal rainforest, you will see plenty of birds and possibly koalas, goannas, dingos, possums and swamp wallabies.

Myall Lakes is 236 km (146 m) north of Sydney and there is plenty of accommodation in the local towns of Bulahdelah, Tea Gardens and Hawkes Nest. Caravans and cabins are provided at Myall Shores Resort and there are camping areas at Mungo Brush, Bombah Point and Violet Hill. Other camping areas can be reached by boat or on foot. There is no entry fee to the park but there is a fee for camping.

Kosciusko National Park is Australia's highest alpine park and a winter playground containing most of the state's ski resorts. Clearing land for ski runs is not in harmony with the philosophy of national parks, however, only 40 500 ha (100 077 a) of the 690 000 ha (1 705 027 a) park is snow-covered during winter, and only a small portion of this is licensed for downhill skiing. Cross-country skiing has less impact on the environment and snow camping is permitted. A waterproof, colour-coded map of the 110 km (68 m) of cross-country trails is available from visitors' centres.

The park rises to 2228 m (7310 ft) at the summit of Mount Kosciusko and is the headwaters of three of Australia's major rivers — the Murray, Snowy and Murrumbidgee. It is a magic place in summer. The wide open spaces, crisp, crunchy air, clear mountain streams and vast vistas are a summertime delight. The high, treeless plains have a recorded 200 species of herbs, heaths and alpine flowers which burst into wonderful colour in spring and summer, the best wildflower display being in late January and February. Lower down the slopes, twisted and gnarled snow gums are lovely to picnic under and make for great photographs. Further down still, the Thredbo River valley is lush and green, with a crystal-clear river and attractive camping areas. The clear, unpolluted, mountain air fills everyone with surprising energy in summer and there is plenty to do. You can join a tour or hire gear to walk, canoe, play tennis or golf, visit caves, fish or ride horses.

Walking trails stretch over the park and most are graded easy to moderate. The most popular is the easy, 6 km (3½ m) raised metal walkway which goes from the top of the Crackenback Chairlift at Thredbo to Mount Kosciusko. You should allow about two-and-a-half hours to reach the summit and a little less for the return journey, which is slightly downhill. This raised walkway is one of the best examples I have seen of how the environment can be protected yet still open to the public. It allows the water to flow without interruption and lets light through so plants can grow underneath. Staff at the Thredbo Alpine Village provide guided walks of this area throughout summer and the park rangers offer walks, talks and night stalks during peak holiday times.

Bush camping is allowed, with some restrictions, and camping areas are established at Sawpit Creek and along the Thredbo River, off Alpine Way. Bush huts, once used by stockmen, can now be used by walkers. Detailed information on walks and camping is available from the park rangers at Sawpit Creek, Tumut, Khancoban, Yarrangobilly Caves, Bullocks Flat, Perisher Valley (winter only) and at the Snowy River Information Centre in Jindabyne.

Northern Territory

To many people the Northern Territory is the soul of Australia. This is where the red desert sands, speckled with scrubby bush, stretch from one horizon to another. It is where the famous features — Uluru (Ayers Rock), Katherine Gorge and the wetlands of Kakadu — materialise in unexpected splendour from an otherwise monotonous landscape. This is where escarpments slash the land with great drama and cattle stations are so large they are measured in thousands of square kilometres.

Even the climate is theatrical, crashing from one extreme to another. As the summer wet season approaches, sensational electrical storms fire the sky and thick clouds rumble across the sun. The rain falls so heavily you cannot see your hand in front of your face and, in minutes, all but sealed roads are slippery and often impassable. The dry plains become shimmering oceans and hundreds of thousands of birds arrive to bicker and breed. Trees and grasslands turn green and wildflowers burst into brilliant colour. The wet is a time of rich abundance, but before venturing forth you should check on road conditions with the Northern Territory Emergency Service at Darwin (089) 84 4455 or Alice Springs (089) 52 7111.

By contrast, the dry turns the fine particles of clay into 'bulldust', which fluffs up and fills your car and nostrils with a pink, powder-like dust. As the wetlands shrink, the water birds and crocodiles have less habitat and you see them in greater concentrations. Thousands of birds migrate to other wetlands during the dry and many fish bury themselves to await the next rainfall. This is the most comfortable time of the year to visit the northern areas of the state but it is also the time for bushfires. Always take extreme care — no cigarettes flicked out of car windows and portable gas or fuel stoves should be used for cooking.

The Northern Territory has 4.4 million ha (10.8 million a) listed as parks and reserves and 229 000 ha (565 871 a) as marine parks. The water in the parks is not usually treated for drinking so you should carry your own — the minimum recommended quantity for a walker in this heat is 4 litres (8½ pints) a day.

The Territory is basically divided into two regions: the Top End in the north, and the Red Centre in the south and each is totally different to the other.

The Top End is where you experience the extremes of the wet and the dry mentioned above. Its steamy, tropical climate produces richly vegetated coastlands, patches of lush rainforest and long, spectacular waterfalls that tumble over sheer escarpments after rain. It has many gorges gouged by raging rivers during the wet, which provide cool swimming holes during the dry.

Kakadu National Park is the Top End's largest national park and is described in detail in the chapter on World Heritage Areas (see page 13).

A magnificent Top End park is **Litchfield**, an easy 2-hour drive from Darwin along a gravel road via the Cox Peninsula Road, or by a sealed road through Batchelor. This beautiful park has gorgeous waterfalls that cascade from the Tabletop Range into deep, clear waterholes where it is safe to swim. Buley Rockhole is also fabulous for a dip, especially if you like tumbling about among frothing rapids. The marked walking trails that lead you along the tabletop provide breathtaking views down into the green valleys and over waterfalls.

Near the Tolmer Falls there are rock arches which form natural bridges across the deep gorge. You can take the easy track to the lookout over the falls, or the more difficult but stunning walk to the top of the waterfall. Florence Falls is the most beautiful of them all and you reach its pool down a steep track from the car park. The most suitable for families is Wangi Falls, which is close to the car park and picnic area.

The main roads in Litchfield are sealed but if you take the side track to the Lost City, a mythical metropolis of tall rocks, you will need a four-wheel drive and some experience of bush-track driving.

The park has camping areas near Wangi, Florence and Tjaynera Falls (Sandy Creek) and Buley Rockhole. Information on camping and walking trails can be obtained from the Conservation Commission offices at Batchelor before you enter the park.

Gurig National Park and

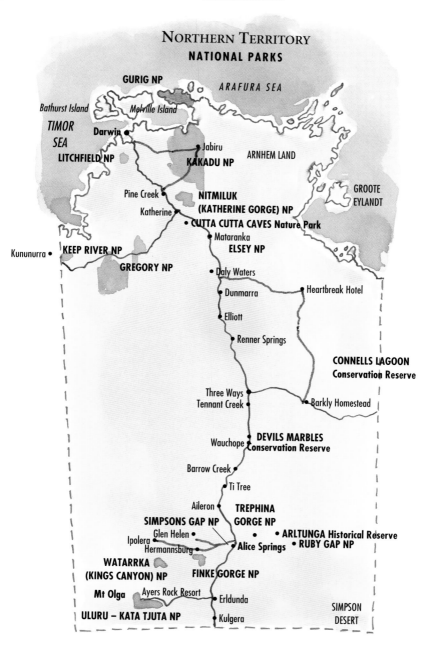

NORTHERN TERRITORY
NATIONAL PARKS

GURIG NP

ARAFURA SEA

Bathurst Island

Melville Island

**TIMOR
SEA**

Darwin

LITCHFIELD NP

Jabiru

ARNHEM LAND

KAKADU NP

Pine Creek

NITMILUK
(KATHERINE GORGE) NP

GROOTE
EYLANDT

Katherine

CUTTA CUTTA CAVES Nature Park

Mataranka

Kununurra

KEEP RIVER NP

ELSEY NP

GREGORY NP

Daly Waters

Dunmarra

Heartbreak Hotel

Elliott

Renner Springs

CONNELLS LAGOON
Conservation Reserve

Three Ways
Tennant Creek

Barkly Homestead

DEVILS MARBLES
Conservation Reserve

Wauchope

Barrow Creek

Ti Tree

Aileron

TREPHINA
GORGE NP

SIMPSONS GAP NP

Glen Helen

ARLTUNGA Historical Reserve

Ipolera

RUBY GAP NP

Hermannsburg

Alice Springs

WATARRKA
(KINGS CANYON) NP

FINKE GORGE NP

Mt Olga

Ayers Rock Resort

Erldunda

ULURU – KATA TJUTA NP

Kulgera

SIMPSON
DESERT

Cobourg Marine Park, 570 km (354 m) northeast of Darwin, are not easily reached but are worth the trip. The only way to get here is by four-wheel drive, boat or light aircraft. The coastline is mostly flat with coral reefs, clear water, safe anchorage and sandy beaches where you will find goannas and turtles. Many lagoons, swamps and streams are surrounded by paperbark forests and support birds such as egrets, rajah, shelducks, whistling ducks, geese, plovers and pied herons. The estuarine crocodile also lives here and often travels to inland creeks and lagoons. Other wildlife you can expect to see includes bandicoots, possums, wallabies, antelope kangaroos and introduced buffalo, pigs and banteng (Bali cattle).

Gurig is owned by the Aboriginal people and you need an entry permit which can be obtained from the Central Land Council in Alice Springs. The number of vehicles allowed into the park is limited so it is best to apply for a permit well in advance of when you intend to travel. Camping is allowed at Smith Point, and the only resort accommodation in the region is at Seven Spirit Bay (see Accommodation, page 188), an up-market property developed with the permission and assistance of the Aboriginal people.

Driving south from Darwin through the monotonous landscape of scruffy eucalypts and spear grass tussocks does not prepare you for the grandeur of **Nitmiluk (Katherine Gorge) National Park**, with the Edith Falls in its northwest corner and the deeply cut Katherine Gorge in the south. Gouged out of an ancient sandstone plateau over thousands of years by the Katherine River, the zigzag series of 13 gorges is fringed with silver paperbark trees, mangroves and pandanus palms. Ferns and mosses grow in moist crevices along the orange-red cliffs lining the gorge.

The best way to experience the 10.5 km (6½ m) gorge system is from the water. You can use your own boat, hire a canoe or take a cruise. Canoeing is the nicest way to travel but does involve some effort in lugging the canoe over the shallow areas of water. If you take a cruise, choose one that will take you as far as one of the beautiful waterfalls, which drop from the plateau in a long streams of silver into a clear pools where you can have a refreshing swim. It is difficult to imagine that this tranquil river becomes a raging torrent in the wet, resulting in the Gorge being closed to boats.

The park has more than 100 km (62 m) of marked walking trails, taking from one hour to a few days to complete. The walk above Edith Falls leads to rockpools and waterfalls. Fit walkers could undertake the five-day walk from the Gorge to Edith Falls.

The wildlife includes rock wallabies, euros, kangaroos, echidnas, dingos and lizards on the ground, and red-tailed black cockatoos, parrots, rosellas, honeyeaters, the great bowerbird and bright little finches in the air. The birds are particularly prolific during June and July when the gums are flowering.

Emus and wallabies hang around the camping areas looking for food but, as in all national parks, wildlife should not be fed. The most interesting of the fish in the area is a character called the archer (or rifle) fish, so named because it shoots down insects with a jet of water and then eats them. Freshwater crocodiles live in the rivers but they are not aggressive and will not harm you if leave them alone.

Bush camping is allowed in the park and there are commercially operated camping facilities at Katherine Gorge and Edith Falls. A caravan park, information centre and shop are located at the entrance to Katherine Gorge. The town of Katherine, 32 km (20 m) from the Gorge and 330 km (205 m) south of Darwin, has an airport and a good selection of motel and hostel accommodation.

As you drive south from Katherine Gorge you come to the Red Centre, which is much drier than the Top End. Here the vegetation is low and hardy, the desert sands are a rich red, and jagged ranges glow faintly purple in the heat. Occasionally you come across gorges and waterholes that are fringed with an astonishing variety of gums, palms, cycads, ferns and other tropical vegetation left over from a much wetter period in history. Many of the desert plants only bloom after rain and there are fish that survive by burying themselves during the dry periods and not emerging until it has rained. Amazingly, the desert gets quite cool at night but is extremely hot during the day. The best time to visit is in the cooler winter months.

Aboriginal people have learnt how to survive in the desert and there is evidence to indicate they lived here up to 50 000 years ago. Today many Aboriginal people work as guides in the national parks and some of their communities are open to visitors. Their tours give a fascinating insight into how they found food, water and medicine in such a harsh environment.

The most visited and photographed feature of the Red Centre is the strangely isolated Ayers Rock, which rises like a big plum pudding from the flat, red, desert floor. The Rock is so famous it has icon status, along with the Great Barrier Reef, the Sydney Opera House and the Sydney Harbour Bridge. It is located within the **Uluru–Kata Tjuta National Park**, which is more fully described in the chapter on World Heritage Areas (see page 13).

An excellent driving tour of the Red Centre is the Mereenie Loop Road. Starting from Alice Springs, this loop goes via Simpsons Gap, Standley Chasm, Ellery Big Hole, Serpentine Gorge, the Ochre Pits, Ormiston Gorge, Glen Helen Gorge, Mount Sonder, Redbank Gorge, Gosse Bluff, Watarrka National Park (which includes Kings Canyon) and Uluru–Kata Tjuta National Park (which includes Ayers Rock), and returns via the Lasseter and Stuart highways. This scenic route of about 1100 km (683 m) was upgraded in 1994 to make it accessible to all vehicles; previously only four-wheel-drive vehicles could pass some sections.

The Mereenie Loop Road passes near two Aboriginal communities which welcome visitors — Ipolera near Gosse Bluff and the Hermannsburg Mission. As an alternative to the complete loop, you could turn off at Gosse Bluff and return to Alice Springs via the Hermannsburg Mission and the Larapinta Highway. This shorter loop could be done comfortably in two days with a camp at either Glen Helen or Ipolera.

Following the Mereenie Loop Road west from Alice Springs you come to the **West MacDonnell National Park**, an area of arid landscapes, gorges, craggy red cliffs, panoramic views, white ghost gums along dried riverbeds and waterholes of astonishingly cold water. Very often ferns and palms fringe the waterholes and dingos visit camping areas looking for food scraps.

There are several gorges within the park, which you can visit by car or on a commercial tour from Alice Springs. The closest is Simpsons Gap which can be reached along a sealed road or a 24 km (15 m) cycle path. It took an estimated 60 million years for the creek to carve Simpsons Gap through the quartzite, which now appears as roughly hewn layers of red rock rising above a small waterhole. You can walk to the Gap from the visitors' centre at the end of the

Wangi Falls, Litchfield National Park, Northern Territory

road and there is a dry river with lovely ghost gums to picnic under. Black-flanked rock wallabies live along the rocky cliffs but they are difficult to see unless they move; they are most active in the morning and late afternoon.

Ormiston Gorge, 132 km (82 m) west of Alice Springs, was gouged out by the floodwaters of the Ormiston Creek. Although mostly dry in the winter it floods quite often in summer and some waterholes remain all year providing a welcome swim on a hot day. The best way to see the gorge is to walk. Some walks are quite short although they involve a bit of effort in this heat. The visitors' centre at the car park will supply information on the ten-minute walk to the waterhole, and the three-hour walk into Ormiston

Simpsons Gap, Northern Territory

Pound, a natural amphitheatre surrounded by high ridges.

Bush camping is allowed and is free, but there is a small fee to use the camping area near the car park. Nearby Glen Helen Homestead has cabins, backpacker rooms and a camping area. The Glen Helen Gorge is also stunningly beautiful with tall, coloured cliffs and a deep waterhole.

Still following the Mereenie Loop Road you come to the **Watarrka National Park** which encompasses Kings Canyon, an enormous and ancient chasm of 300 m (984 ft) high cliffs sculptured out of sheer sandstone. The views from the rim of the Canyon are spectacular and on the valley floor is the Garden of Eden, a unique waterhole surrounded by palms and ferns. Within the canyon there is an amazing diversity

of plantlife and wildlife. There is a walk around the rim which is a must, and a shorter one-and-a-half-hour walk along the rocky creek bed for a different perspective of the towering rock formations.

Frontier Kings Canyon resort, 7 km (4 m) from the Canyon, has hotel rooms, backpacker rooms, caravan sites and camping areas. The complex has been built to strict environmental guidelines in conjunction with the Conservation Commission of the Northern Territory. It is fully self-sufficient for power, water and waste disposal and the water from the sewerage treatment plant is used to irrigate a plantation growing firewood for use in campfires. Some 25 000 plants native to the area were re-planted in a major rehabilitation program after construction was completed.

Queensland

Known as the Sunshine State because of its good weather, Queensland is also a state of great natural beauty. It contains dripping rainforests, golden beaches, coral reefs, dreamy islands, spectacular waterfalls, crisp green

Katherine Gorge, Northern Territory

mountains, vast scrub and grass-covered plains and abundant wildlife. Two-thirds of Australia's native mammals (205 species), three-quarters of its birds (612 species), just over half of its reptiles (402 species) and 113 frog species live here. It has three areas that have been World Heritage listed for their outstanding natural qualities: the Great Barrier Reef, the Wet Tropics and Fraser Island. The Great Dividing Range runs north–south, roughly parallel with the coast, creating a natural barrier between the wet coastal strip and the drier interior.

About 60% of the state lies north of the Tropic of Capricorn and has a typically tropical climate. December to March is the peak of the wet season, when torrential downpours turn rivers into inland seas and many roads become impassable. In the dry winter season the waterholes shrink, swamps dry up and there is a high risk of bushfires. By late November the wildlife is gathering around the dwindling water holes and this is a good time to go wildlife viewing. Nearly 4% of the state is designated as national park or other conservation reserve. Queensland has more than 300 national parks, but some are tiny and there is a proposal to consolidate them to create larger individual parks. No national parks charge an entry fee but there is a small fee for camping.

Starting from the north, there is Cape York Peninsula, a wonderful wilderness area for the intrepid traveller. The peninsula is sparsely populated and few roads are sealed so you will need a reliable four-wheel drive and to carry all your own supplies, including mechanical spares. Plan to travel during the dry winter months as the roads can become boggy during summer, and often as late as June. Quite a lot of land on the Peninsula is owned by the Aboriginal people and you will need a permit to enter onto their land. Check for details with the Queensland Department of Family Services and Aboriginal and Islander Affairs.

Near the northern tip of the Peninsula is the remote **Jardine River National Park**. The early explorers found this whole area difficult and unpleasant and named it the 'wet desert'; Frank Jardine, an explorer who spent many years at Somerset on Cape York, cursed 'the mosquitoes and the bogs and scrubs of this villainous country'. However, if you are well equipped and enjoy an adventure it is a great challenge, and the vegetation and wildlife are varied and interesting. A vehicular ferry operates on the Jardine River when the roads are passable, which is usually from July to November. Camping is permitted but be very careful of where you swim because the crocodiles here are numerous and dangerous.

A more accessible park on the Peninsula is **Lakefield National Park**, 390 km (242 m) north of Cairns. It is the state's second-largest national park and provides a semi-wilderness experience with good opportunities to photograph wildlife. Lakefield has an extensive river system and is a major habitat for birds and crocodiles, both the freshwater and the estuarine variety. In the dry winter months the waterways shrink noticeably, but there are still many swamps, creeks and lily-covered lagoons to attract birds. The diverse vegetation, which includes rainforest, stringybark forest, paperbark woodland, mangroves, mud flats, open grassy plains and swamps, attracts a huge variety of animals and birds.

You can reach the park in a standard vehicle along the Peninsula Development Road to Laura where you turn off to New Laura. If entering from Cooktown via Battlecamp or Coen via Musgrave and Saltwater Creek, you will need a four-wheel-drive vehicle.

Bush camping is allowed and you can collect your permit from the rangers at Lakefield or New Laura (both within the park). There is a good camping area at Kalpowar Crossing located approximately in the middle of the park and a boat ramp near Bizant.

Travelling south down the coast from Cairns you come to many parks offering a variety of experiences, including golden beaches, mangroves, rainforests and tall, wet, heavily vegetated hills. A short ferry ride from Townsville takes you to the delightful **Magnetic Island National Park**, a paradise of golden sandy beaches, transparent warm water, granite headlands and walks through native bushland where koalas and possums live contentedly in the trees. Camping is not allowed in the park, but there is a wide choice of

accommodation in the little settlements along the beaches outside the park boundaries, and the town where the ferry stops. You can take your own vehicle across on the ferry, or go mad for a few days and hire a colourful, open-sided Mini Moke.

The **Eungella National Park** is an outstanding park of lush tropical and subtropical rainforest with abundant wildlife including some half a dozen wildlife species which are endemic to its boundaries. Its lowlands offer a tropical climate and vegetation while the higher peaks (Mount Dalrymple is 1280 m (4199 ft) above sea level) are cooler and often shrouded in cloud. Most of the northern section has stunning forests and great gorges but it is difficult countryside and is only suitable for experienced walkers.

On the western slopes — where less rain falls — there are open eucalypt woodlands.

Australia's unique duck-billed platypus lives in Broken River, quite near the picnic and camping area. If you sit here of an early morning or late afternoon you may see them, and tortoises, feeding; look for bubbles on the surface to indicate platypuses feeding on the river bottom. The river is also home to a great variety of fish and eels and a feeding ground for graceful egrets and herons.

Most of the walking trails start from the Broken River and Finch Hatton Creek camping areas and lead through moist, green rainforest with hundreds of birds, lizards, frogs and snakes. The walks lead to fabulous lookouts and waterfalls where you can swim and possibly see the

Eungella day frog, a little brown fellow endemic to the park.

The park is 80 km (50 m) inland from Mackay and camping areas in the park fill quickly during holiday periods so it is wise to book. There is a kiosk and ranger station at the Broken River camping area and accommodation and supplies at Eungella township. Broken River Mountain Retreat near the ranger station, has self-contained cabins and motel-style rooms and offers free transport to the start of various walks in the national park.

The **Whitsunday Islands National Parks** off the coast east of Proserpine are utopia for boating enthusiasts. More than 70 islands and clear, warm waters offer the romance of cruising in relatively safe waters and overnighting in secluded bays. Most of the islands — and large chunks of the water — are designated national and marine parks.

If you do not have a boat of your own you can easily hire one. Coastal towns like Airlie Beach have charter craft ranging from cruisers to yachts, with or without a skipper and with or without provisions. The winds and tides around the island are a bit tricky, but you are given very clear instructions; follow them and you will have no trouble.

One of the great charms of the Whitsundays is the variety of landscape. Some islands are steep and craggy, rising sharply from a vibrant blue ocean; others are low green mounds with pale, sandy beaches fringed by rainforest. Fringing reefs provide great snorkelling and diving,

especially around Hook, Border, Deloraine and Langford islands. Some reefs are exposed at low tide and are interesting to explore, but be careful not to damage live coral and always replace any pieces you pick up. Around the shores oysters, snails and crabs attract sea birds galore.

Resort development has been permitted on some islands, and three — Hayman, Hamilton and Dent — are not national parks. Anchoring offshore and calling in at the island resorts is part of the fun of cruising the Whitsundays. There are marked walks on South Molle, Lindeman, Long and Whitsunday islands. Elsewhere you can explore the rocky shores and wooded slopes at your leisure.

Camping is allowed but you need a permit, which can be collected from the Department of Environment and Heritage office at Airlie Beach. A few things to note: there is no water on most of the islands; you must use a portable stove; and the sun and insects can be relentless so take plenty of sunscreen lotion, insect repellent and vinegar to treat marine stingers.

Further south and 510 km (317 m) inland from Gladstone, the **Carnarvon National Park** materialises as a sanctuary of lush vegetation and extraordinary beauty. The Carnarvon Gorge is only a small portion of this large national park, but it is so varied and abundant that many people travel no further. The main gorge and side gorges have been gouged out over millions of years by the Carnarvon Creek and its tributaries. The

QUEENSLAND
NATIONAL PARKS

Thursday Island

GREAT

Cape
York
Peninsula

Cape Melville
LIZARD ISLAND NP
LAKEFIELD NP **CAPE TRIBULATION NP**

Mornington Island.

Cooktown
CHILLAGOE-MUNGANA Daintree
CAVES NP Cairns
Innisfail
Tully
HINCHINBROOK ISLAND NP

BARRIER

MOUNT SPEC NP
MAGNETIC ISLAND NP
Townsville

CAMOOWEAL NP **WHITSUNDAY ISLAND NP**
CONWAY NP **CUMBERLAND ISLAND NP**
Mt Isa **EUNGELLA NP**
Mackay

REEF

Longreach Rockhampton
BLACKDOWN TABLELAND NP

SIMPSON DESERT NP **CARNARVON NP** Fraser
Island.
Birdsville
COOLOOLA NP
NOOSA NP
Moreton
Island
BUNYA MOUNTAINS NP
Toowoomba Brisbane
LAMINGTON NP Surfers
GIRRAWEEN NP Pardise
SPRINGBROOK NP

consistent moisture they provide supports a wide variety of trees, ferns and mosses, which in turn nurture and shelter numerous mammals, reptiles and birds. The bird population swells during spring when the wildlfowers are out — the bright red flowers of the bottlebrush being a favourite of the yellow-

tufted honeyeater.

Aboriginal rock carvings and paintings are found in many of the caves along the gorges. The two main rock art sites are at the Art Gallery and Cathedral Cave and walking trails lead to these and to lookouts and other areas of interest. The Consuelo Tableland and the Great

Dividing Range on the higher, drier areas are only suitable for experienced walkers.

Bush camping is allowed and there are two designated camping areas — the one at the park entrance has good facilities, the other, Big Bend, has toilets only and is a 10 km (6.2 m) walk from the nearest carpark. The information centre is at the park entrance. The park is popular so you should book early.

The Oasis Lodge, just outside the entrance, has comfortable safari-style cabins with ensuite. From April to November, Lodge staff run a program of day and evening guided walks, as well as a variety of activities such as abseiling, birdwatching, platypus viewing and bush breakfasts. For those without a car, the Lodge offers a weekly bus service from Roma (250 km (155 m)). Alternatively, you could fly. There is a light airstrip at Ingelara, 3 km (1.6 m) from the Lodge.

At the southern end of Queensland's coast are the famous resort towns of Noosa and Surfers Paradise. Both towns have an abundance of accommodation, camping areas and eateries. They are also close to outstanding national parks.

Noosa National Park is a small coastal park only 1 km (½ m) from the centre of Noosa Heads. You can walk to it easily and spend a day exploring its 454 ha (1122 a) of rainforest, open forest, wallum heathlands, shrublands and grasslands, or find a beach and explore the rock pools. Camping is

not allowed because the park is so small but there are lovely picnic areas and breathtaking ocean views.

Lamington National Park and **Springbrook National Park**, inland from Surfers Paradise, are mountainous, with spectacular escarpments, rainforests, woodlands, cool streams, waterfalls and thrilling views. An extensive network of well-marked walking trails leads to the lookouts, creeks, waterfalls and picnic areas. You will see and hear some of the most beautiful birds in the country: the black and gold regent bowerbird, eastern spinebills, pied currawongs, satin bowerbirds, Australian brush turkeys, king parrots, crimson rosellas, wompoo pigeons (listen for their distinctive 'wom-poo' call), eastern yellow robins — the list goes on. Most rainforest mammals are nocturnal so take a spotlight walk to see mountain brushtail possums, bush rats, bandicoots, glider possums and ringtail possums. In the early morning and at dusk the red-necked pademelons come out to graze.

Both parks are within a one- to two-hour drive from Surfers Paradise so you can either stay on the coast or at one of several mountain lodges. You will have no difficulty getting maps and information on the parks from travel agents and accommodation houses in Surfers Paradise. Many tour operators run day and half-day trips by coach or four-wheel drive into the parks.

Bush camping is allowed with a permit, but open fires are banned. The parks are well above sea level, about 1000 m (3281 ft), so they can be quite chilly in winter and wet at any time. The ranger stations for the Springbrook National Park are on Springbrook Road and the Murwillumbah–Nerang Road, near the entrance to Natural Bridge. Lamington has ranger stations at Binna Burra and Green Mountains.

As you move inland from the coast, you leave behind the rains which nurture the rainforests and the mountains with their deep river gorges and you come to a measureless, flat landscape. The climate is dry, the vegetation is sparse and scrubby, and the temperatures are hot during the day and near freezing some winter nights. This is open country for people who like plenty of space and huge, starry night skies.

In the southwest corner of Queensland the **Simpson Desert National Park** spreads for 200 000 km² (77 220 m²) across Queensland, South Australia and the Northern Territory. It is waterless and uninhabited and should only be traversed by people experienced in remote travel and good at repairing four-wheel-drive vehicles. There are no facilities in the park and no roads other than old mining or seismic exploration tracks. Some of the sand dunes are 20 m (65 ft) high and, although beautiful to see, they are difficult to cross. The temperature varies significantly — summer days at Birdsville average 35°C (95°F), but winter can bring bitterly cold nights.

Once in the park you will be amazed at how such arid conditions can support so much plantlife and wildlife. Sandhill canegrass, lobed spinifex, wattle and grevillea grow here and 41 bird species have been identified, ranging from tiny insect- and seed-eating wrens to the grand wedge-tailed eagle. Other creatures that have adapted to the harsh environment are snakes, lizards and small marsupials, such as mulgaras and dunnarts.

The nearest town for supplies is Birdsville but you should equip yourself from a larger town before heading west. You need a permit to enter and camp in the park and can get this from the Queensland National Parks and Wildlife Service at Longreach. If you plan to go over the border into South Australia you will need the South Australia National Parks and Wildlife Service handbook and pass.

In the north you come to the unique **Undara Volcanic National Park**. This park contains huge lava tubes that were formed 190 000 years ago when, during a series of volcanic eruptions, the molten lava from the Undara crater flowed along an old watercourse. As it flowed, the lava cooled and hardened along the base and sides of the watercourse and formed a roof overhead. The molten lava continued to flow through this natural tunnel until the eruption stopped. Then, like a tap being turned off, the lava continued flowing until all of it had passed out and the hollow tube was left. The lava tubes formed for some 60 km (37 m) of the 160-km (99-m) length of the lava flow. Some sections of the tube have since collapsed and these collapsed areas have become pockets where a type of rainforest has been able to grow. These patches of dark rainforest can seen from the air and highlight the wavy route the lava took as it flowed though the open woodland.

The only accommodation in the park is at the Undara Lodge, which offers motel-style rooms in old railway carriages, as well as camping areas. Tours to the lava tubes leave the Lodge throughout the day and are led by Savannah Guides who give an excellent interpretation of the plants, wildlife, the lava tubes and the history of the area. You reach the lava tubes down quite steep paths through the heavily vegetated collapsed areas. It is an eerie feeling to leave the hot outdoors and enter the tubes, which are cavernous and streaked in various shades of ochre, black, yellow and white. Nothing lives in them other than a few bats, and nothing grows inside them other than tiny patches of cave coral which are a build-up of mineral salts.

This is beautiful open savannah country with some tall granite peaks which you can climb for sweeping views, and numerous euros, kangaroos and birds. To reach the park, turn off at the sign on the Gulf Developmental Road, 275 km (171 m) southwest of Cairns.

South Australia

Through the southeast corner of South Australia flows the Murray River — the largest river system in Australia. This fertile corner of the state is where most of the population lives; elsewhere it is hot and dry and often barren.

Inland and north of Adelaide stretch the rugged Flinders and Gammon ranges where moist gorges support plant and wildlife and masses of wildflowers bloom in spring. Beyond these ranges lie the vast reaches of the Outback with shimmering plains, dried lakes and riverbeds, and occasional water holes. As you move further out you reach the arid terrain of the Great Victoria Desert and the Nullarbor Plain which spread into Western Australia, and the Simpson Desert which crosses the northern borders into the Northern Territory and Queensland.

South Australia has 16 national parks and more than 200 conservation areas and other reserves, encompassing nearly 20.2 million ha (49 915 287 a).

Camping and bush camping are allowed in most national parks, however, be aware that this is a very dry state and there will be times when a total fire ban will be in force. Also there is very little fallen wood for fuel away from the coast, and most of it is protected, so you should carry a gas or fuel stove. There is an entry fee to most parks and a special Desert Park Pass for the desert parks, which cover nearly 8 million ha (19 768 430 a) of the state (this is one of the largest arid region park systems in the world). The Pass costs $50 per vehicle for 12 months and can be purchased from National Parks and Wildlife Service offices, park visitors' centres and most shops and service stations in Outback towns.

The best time to visit the coastal parks is during the summer or autumn months when the winds coming off the cold Southern Ocean have less bite. The mountains are best visited during winter and spring when the temperatures are cooler and the wildflowers are in bloom. The desert parks should only be visited in winter.

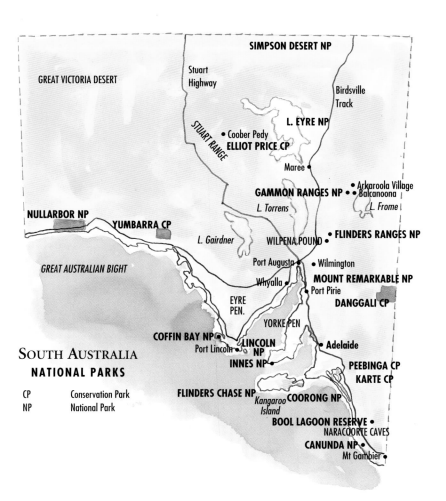

One of the great desert parks is the 1.2 million ha (2.9 million a) **Lake Eyre National Park**, 650 km (404 m) north of Adelaide. This is a huge 'salt sink' left by the evaporation of floodwaters over thousands of years. It has water in it about once every eight years, and has been full to capacity only three times over the past 150 years. Mostly the lake is dry and the landscape stark and sparsely vegetated. You should only come here if you are well prepared for a truly remote desert experience — some people fall in love with its stark beauty, but some are frightened by its size and apparent barrenness.

If you strike it lucky and arrive during or just after rain you will encounter a desert ablaze with colour. The ground will be covered in dense green foliage and ephemeral wildflowers of yellow, orange, pink and mauve will be spread out in patches of brilliant colour. The nectar and seeds of these flowers attract many insects, and all this abundance attracts flocks of birds, especially pelicans, silver gulls, avocets, banded stilts and gull-billed terns.

You can enter the park from a track about 7 km (4.3 m) southeast of William Creek (it is another 57 km (35 m) to the park boundary) or from Marree (94 km (58 m) from the boundary). Both townships have fuel and a Desert Parks Pass agency. To travel in the park you will need a four-wheel drive and must be totally self reliant as there are no services, designated camping areas or reliable water supplies. The only designated bush camping area is at Muloorina Bore on the road from Marree — ask for permission from the station owner at the homestead, use the water with care and do not disturb the stock.

Closer to Adelaide is the **Flinders Ranges National Park,** which rises from the parched plains like a ragged, red wall along a hazy horizon. The mountains of this 95 000 ha (234 750 a) park have many gorges and ancient geological features to explore, as well as a wealth of vegetation and wildlife. Its rugged charm makes it popular with bushwalkers but it has a harsh terrain and a hot, dry climate so you must travel well-supplied with water and good, sturdy footwear.

The best time to see wildflowers here is from July to October, although rain will produce unexpectedly brilliant displays at other times. You should be able to see the Sturt desert pea, South Australia's floral emblem; desert wattles; river red gums; Sturt's desert rose and many herbs. Red kangaroos and emus live on the plains and low hills, while euros (mountain kangaroos), lizards, snakes and yellow-footed rock wallabies (once hunted for their beautiful fur) live in the mountains and gorges. More than 100 species of birds have been identified, including corellas, mallee ringneck parrots, galahs, wedge-tailed eagles, pied butcherbirds, Australian kestrels, honeyeaters and pretty little blue and white wrens.

One of the outstanding features of the park is Wilpena Pound, a crater-like basin encircled by high cliffs. Wilpena is an Aboriginal word meaning 'bent fingers' and the Pound looks like a cupped hand. The open country of the central basin was farmed by the early settlers. The slopes are wooded and crossed with walking trails that lead to lookouts with breathtaking views. *Bushwalking in the Flinders Ranges* is a good guide to the park and is available from the park headquarters at Wilpena or the regional office at Hawker. A section of one of Australia's great long walks, the Heysen Trail, crosses the park from Black Gap in the south to Aroona in the north.

The entry road from Hawker is sealed as far as the campground at Wilpena. This is the main camping area but there are others within the park that can be reached by most vehicles. It is not necessary to make a booking to camp at Wilpena but it is necessary to book the motel units. Check with the rangers if it has been raining because some roads become boggy and impassable. Bush camping is allowed, although it is restricted during total fire bans. A camping fee applies. The best time to visit is during winter and spring (April to October).

Mount Remarkable National Park is at the southern end of the Flinders Ranges. It is wetter than the Flinders Ranges National Park and has a more dense vegetation with brilliant wildflowers in spring. The Mambray and Alligator creeks flow through gorges of white to reddish-brown quartzite and sandstone in an oval basin, somewhat similar to Wilpena Pound. The wildlife is abundant and there are excellent walking trails. A National Parks and Wildlife leaflet called 'Walking Trails in Mount Remarkable National Park' details some of the walks and is available from the ranger station at Mambray Creek.

The park can be divided into three sections: Alligator Gorge, Mambray Creek and Mount Remarkable, each reached by a different route. All sections have walking trails varying in duration from two hours to two days. The walking trail to the Mount Remarkable Summit is part of the Heysen Trail.

Alligator Gorge is in the northern part of the park and is reached from Wilmington. It is a day visitor area and a vehicle entry fee applies. Although there is no designated camping area here, bush camping is permitted. Mambray Creek is the main entrance and has an excellent camping area near the park headquarters. There is no entry fee but a camping fee does apply.

Bush camping areas have been established throughout the park and the rangers will give you a useful Bushcamping Guideline Sheet. There is a wood fire ban from 1 November to 30 April and it is advisable to carry water, which you can get from the picnic grounds at Mambray Creek and Alligator Gorge.

On the southern tip of Eyre Peninsula, southwest of Adelaide, are two ruggedly beautiful coastal parks — Coffin Bay and Lincoln. Both are quite rugged and most suitable for keen wilderness bushwalkers and four-wheel drive enthusiasts.

Coffin Bay National Park is large and wild, receiving the full fury of the Great Australian Bight on its western shore. It is a birder's paradise with 148 species of both shore and sea birds, including white-bellied sea eagles, osprey, albatross, petrels and shearwater along the coast, and several species of parrots and colourful lorikeets inland. Western grey kangaroos, bush rats, dunnarts, western pigmy possums, bats, lizards and snakes also live here. Avoid swimming near Point Avoid because the seal colony attracts the large and dangerous white pointer shark.

The park is 50 km (31 m) west of Port Lincoln and 2 km (1.2 m) west of Coffin Bay township, along a well signposted road. The ranger station at the entrance can supply you with information on the park's many

Koala

walking trails and camping areas and can issue camping permits. You will need to check at the ranger station if you are towing a caravan as some areas are only accessible by four-wheel drive and may be closed during wet weather. There are boat ramps at Coffin Bay and Point Avoid (four-wheel drive only).

The **Coorong National Park** is one of the Australia's most important wading bird breeding areas. It is isolated, undeveloped and quietly beautiful in the way that low landforms interspersed with arms of water can be — sometimes calm and reflective, at other times stormy and grey. The highway runs along the park's eastern border and most people rush by, not taking the time to branch off onto the dirt roads to visit the quiet bays and rocky outcrops that grace the shores of Coorong Lagoon.

The dramatic sand dunes of the Coorong National Park, South Australia

The park is a narrow strip of nearly 40 000 ha (98 842 a) running south from the mouth of the Murray River. There are two main areas to visit: the low-lying mainland section where many people camp, and the Coorong Lagoon which is home to thousands of pelicans, seagulls, black swans, Cape Barren geese, stilts, rare shoreline birds and many land birds. You see them not in singles or pairs but in huge flocks that darken the waters and fill the skies. The migratory species arrive in November and leave again in early April. Be careful if you go boating because it is very shallow and when windy becomes choppy and dangerous.

These two inland areas are protected from the worst of the Southern Ocean storms by Younghusband Peninsula, a long narrow (average 2 km (1.2 m) wide) strip of tall sand dunes and dense coastal scrubland. The Aboriginal people fished on the Peninsula and their middens are spread over the dune valleys in a white sheet of empty shells. When the European settlers arrived about 850 Aboriginal people lived on the peninsula but nowadays only emus, birds and occasional human visitors come here.

The narrowest point for a boat crossing to the Peninsula is Parnaka Point, or you can drive across at one of four crossings at the southern end of the lagoon. Check with the rangers because these may be closed at high tide and are not always suitable for standard vehicles. You will need a four-wheel-drive vehicle to drive along Younghusband Peninsula — or you can walk, which is the better way to experience the dunes.

The Ngarrindjeri people have a permanent base at Camp Coorong just south of Meningie, from where they run guided nature and cultural tours. The Camp has excellent dormitory accommodation for groups as well as self-contained cabins.

Camping is allowed throughout the park, although no camping areas have water or toilets. Caravan parks and other accommodation are available in the local townships of Meningie, Woods Well, Policemans Point and Kingston. Poltalloch, built in 1876, at the northern end of the park offers accommodation in charming, refurbished cottages. The former ranger station at Noonameena has self-contained accommodation for groups.

The main ranger station is at Meningie, but about 20 outlets (mostly local service stations) sell camping permits and can supply maps and information. The free *Coorong Tattler* is very informative and you should be able to pick up a copy quite easily.

On the western tip of Kangaroo Island is **Flinders Chase National Park**, a 74 000 ha (182 858 a) gem with many facets — open spaces, sculptured boulders of uncommon beauty, steep cliffs and rocky outcrops pounded by raging southern seas, dense low vegetation that hides hundreds of birds and little mammals, sandy beaches, old lighthouses, gliding osprey and sheltered camping areas.

The park has wonderful coastal walks and abundant wildlife, including kangaroos, tammar wallabies, possums, bandicoots, koalas, goannas, snakes, seals and 120 species of birds. At Rocky River picnic and camping area wallabies, kangaroos, two emus and Cape Barren geese come to your table with pleading eyes. This is an example of where wild animals have been fed until they are totally dependent on human hand-outs. Park authorities want to phase out the feeding, but a whole generation has lived this way and would not know how to survive. To prevent further harm, the rangers sell special pellets suitable for the animals' digestive systems.

The Remarkable Rocks at Kirkpatrick Point are an outstanding example of how nature can outperform humans at art. The gigantic rocks have been sculptured over aeons by wind and rain eroding their soft areas to create cavernous hollows, narrow walk-throughs, menacing overhangs and flat faces gouged with hollows until they look like Emmental cheese. To add to the drama, the rocks are piled upon a smooth hump of granite that overlooks the ocean at the end of a long cliff. And finally, red ironstone and yellow-orange lichen have spread over the surfaces to add a touch of colour to the whole design.

There are marked walking trails and picnic areas throughout the park. Camping areas are provided at Rocky River, Harvey's Return, Snake Lagoon and West Bay. Historic accommodation is available at Rocky River in the Old Homestead (sleeps six) and Postman's Cottage (sleeps four), and in original lighthouse keepers' cottages at Cape du Couedic and Cape Borda. The entry fee to the park and accommodation bookings can be made at park headquarters at the Rocky River entrance.

However, you would not come to Kangaroo Island just to visit one park. The whole island is delightful with many parks, reserves, beaches and rocky outcrops. It separated from the mainland 10 000 years ago and is still the quite domain of 4300 people who live a healthy rural lifestyle that is the envy of all who visit. For example, you would not come to the island without visiting the sea lions at Seal Bay on the south coast. This is one of the few places in the country where they come ashore and can be seen at such close range. Nor would you fail to spend an evening on one of the shores watching the little penguins come ashore.

Experienced walkers could take a wilderness walk through Cape Gantheaume Conservation Park. Start at one end, say Bales Bay, and follow the coast past spectacular cliffs, caves, coves, rock platforms and tightly packed, low vegetation to D'Estrees Bay. At the northern end of the park is Murray Lagoon, home to hundreds of water birds such as black swans, chestnut teals, Australian grey teals, egrets and spoonbills.

You reach Kangaroo Island by air or coach from Adelaide, or by car ferry from Cape Jervis (one-and-a-half hours from Adelaide) or Port Adelaide. The island is 150 km (93 m) long, 50 km (31 m) wide and has 1600 km (994 m) of roads, most of which are not sealed. You must

pay a camping fee for all designated camping sites but if you are intending to be on the island for a few days, you can buy an Island Pass which entitles you to free entry into Flinders Chase National Park and to all National Park and Wildlife tours.

Tourism is a major industry, so the island has plenty of good accommodation and some excellent tour operators. Kate Stanton conducts a one- to two-hour bushwalk through land owned by her family. She grew up here and will show you many rare and endemic plants, orchids, snotty gobble, centuries old yaccas (similar to a blackboy or grasstree), kangaroos, tammar wallabies, echidnas, birds, koalas and yabbies that live in and along the creek.

Tom and Liz Bettess gave up sheep farming to run Kangaroo Island Wilderness Tours and Wedgwood Host Farm. Tom knows all the island's beauty spots and most of its secrets, and Liz provides the warm country hospitality and meals one dreams of.

Craig Wickham, a former National Parks and Wildlife ranger, owns Adventure Charters of Kangaroo Island and he — or one of his guides — give a knowledgeable interpretation of the flora, fauna and social aspects of island living.

Anna Howard, a fourth-generation islander, operates Australian Odysseys and offers one- to six-day tours with accommodation in cottages, motels or camping. She also offers the visually impaired a unique experience of the island through the senses of taste, touch, scent and sound.

Tasmania

Tasmania is an island state — roughly the size of Switzerland and a littler larger than West Virginia in the United States — lying 240 km (149 m) off the south coast of Australia. Its landscapes are widely varied, rising gradually in some areas from clean, white, sandy beaches and in others from dramatic coastal cliffs. It is renowned for its spectacular wilderness areas and wild rivers, which draw people from around the world to experience its remoteness, to walk its tracks, to ride its rivers and to photograph its stark splendour. Steeply wooded hillsides, plateaus covered in bog and low, dense shrubs, crater lakes and jagged mountains that disappear into soft grey clouds are a magnet to bushwalkers. Yet it is not all wilderness. There are many areas of gently rolling farmland dotted with historic homes and old stone bridges. Long sandy beaches and coastal waters abound with fish and shipwrecks and its tall forests are acclaimed for their magnificence.

The climate has four distinct seasons, but it can change rapidly and unseasonably. The most attractive seasons are spring when the wildflowers bloom, and autumn when the leaves change colour, but summer is the best time to visit. Winter can be cold with snow and low-hanging clouds.

Because Tasmania is compact, with light traffic and a small population (less than 500 000), it is easy to travel around by car or bicycle and both can be hired in main cities and towns. Scenic flights are also popular, especially for day trips over and into wilderness areas. Most of the state's national parks have designated camping areas and allow bush camping. There is an entry fee to each park, however, there are multi-day passes available which offer a worthwhile saving.

About 30% of the state is protected by a World Heritage listing or is designated as some form of conservation park or reserve. Nearly 1.4 million ha (3½ million a) (more than one-fifth of the island) is World Heritage listed, encompassing three of the state's most spectacular national parks: **Cradle Mountain–Lake St Clair National Park, Franklin–Gordon Wild Rivers National Park** and **Southwest National Park**. (see World Heritage Areas, page 13). One of this country's most famous fights to save the environment was the battle to stop the damming of the Gordon River during the late 1970s and early 1980s. It was argued that the dam would flood the Gordon and Franklin rivers, hectares of virgin bush and caves full of Aboriginal artefacts. The fight was long and bitter, but successful.

Tasmania's northwest coast features lovely capes, headlands and beaches, safe for swimming and diving. **Rocky Cape National Park**, about two-hours' drive west of Devonport has wonderful wave-shaped caves that contain traces of early Aboriginal activity. The park's varied and unique heath vegetation makes it a popular nature study area and the woodlands have many different bird species and wildflowers in spring. There are reefs off the beaches and the sheltered bays are good for swimming and boating. There are picnic areas but no camping facilities. Motel accommodation and camping areas are available at Boat Harbour nearby.

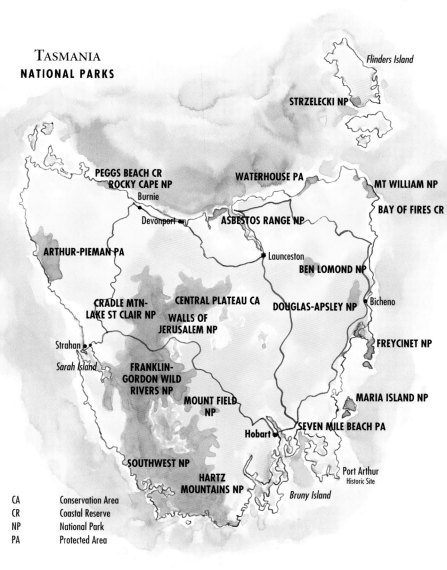

TASMANIA
NATIONAL PARKS

Flinders Island

STRZELECKI NP

PEGGS BEACH CR
ROCKY CAPE NP
Burnie

WATERHOUSE PA

MT WILLIAM NP

BAY OF FIRES CR

Devonport

ASBESTOS RANGE NP

ARTHUR-PIEMAN PA

Launceston

BEN LOMOND NP

CRADLE MTN-
LAKE ST CLAIR NP

CENTRAL PLATEAU CA

WALLS OF
JERUSALEM NP

DOUGLAS-APSLEY NP

Bicheno

Strahan

Sarah Island

FREYCINET NP

FRANKLIN-
GORDON WILD
RIVERS NP

MOUNT FIELD
NP

MARIA ISLAND NP

Hobart

SEVEN MILE BEACH PA

SOUTHWEST NP

HARTZ
MOUNTAINS NP

Bruny Island

Port Arthur
Historic Site

CA	Conservation Area
CR	Coastal Reserve
NP	National Park
PA	Protected Area

Freycinet National Park is a spectacular peninsula about halfway along the east coast. A ridge of granite hills known as the Hazards gives the peninsula a rugged, isolated appearance and it is popular with bushwalkers who take off down its arm, camping beside the clear, clean waters that lap its sandy bays. The peninsula's climate is slightly warmer and has less rainfall than the rest of the state, which has made it a popular holiday spot since the beginning of the century.

There are a number of walking trails, the most popular — and a must if you haven't been here before — is the winding, half-hour climb up numerous steps to the lookout in the saddle between Mount Amos and Mount Mayson. From here you can see in all directions, but the main reason for doing this climb is to gaze down upon Wineglass Bay, the most idyllic of beaches, with not a building in sight. Its long, half-moon sweep of white sand gently separates the frothy white waves from the deep green of the surrounding hills. A path from the lookout leads down to the Bay and returns to the carpark via Isthmus Track and Hazards Beach Track (about 10 km (6.2 m)). Take your swimsuit — the water is crystal clear and tempting after a hot walk.

Bush camping is allowed within the park although the rangers like you to use the areas where pit toilets have been placed. Within the park there are designated beachfront camping areas and Freycinet Lodge offers high-quality cabin accommodation and a central lodge with restaurant and bar. A four-wheel-drive track leads to the lighthouse at Cape Tourville which has stunning coastal views and you can camp among the trees.

Just before you enter the park you come to Coles Bay, a charming waterfront town with a permanent population of three hundred. It has camping areas, motel, self-contained villas, a store, fuel and a boat ramp. The ranger station is located on the only entrance road. If it is closed, there is an information booth near the entrance to the park and another before you enter Coles Bay.

Mount Field National Park is only an hour's drive from Hobart, which makes it a popular retreat for the city's residents. It has some of the finest tall forest and alpine scenery in the state. The park's ancient rocks were worn and weathered during the last ice age, forming calm glacial lakes and pools and deep gullies where dense forests and dripping ferns fringe cold water streams and spectacular waterfalls. At the entrance there is a camping area, kiosk, visitor centre, youth hostel, pub and ranger station. From the car park it is about five minute's walk along a sealed track (suitable for wheelchairs) to Russell Falls, which sprays over layers of rock in two stages. There are several other easy walks from the car park or a two-hour walk that links them all.

To visit the higher alpine areas continue on along Lake Dobson Road for another 16 km (10 m) to Lake Dobson car park and shelter. As you drive the vegetation will change from tall forests to the shorter, more hardy, alpine bushes and moorlands. From here you can do the Pandani Grove Nature Walk (one hour return), which passes along the lake's edge and through groves of ancient pencil pine and tall pandani. Longer walks go past glacial lakes, across open moorland and provide panoramic views. Serious walkers can go to the top of Mount Field West, the highest peak in the park, which takes about eight hours return.

Hikers planning to stay overnight will find some huts along these walks but these cannot be booked so it is wise to carry a tent in case they are full. Three government huts accommodating six people each are about a 500 m (547 yd) walk from the car park and can be booked in advance.

Maria Island National Park is reached by ferry from Triabunna and Louisville Point, a little more than an hour northeast of Hobart. Maria Island's history has gone from peace to turbulence and back to peace. Its first visitors were the Aboriginal people who left it as they found it. Then came the Europeans who established a penal colony and a cement works (the ruins of both are interesting to explore).

Today the island is a sanctuary where endangered plant and animal species have been introduced to build up their numbers. Forester kangaroos, Bennetts wallabies, Cape Barren geese, emus and native hens have been introduced to the island. Mostly they live in peace with the native pademelon and the forty-spotted pardalote, although the kangaroos

have thrived so well that they are now a bit of a problem. Some of the waters are marine reserves where you can snorkel and scuba dive, but not fish. There are also the Fossil Cliffs and Painted Cliffs to visit, and longer walks can be taken to the mountains and the little-visited southern parts of the island.

The information centre near the jetty will supply maps and information. Basic bunk-room accommodation is available in the old penitentiary at Darlington. Camping is allowed at Darlington or take the three to four-hour walk to French's Farm and Encampment Cove and camp there. There is a park entry fee and camping fees.

Victoria

Victoria is the most southern mainland state and the most populous. It has an interestingly diverse landscape containing alpine areas, deserts, rolling farmlands, forested foothills and a spectacular coastline. For all this diversity it is a compact state and you can easily see a variety of landscapes in just a few days of driving. About 12% of the state is protected within its 32 national parks and other reserves.

The Victorian coastline varies from spectacular jagged outcrops that have caused the death of many fine sailing ships, to stretches of golden sand and quiet inlets that are a sanctuary for wading birds.

Port Campbell National Park lies between Princetown and Peterborough along the Great Ocean

Road, southwest of Melbourne. This road is considered to be the most spectacular and dramatic coastal road in the country. It is a rugged coast of steep limestone cliffs which have been sculptured by stormy seas and weathered into caves, gorges and the famous formations: the Twelve Apostles, Loch Ard Gorge and London Bridge. Many ships lie here — historic reminders of the rough seas and journeys which ended in tragedy.

Camping and accommodation are available at Princetown, Peterborough and Port Campbell (you need to book camping sites during peak holiday times). The park ranger's office is at Port Campbell, which is located 249 km (155 m) west of Melbourne and is about the centre of the park. There is no park entry fee.

By contrast, **The Lakes National Park** is within a vast inland system of rivers, lakes, lagoons and islands which have gentle waters suitable for canoeing, sailing, fishing, swimming and birdwatching. This 2390 ha (5906 a) park is separated from the sea by a long, narrow strip of secluded coastline known as Ninety Mile Beach. The park is set on Sperm Whale Head, which has a large population of kangaroos and more than 140 native bird species. It lies 330 km (205 m) east of Melbourne and there is no entry fee. It has a basic camping area, or you can stay at nearby Rotamah Island Bird Observatory on the shores of Lake Victoria. The Observatory offers basic accommodation and special

programs for nature lovers (see Birdwatching, page 108).

About an hour's drive north of Melbourne you come to the Great Dividing Range, which stretches all the way to north Queensland. The romance of these mountains and the cattlemen on their sturdy mountain ponies was told to the world through the movie *The Man From Snowy River*. In summer, wildflowers cover the countryside and in winter, deep snow softens the ridges.

At one time the high country was

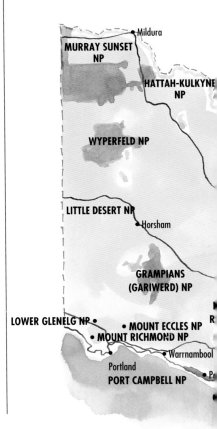

protected by a number of different national parks and reserves, but in 1989 these were merged and became the **Alpine National Park.** This immense and breathtaking 646 000 ha (1 596 300 a) of alpine reserve comprises the area from central Gippsland to the New South Wales border and beyond. It is a fantastic area for nature and adventure holidays offering walking, bush camping, car touring, four-wheel driving, cross-country skiing, horse riding, fishing, canoeing, wildflowers and more. The Department of Conservation & Environment has produced an informative guide entitled *Into the High Country,* which can be bought from its offices in local townships.

A good range of nature and adventure tours are offered into the high country by tour companies in the area, or from Melbourne. Bush camping is allowed in the park or you can stay at a camping area or in accommodation in any of the local towns. Ski resorts stay open during summer and provide comfortable lodge accommodation. There is no entry fee into the park.

Mount Buffalo National Park, about four hours' drive northeast of Melbourne, is one of the city's favourite parks for winter skiing and summer walking. It offers 90 km (56 m) of well-marked walking trails with spectacular views, dancing waterfalls and glorious wildflowers from November to March. The park has some 400 species of plants, most of which have adapted to the sub-alpine conditions. It is also known for its challenging rock climbs and has been a site for World Championship hang-gliding.

Map: **VICTORIA NATIONAL PARKS**

Echuca • — Wodonga — River
BURROWA PINE MOUNTAIN NP
• Bendigo — MOUNT BUFFALO NP
FRASER NP — ALPINE NP — SNOWY RIVER NP
ORGAN PIPES NP — • KINGLAKE NP — • ERRINUNDRA NP
urat — • COOPRACAMBRA NP
Orbost
HURCHILL NP — Melbourne • BAW BAW NP
DANDENONG RANGES NP — CROAJINGOLONG NP
THE LAKES NP
• MORWELL NP
OINT NEPEAN NP — • TARA-BULGA NP
WILSONS PROMONTORY NP
ASS — STRAIT

There is an entry fee into the park and basic camping facilities are provided at Lake Catani. It is open November to May and is often heavily booked so you need to reserve a site. Motel and lodge accommodation is available at Tatra Inn and guesthouse accommodation is available at the Chalet. Both places provide a range of activities and information on the park, or you can call in at the park office, which is normally open on weekdays. Lake Catani is good for fishing, swimming and canoeing.

The Grampians National Park, 260 km (161 m) west of Melbourne, rises out of the west Victorian farmlands as an oasis of green hillsides and deeply etched gorges. This weathered mass of sandstone is considered to be the westernmost outlier of the Great Dividing Range. The vegetation is rich and varied, with heaths on the plateaus, eucalypt forests and woodlands on the slopes, and streams, lakes and waterfalls in the valleys. It has 900 native plant species, enough to keep the botanists happy for many days. More than 160 km (99 m) of well-maintained walking tracks offer everything from a short stroll to long treks requiring overnight camps. Most of the park and many picnic areas can be reached by car and there are some very scenic drives.

Most of the state's rock art is found here and can be seen on a guided tour or by following well-marked walking trails. The largest single overhang, with more than 2000 Aboriginal motifs, is at Billimina shelter. Brambuk Cultural Centre at Halls Gap has displays of the cultural heritage of the five Aboriginal communities of the region.

The best time to visit the Grampians is during spring or late summer; winter can be cold and wet and midsummer hot and dry. Accommodation is available at Halls Gap and other regional towns. There are good camping areas in the park, for which there is a small fee, however, these cannot be booked ahead and unfortunately it is first in, first served. Bush camping is allowed and park entry is free. The visitors' centre on Grampians Road, south of Halls Gap, has information, maps and displays.

Wilsons Promontory National Park — the Prom — 250 km (155 m) southeast of Melbourne, is a favourite with Victorians. Although thousands of people come here, the Prom's rugged ranges and 130 km (81 m) coastline allow plenty of room for a peaceful picnic or a solitary walk. The park has numerous walking trails and self-guided nature walks, which range from a short amble to a four-day trek with camping. The vegetation includes fern gullies, salt marshes, tall forests, rainforest and heathlands. This diverse range of vegetation provides habitats for a wide variety of birds and other wildlife.

Around the coast, big granite boulders border sheltered inlets and coves and are a photographer's delight. Marine reserves around the coast protect these waters and provide good snorkelling, sailing and scuba diving. Fishing is allowed, but check with the rangers first for there are some restrictions.

You enter the park across Yanakie Isthmus, a sandy bar which joins the Promontory to the mainland (there is an entry fee). Thirty-two kilometres (20 m) into the park you come to Tidal River, which has camping, accommodation, food and fuel (not LPG) and a comprehensive visitors' centre with displays, audiovisuals, maps and publications. Do not rush this drive because it has some spectacular views, walking tracks and picnic spots along the way.

Bush camping is allowed at defined sites within the park and you will need a permit if you wish to camp away from Tidal River. Tidal River is booked out long before holiday periods, so if you are planning to stay here you would be wise to book early.

Croajingolong National Park in the far eastern reaches of the Victorian coast runs for 100 km (62 m), from Sydenham Inlet to the New South Wales border. It is cut by many creeks, which tumble through steep forested slopes and across low coastal plains to the ocean. The coastline is constantly being transformed by moving sand dunes which create inlets and estuaries that are then destroyed by the next big storm.

A variety of landforms and a mild climate have endowed this park with a vast array of vegetation which in turn supports a diverse wildlife, making this a fabulous haunt for naturalists. Australian fur seals and little penguins share the coast and offshore islands with thousands of sea birds. Further inland, the forests are home to kangaroos, possums, lyrebirds, kookaburras and the interesting whipbird, which ends its whistle in a distinctive whipcrack note.

There are two designated wilderness areas in the park: Sandpatch (15 600 ha (38 548 a)) and Cape Howe (7100 ha (17 544 a)). Both offer self-reliant visitors an opportunity to see nature at its undisturbed best.

The park is popular for camping, picnicking, walking, boating, fishing, swimming and for just doing nothing. Sometimes the roads are affected by bad weather and there is no drinking water at some picnic sites so check both these points with the rangers before venturing out. Park information centres are at Cann River and Mallacoota. Basic campsites are provided at Wingan River, Shipwreck Creek, Tamboon Inlet, Thurra River and Mueller River. There is no park entry fee but a small fee for camping and you need to book during school holidays.

For visitors to Melbourne with only a little time to spare there are two excellent national parks that can be visited easily in a day.

The **Dandenong Ranges National Park** is easily reached by car, or you can take the train to Upper Ferntree Gully and walk to a forested picnic spot from there. Mountain ash forests, eucalypt woodlands and fern-filled gullies provide interesting and varied walks and scenic drives. There is an entrance fee into parts of the park and camping is not allowed. While here you can combine your enjoyment of nature with a browse through the tiny townships and the many arts and craft centres and antique shops. And you can rest a while at any one of several historic homes, now teahouses serving country-style lunches and afternoon teas.

The **Brisbane Ranges National Park,** a short drive west of Melbourne, is renowned for its flora and wildflowers. Many of the park's 475 plant species are either rare or remote from their normal localities. The flora is interesting throughout the year but if it is wildflowers you want to see, then visit the park from August to November. Koalas were once present only in small numbers, but restocking has lead to an abundance and you can be sure of seeing these sleepy creatures curled up high in the trees. And, while looking up into the trees, take note of the birds — more than 170 species of native birds have been identified in the park. Those of particular interest to birdwatchers are the yellow-tufted honeyeater, white-throated nightjar and rainbow bee-eater.

In the 1850s and 1860s gold was found in the Ranges and the rush was on. After it was over, the town of Steiglitz, once home to 600 miners, died and has been turned into a historic park adjoining the national park. Many of the old buildings are gone and the mines filled, but it is interesting to visit, and the old courthouse, which is open Sundays and public holidays, has a display of old photographs of Steiglitz.

Entry to the national park is free. There is a camping area at Boar Gully and information on this as well as walks, picnic sites and other features of the park can be obtained from the park office at Anakie.

The northwest of Victoria is semi-arid and the vegetation is vastly different to that of the high country. This is mallee country, where low eucalypt trees flourish, the malleefowl builds its nesting mound in the sand, and wildflowers and birds arrive in their thousands after rain. At night the air is so clear the stars seem to jump out of the sky. The wildlife includes emus, western grey kangaroos, lizards, goannas and many species of birds. The three main mallee parks are Wyperfeld, Murray–Sunset and Hattah–Kulkyne.

Wyperfeld National Park, 450 km (280 m) northwest of Melbourne is the state's third largest national park covering 356 800 ha (881 672 a) of normally dry lakes and mallee in the eastern section, and rolling sand plains in the west. It has 450 species of plants native to the area and is a bird-watcher's delight, with more than 200 species, including sulphur-crested cockatoos, mallee ringneck parrots, galahs, red-rumped parrots, variegated fairy-wrens and red-capped robins. Other wildlife includes western grey kangaroos, stumpy-tail lizards and sand goannas. You can walk, cycle, drive and camp in the park. However, you will need a four-wheel-

Sulphur-crested cockatoo

A bush camp

drive vehicle to access the wilderness areas in the west and the tracks may be impassable if it has rained.

Collect information and maps at the information centre near the southern entrance or at the ranger station at Yaapeet; there is no entry fee. The main camping area is in the south of the park and there are two basic camping areas in the north. Because there is so little water in the region, none of the camping areas have showers and you must carry your own drinking water if you intend driving off sealed roads. Supplies and accommodation are available at Hopetoun and Rainbow near the southern entrance, and Patchewollock in the north.

The 633 000 ha (1 564 177 a) **Murray–Sunset National Park** is less developed than Wyperfeld and you will need to be well equipped to venture far. It has only a small camping area with basic facilities. The nearest ranger stations for information are at Mildura and Ouyen. However, for the adventurous it has vast open spaces, pink salt lakes, spring wildflowers and all the pleasures of camping far from city lights and other people.

Western Australia

No other state combines so many contrasts and so much that is unique. Cut off from the rest of Australia by a vast desert the flora and fauna has developed in isolation, sometimes changing to survive the environment and very often unaffected by changes elsewhere in the country. Even within the state there is a great variety of landforms and environments. Its long coastline extends for 12 500 km (7767 m) from the cool climes of the south where the land is fertile and most of the population lives, to the hot, barren, tropical regions of the Kimberley in the north. Most of the eastern side of the state is desert, and a band of desert stretching across to the coast forms a natural barrier between the Kimberley and the central and southern regions. Travelling here entails long distances through sparsely populated areas. However, the state is magic and the sights you will see will dwell in your memory forever.

In the north you will find the mysterious Bungle Bungle mounds, 12 m (39 ft) tides that crash and boil across reefs, the remains of an ancient coral reef and chasms lacerated by raging rivers in the wet and parched during the dry. In the centre, calm beaches, friendly wild dolphins and whale sharks on the coast and deep gorges with rocks dating back 2000 million years, arid ranges and lush vegetation around spring-fed water holes and occasional rivers further inland. In the south, forests of karri and jarrah rising to 80 m (262 ft), a beautiful coast with beaches, bays and sand dunes, and wildflowers galore — blankets of them extending as far as the eye can see.

Western Australia is rated as one of the best places in the world to see wildflowers. Of its 12 000 flowering plant species some two-thirds are endemic (see Wildflowers, page 118). The best national parks to visit during spring to see wildflowers are: **John Forrest National Park** and **Kalamunda National Park**, both 25 km (15½ m) east of Perth; **Moore River National Park, Badgingarra National Park, Watheroo National Park, Alexander Morrison National Park, Tathra National Park** which are, respectively, from 120 to 300 km (74 to 186 m) north of Perth; and **Stirling Range National Park**, 450 km (280 m) southeast of Perth.

Travelling by land to Western Australia is an adventure in itself. From the southeast you cross the monotonous Nullarbor Plain, which takes about three days from Adelaide. From the north, you cross from Darwin to Kununurra through semi-arid terrain. Travelling north and south within the state is also quite a journey — Kununurra is 3214 km (1997 m) northeast of Perth. If travelling in the northern regions you will need a four-wheel drive if you plan to leave the main highways. Also carry your own water and a gas or fuel stove because both water and wood fuel are in very short supply.

Western Australia has 63 national parks covering 5.1 million ha (12.5 million a). In total, 20.1 million ha (49 million a) (7.5%) of the state is protected by various parks and reserves and another 1.1 million ha (2¾ million a) is part of marine reserves.

Perth is a beautiful city with the Swan River wandering through its centre and five national parks within a 25 km (15½ m) radius. Literally within the city suburbs is the **John Forrest National Park**, a nature haven with many lovely walks. The walks pass jarrah forest, open woodland, waterfalls and streams. A pool has been created by a dam across Jane Brook and facilities have been erected for swimmers and picnickers. This is one of the areas closest to Perth to see wildflowers, which are at their best from July to October.

One of the great natural attractions of the southwest is its magnificent trees — great stands of karri, jarrah and marri. Sadly, their grand height was no defence against the European thirst for timber and millions have been lost to the saw and are still falling. However, there is today a greater appreciation of the need to preserve some of these trees and many of the timber towns are benefiting from their tourist value.

The gateway to the timber county is Manjimup, 304 km (189 m) south of Perth. It has a timber museum and a timber park with tours of the mill and surrounding bush. Further south is Pemberton, which has a replica of a 1907 tram that does a scenic run through the forests, crossing rivers and rustic wooden bridges. Numerous parks and reserves protect the tall forests in this region. Enquire at the local tourist offices for information on drives, walks, picnic and camping areas.

Warren National Park, near Pemberton, is a small, easily accessible park of virgin karri forest. You can drive through the park but you should allow time to stop and walk around to enable you to feel the greatness of these giants and to see the tiny flora and fauna that lives within their shadow. Some of the trees are estimated to be 400 years old and some reach an amazing 89 m (292 ft) in height. The park has delightful picnic and camping areas and the Warren River is good for swimming, canoeing and trout fishing.

Further south, the giant trees meet the ocean and tower above lovely bays and protected inlets. Here the **D'Entrecasteaux National Park** and the **Walpole–Nornalup National Park** have been established to protect the trees and abundant wildlife and flora. Walpole–Nornalup National Park covers 18 000 ha (44 479 a) of diverse terrain, including karri forests, coastal cliffs, solitary beaches, heathlands, scrubland, rivers for canoeing and the Nuyts Wilderness Area. The birdlife changes from sea birds, such as pelicans, waders and black swans along the coast, to a host of small colourful inland birds that flit below the forest canopy.

The best time to visit is during spring and summer when the wildflowers are out and there is little rain. This is also the best time for canoeing. The park ranger's office is at Crystal Spring and there is a designated camping area here, as well as a privately managed camping/caravan area at Coalmine Beach. There is no fee to enter the park but a fee for camping.

North of Perth is the Pinnacles Desert in the **Nambung National Park**. Scattered across the sands, the Pinnacles look like tombstones or pieces of debris scattered from outer space. They are, in fact, limestone pillars formed by erosion over aeons. They are the main reason to visit this park although the beach provides good fishing and swimming. The wildflowers bloom in September.

You enter the park near Cervantes, 245 km (152 m) north of Perth, along a road that is not suitable for caravans. From the carpark you can take the 500 m (547 yd) walking trail, which loops through the Pinnacles. Camping is not permitted but there is accommodation at Cervantes, and while in Cervantes call into the Department of Conservation and Land Management (CALM) office for park information. Picnic areas have been set up at Kangaroo Point and Hangover Bay on the coast but there is no drinking water so you should take your own.

About 1400 km (870 m) north of Perth you come to the **Karijini (Hamersley Range) National Park**, which, at 6 million ha (14¾ million a) the second largest park in the state. The southern section is not easily accessed and has no walking trails or facilities for camping, however, the north has enough precipitous gorges, rock pools, plunging waterfalls, plateaus, plants and wildlife to fill in many hours of walking. Trails with spectacular views range from easy, to long and difficult and recommended only for experienced walkers.

This is an old part of the world with some rocks estimated to be about 2000 million years old. The vegetation on the arid plateaus is mostly spinifex and eucalypt, but the lower areas have mulga woodlands and wildflowers, which bloom in a profusion of yellow-flowering sennas (cassias), acacias, northern bluebells and purple mulla-mullas. The best wildflower displays happen immediately after rain. The best time to visit is winter and spring when there is less likelihood of heavy rainstorms and the days are warm and clear. However, the nights can be cold so take some warm clothing.

The park can be entered from the west, east and north. The western entry is from Tom Price Road onto the Marandoo Road (sealed), or from the Nanutarra Wittenoom Road onto the Hamersley Mount Bruce Road (unsealed). The eastern entry is from the Great Northern Highway onto Packsaddle Road (unsealed). The northern entry is from the north through Yampire Gorge from the Roy Hill Wittenoom Road. Camping areas are located in the north, at Fortescue to the west and Joffre to the east. Bush camping is not encouraged. Information is available at camping areas, the starting points of walking trails, the ranger station and the new seasonal visitors' centre, north of the Falls Road and Juna Road intersection. The visitors' centre is staffed by the Karijini Aboriginal Corporation and provides park and cultural information to visitors.

Northwest from Karijini is the 200 000 ha (494 211 a) **Millstream–**

Chichester National Park, which has a landscape of rolling spinifex hills, spectacular escarpments and winding tree-lined watercourses. The lush oasis of the Millstream wetlands is fed by the aquifer of the Fortescue River catchment. Millstream offers shady camping areas at Deep Reach, Crossing Pool and Snake Creek. The deep pools are an ideal place to swim, walk and relax. Information is available from the Millstream Homestead, built in 1920 and now the visitors' centre.

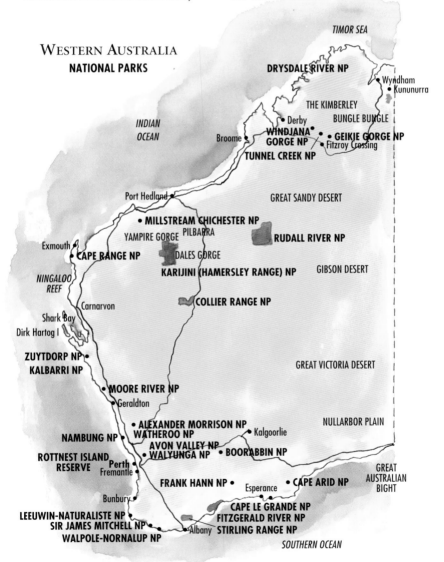

WESTERN AUSTRALIA
NATIONAL PARKS

TIMOR SEA

INDIAN OCEAN

DRYSDALE RIVER NP

Wyndham
Kununurra

THE KIMBERLEY
BUNGLE BUNGLE

Derby
Broome
WINDJANA GORGE NP
GEIKIE GORGE NP
Fitzroy Crossing
TUNNEL CREEK NP

Port Hedland

GREAT SANDY DESERT

MILLSTREAM CHICHESTER NP
YAMPIRE GORGE
PILBARRA
RUDALL RIVER NP

Exmouth
CAPE RANGE NP
DALES GORGE
KARIJINI (HAMERSLEY RANGE) NP
GIBSON DESERT

NINGALOO REEF

Carnarvon
COLLIER RANGE NP

Shark Bay
Dirk Hartog I

ZUYTDORP NP
KALBARRI NP

GREAT VICTORIA DESERT

MOORE RIVER NP
Geraldton

ALEXANDER MORRISON NP
WATHEROO NP
NULLARBOR PLAIN

NAMBUNG NP
Kalgoorlie
AVON VALLEY NP
WALYUNGA NP
BOORABBIN NP

ROTTNEST ISLAND RESERVE
Perth
Fremantle

FRANK HANN NP
Esperance
CAPE ARID NP
GREAT AUSTRALIAN BIGHT

Bunbury

LEEUWIN-NATURALISTE NP
SIR JAMES MITCHELL NP
WALPOLE-NORNALUP NP
Albany
CAPE LE GRANDE NP
FITZGERALD RIVER NP
STIRLING RANGE NP

SOUTHERN OCEAN

STEPPING LIGHTLY ON AUSTRALIA

The Kimberley region provides a totally different experience. Here the tropical heat, the extremes between the wet and dry seasons, the unfamiliar vegetation and the isolation broke the heart of many an early settler. Even today you need a reliable four-wheel drive, a good supply of water and fuel and a stout constitution. However, it is an awesome area and its power and mystery will enthral you.

Deeply carved gorges, plateaus, pools of crystal-clear water, towering cliffs embedded with fossilised ancient marine life, open savannah woodland, deserts, pockets of rainforest, drought and flood — this is the Kimberley. And the coast is just as dramatic, with intimidating tides of terrible power that often exceed 8 m (26 ft) and reach up to 10 m (33 ft) during the equinox.

There is evidence that the Aboriginal people lived or visited this region as long as 20 000 years ago. Now, local communities work with the state government to develop tourism that is both environmentally sensitive and culturally inspiring.

The Kimberley region covers an area of 320 000 km^2 (123 553 m^2). In the south is the old pearling town of Broome, now a beachside resort with good facilities. In the north is Kununurra, a modern tropical town surrounded by irrigated farmland. South of Kununurra is man-made Lake Argyle, which holds nine times the volume of Sydney Harbour and is home to some 25 000 freshwater crocodiles. Near here is the Argyle Diamond Mine with one of the world's largest deposit of diamonds

— this is a region of surprises.

Derby in the west, and Kununurra are good base towns to stock up on supplies and collect maps and information, or to join a commercial tour. Slingair has a selection of charter flights in small aeroplanes and helicopters for people in a hurry. But, although the countryside is spectacular from the air, you can only get to know it by walking on the ground.

The **Purnululu (Bungle Bungle) National Park** is strange and quite unique. The park covers 3000 km^2 (1158 m^2) but the main attraction is the Bungle Bungle massif, estimated to be 360 million years old and covering 45 000 ha (111 197 a).

The Bungle Bungle domes (sometimes described as beehives) are mounds of sandstone, which rise tall and naked except for the encircling stripes of black lichen and orange silica. The lichen and silica form a hard outer rim that protects the soft sandstone inside. If the edge is damaged, the soft sandstone will crumble and the whole formation will gradually erode. This is why you must not clamber over the domes.

Between the mounds lives a diversity of vegetation, including the Bungle Bungle fan palm. There are also a few water holes which, in the dry winter season, shrink to dark pools of doubtful quality. When I was at the water hole in Cathedral Gorge along the Piccaninny Creek walk, it was covered in a green slime and, although I was told the slime was harmless, I chose not to swim. However, another person in my group did and suffered no ill effects. The rock formations along this walk are spectacular and you will be tempted to explore other gorges which branch off from the walking trail. Allow an hour each way without any side trips. Remember to take drinking water for the creek is dry and the heat intense.

On the walk to Frog Hole you have to climb over, and squeeze around, large rocks but it is well worthwhile. Some of the Livistona Palms growing here are more than 200 years old and thousands of tiny frogs live in the water hole.

The entrance to the park is off the Great Northern Highway, 250 km (155 m) south of Kununurra, or 109 km (68 m) north of Halls Creek. The roads in the park are unsealed and only suitable for four-wheel-drive vehicles without caravans. Camping is allowed and there is a self-registration fee collection centre at the ranger base near Three Ways Track. The best time to visit is from May to September and the park is closed from January to March. You should collect maps and information on road conditions from CALM offices before leaving the nearest town.

The **Geikie Gorge National Park** contains narrow limestone cliffs that have been gouged over millions of years by the waters of the Fitzroy River. The catchment area above the gorge is unable to hold all of the water that falls during the wet season. With few ways out, it tears through gorges like the Geikie in a chaotic fury.

In the dry season the river rests and the camping areas are open. You can take a boat tour up the river or just sit on the banks and wonder at the fury that has been. The still water reflects the soft cream and red of the limestone cliffs which tower upwards to 60 m (197 ft), where hundreds of birds and flying-foxes chatter and squabble among themselves. Most of the trees here are tropical paperbarks and river gums, with some native figs and freshwater mangroves. If a freshwater crocodile slides out of the water to sunbathe — leave it in peace and it will leave you in one piece.

Along the gorge you will see fossilised samples of ancient marine life left by a coral reef system which grew here about 350 million years ago during the Devonian geological period.

The water is fresh, isolated for millions of years from the ocean, yet the mangroves and some of the fish — sawfish and stingray — are species normally found only in salt water. You may also see the archer fish which shoots down insects with a jet of water before eating them.

Geikie Gorge is 16 km (10 m) from Fitzroy Crossing where the camping and caravan sites are. It usually opens in early to mid-April, after the rain. There is an information centre within the park and rangers are based in the park during the season.

About 180 km (112 m) northwest of Geikie Gorge is the **Windjana Gorge National Park**. It has some good walks and areas where you can closely examine the ancient barrier reef. Camping and caravan areas are provided and there is a fee. Rangers are based at the park during the dry season, from April to October.

WILDLIFE PARKS AND SANCTUARIES

In choosing from Australia's many wildlife parks, zoos and sanctuaries, I have selected those that provide a home to native wildlife in natural environments. In a perfect world we would not want to see wildlife in anything but its natural environment, but we do not live in a perfect world.

Most of the parks and sanctuaries listed here have important research and breeding programs and these are producing the knowledge needed to save some of our endangered species. Some nurse and rehabilitate wildlife injured by traffic, drought, fire, feral animals and other hazards. Many breed endangered species for rehabilitation into the wilds — surely one of the most worthwhile programs undertaken by any conservation group.

Sadly, many wildlife habitats no longer exist. They have been filled in, flooded, burnt or smothered under concrete and brick. Where habitats no longer exist, or are too small to sustain wildlife, the wildlife they normally support must live in a sanctuary. Hopefully, we will one day be able to revive these habitats and the captive wildlife can be returned to the wild.

Most parks and sanctuaries charge a fee and the general rate is from $4.50 to $8.50 for adults (only Currumbin Sanctuary in Queensland and Healesville Sanctuary in Victoria are more expensive) and from $2.50 to $6.50 for children. Ask about concessions for very young children, students, family groups and pensioners.

Australian Wildlife Park

SYDNEY

At this park you can wander among the kangaroos in an open area where they show no concern about being photographed and patted. Less-friendly creatures, such as crocodiles, snakes and Tasmanian devils, are viewed from behind a safety fence or through glass. The Park has emus, dingos, wombats, little penguins, native birds, flying-foxes, pademelons, quolls, echidnas, snakes, waterfowl at the lake, and other birds in a specially designed rainforest aviary. Wildlife talks are given daily or by appointment for groups, and you can have your photo taken with a koala. Underground viewing areas allow you see crocodiles under water, wombats in their burrow, and goannas from a glass dome inside their enclosure.

King parrot

Nocturnal House allows you to see animals that are difficult to find in the wild — 70% of Australian natives are nocturnal. The building has a computerised lighting system that simulates the seasons. The lighting is adjusted to allow nocturnal creatures to live and breed normally, while at the same time enabling you to see them. Wait a few seconds after you enter to allow your eyes to adjust to the dim lighting and you will see rufus rat kangaroos, sugar gliders, tawny frogmouth owls, bandicoots and ring-tailed possums.

The Park has a research and breeding program for koalas, and is studying the gouldian finch, bilby and kowari, all of which are classified as endangered species.

Light meals are available and the park is open 9 a.m.–5 p.m. daily, except Christmas Day.

The Park is 45 minutes from Sydney along the M4 motorway, or by rail to Rooty Hill Station then by bus or taxi. Some coach companies run daily tours.

Ballarat Wildlife Park

VICTORIA

This is a family-run business led by Greg Parker, who has been involved in wildlife conservation, photography and management for more than 20 years. His private collection of reptiles, displayed at the Park, is one of the largest in the country. The tropical reptile house has goannas, dragons, skinks and venomous snakes, such as death adders, taipans, tiger snakes and king browns.

The Park is set in 16 ha (39 a) of eucalypt woodland with free-roaming kangaroos and emus and a lake teeming with waterfowl. Wedge-tailed eagles brought to the park because of injuries now live safely in a spacious aviary. The park has an extensive breeding program and is involved in a worldwide breeding program of the giant tortoise. It was the first park in Victoria to breed the Tasmanian devil in captivity and has successfully bred wombats, saltwater crocodiles and koalas.

One-hour guided tours start at 11 a.m. daily and special arrange-ments can be made for groups. Open 9 a.m.–5.30 p.m. daily, except Christmas day.

About one-and-a-half hours' drive from Melbourne; most major coach companies run daily tours.

Cleland Wildlife Park

ADELAIDE

This 34 ha (84 a) park was established by the South Australian Government in 1964 as a reserve where native South Australian wildlife could be maintained in a natural environment and displayed to the public. It has a policy of educating the public to appreciate and care for native wildlife, as well as displaying local species. It is home to kangaroos, wallabies, wombats, dingos, pelicans, Cape Barren geese, swans, emus, snakes, Tasmanian devils and koalas. Many of the animals are in open areas where you can wander among them and you can have your photo taken with a koala. Guided night walks starting half an hour before sunset, provide an opportunity to see wildlife at its most active.

The Park has a breeding program in conjunction with the Adelaide Zoo for the yellow-footed rock wallaby and koalas are maintained for research at Adelaide University.

Open every day 9.30 a.m.–5 p.m. with extended hours during daylight saving.

The park is in the Adelaide Hills, 20 minutes from the city. Weekdays the route 822 bus leaves from the 'koala stop' in Grenfell Street.

Earth Sanctuaries Ltd

SOUTH AUSTRALIA

Earth Sanctuaries is a public company, established to conserve Australian wildlife in a totally natural environment. The company buys large tracts of land that are then fenced to keep out unwanted animals and are revegetated with native plants. All feral animals are destroyed and native species that have disappeared because of farming or prey by feral animals are reintroduced.

The founder of Warrawong, the first Earth Sanctuary, Dr John Wamsley, says his aim is: 'to give Australian animals a small piece of Australia'. Among the reintroduced species thriving here are brush-tailed bettongs, eastern bettongs, rufus bettongs, long-nosed potoroos, tammar wallabies, red-necked wallabies, platypuses and southern short-nosed bandicoots. Warrawong provides a safe home to more than 50 000 native plants and numerous mammals and birds.

The sanctuary has four walks every day, except Christmas day, at dawn, midday, 2 p.m. and sunset. Visitors are not permitted to wander around alone; you must join a walk and you should book before arriving because they are very popular.

About 25 km (15½ m) southeast of Adelaide; follow the signs from the Stirling roundabout.

Earth Sanctuaries' Yookamurra Sanctuary, also in South Australia, covers 1100 ha (2718 a) of pristine mallee country. Many rare and endangered animals, which once roamed this region in large numbers, have been re-established inside the protective fence. An overnight stay is recommended and is quite inexpensive (about $65). This includes accommodation in cabins, a barbecue dinner and some tours. Optional tours include an exhibition of the ancient world of sea-bed fossils, dinosaurs and early marsupials, or a tour of Aboriginal culture and heritage sites. The native plant nursery can be visited by appointment.

Earth Sanctuaries' Yookamurra Sanctuary is about 120 km (74½ m) northeast of Adelaide.

Two additional sanctuaries are planned: Buckaringa in the Flinders Ranges where 1618 ha (4000 a) will be fenced to provide a safe home for the yellow-footed rock wallaby; and Scotia in western New South Wales, which will be the biggest sanctuary with more than 40 468 ha (100 000 a) fenced.

Currumbin Sanctuary

GOLD COAST

This 27 ha (67 a) sanctuary is famous for the hundreds of multicoloured wild lorikeets that fly in twice a day to be fed. They balance themselves on people's heads, arms and shoulders in a kaleidoscope of colour, to drink a specially prepared nectar mix from flat metal plates. Sometimes the noise and excitement of the lorikeets tends to overshadow the many other aspects of this excellent sanctuary. Every year hundreds of sick, injured or orphaned animals and birds are brought in by the public. If possible, they are nursed back to health and returned to the wild, however, some never regain full fitness and spend the rest of their lives in the safety of the sanctuary. Research, breeding and education programs are running all the time and visitors can go to the nursery and orphanage to learn about these.

More than 1250 animals and birds live in spacious enclosures beautifully shaded by tall trees. In a large natural setting you can wander among tame

Royal spoonbill, ibis and heron feeding together

kangaroos, wallabies and emus. Weaving waterways provide habitats for water birds and a walkway leads you very close to koalas in the trees (they are usually asleep — they sleep about 18 hours a day). Other enclosures house reptiles, dingos, freshwater crocodiles, Tasmanian devils, wombats and flying-foxes and the aviaries are filled with spectacular Australian birds.

You need at least a half a day to see the sanctuary, the theatrette and to join the educational talks and feeding programs. It is open 8 a.m.–5 p.m. daily, except Christmas Day.

It is 7 km (4.3 m) north of Coolangatta and 18 km (11 m) south of Surfers Paradise.

Eagles Heritage Raptor Wildlife Centre

WESTERN AUSTRALIA

This fascinating centre concentrates solely on the conservation, preservation and education of birds of prey. Owner Philip Pain became interested in birds of prey in 1970 while working at Sydney's Taronga Zoo, where he met a British falconer. A decade later, at the Perth Zoo, he continued this interest by rehabilitating injured birds of prey and established the Society for the Preservation of Raptors. By 1988 the number of injured birds coming in was so great he had to either stop what he was doing or open the doors to the public to raise much-needed funds. Thus, Eagles Heritage Raptor Wildlife Centre was born.

On entering the centre you should start with the 1.2 km (¾ m) walk through natural bushland, which is scattered with aviaries, some quite large to allow free flight. Then take a seat in the shade and learn about the birds and the ancient art of falconry. If you wish, you can put on a glove and experience the thrill of a bird lifting off from your arm in free flight. Falconry is part of the rehabilitation program.

The centre has successfully bred and reared wedge-tailed eagles, peregrine falcons, black kites, brown goshawks, barn owls and boobook owls. Pain is currently working on a program to breed the rare red goshawk and the endangered grey falcon, both native and endemic to Australia. The centre is open 10 a.m.–5 p.m. daily, except Christmas Day.

Located about 280 km (174 m) south of Perth.

Fleays Fauna Centre
GOLD COAST

One of Australia's most distinguished environmentalists, Dr David Fleay, arrived on the Gold Coast in the early 1950s looking for a suitable environment to continue his research into wildlife. He bought the land now known as Fleays Fauna Centre in the hills above Burleigh Heads and continued his outstanding work. He was the first person to breed platypuses and wedge-tailed eagles in captivity and has released 17 young eagles into the wild. However, he lacked funding and was only able to continue because of the help of willing volunteers and a small fee from visitors. I used to visit Fleays years ago and enjoyed its earthiness. The animals and birds were unrestrained, the forest was creeping in over the rough fences and the platypuses were in a long, dim shed where Dr Fleay would give a talk.

Turtles

Before his death in 1993, Dr Fleay arranged for the centre to be taken over by the Department of Environment and Heritage and that his work would carry on. And it does. Hundreds of sick and injured animals are still brought in for nursing and rehabilitation, volunteers still help out, and the research goes on.

On a wander around the centre you pass through wetland, rainforest and eucalypt forest habitats and see 250 animals including the fearsome saltwater crocodile. Special tours include 'Creature Features', which brings you face to face with some of Australia's most unusual animals, and 'Aboriginal Talks', which explains the customs and way of life of the Kombumerri people who once lived in this area. The centre is open 9 a.m.– 5 p.m. daily, except Christmas Day.

Fleays Fauna Centre is 2 km (1.2 m) from the surfing beaches of Burleigh Heads; leave the Pacific Highway at the Tallebudgera–Burleigh turn-off and follow the signs.

Healesville Sanctuary

VICTORIA

This sanctuary has the largest collection of Australian wildlife in the world, displaying some 200 species of birds, mammals and reptiles. Over more than 50 years it has established programs for vegetation rehabilitation, for breeding highly endangered and threatened species, and for the care of injured and orphaned animals. All its enclosures are in revitalised settings of native bushland, tall trees and fern gullies — lovely settings for a picnic.

On arrival you should check the times for the talks and close-up viewing of the wombats, reptiles, birds of prey, koalas, platypuses and pelicans, and plan your day around these. The rest of the time you can just stroll around and enjoy close contact with many of Australia's strange and beautiful wildlife. Do not miss the Animals of the Night exhibit where you will see long-footed potoroos, mountain pygmy possums and other rare and endangered animals. The sanctuary is open 9 a.m.–5 p.m. daily.

Healesville is 65 km (40 m) east of Melbourne. For information on daily coach tours from Melbourne, ring (03) 617 0900.

Lone Pine Koala Sanctuary

BRISBANE

Established in 1927, this 20 ha (49 a) sanctuary has more than 50 species of native marsupials, birds, mammals and reptiles. It is home to more than 100 koalas and you can have your photo taken holding one. At the koala education centre you learn that koalas feed on gum leaves, but that they will eat only about 48 species from a total of 600 types of gum tree available. This creates a major problem for sanctuaries that keep large numbers of koalas and Lone Pine has two plantations with a total of 30 000 trees just to feed its koalas.

Seventy kangaroos and wallabies roam freely in a 2 ha (5 a) reserve and are so tame you can hand-feed them. Other natives on display include kookaburras, Tasmanian devils, wombats, possums, emus, parrots and turtles, as well as other birds and reptiles.

The sanctuary is open 8.45 a.m.– 5 p.m. daily, except 25 April (Anzac Day), when it is open 1 p.m.–5 p.m., and is closed on Christmas Day.

It is 11 km (7 m) from Brisbane on the banks of the Brisbane River. Cruise boats depart daily from North Quay travelling along the scenic Brisbane River to the sanctuary. The City Council express bus number 518 runs hourly from the Koala Platform in the Myer Centre in the city and commercial coach tours run twice daily from the Roma Street Transit Centre.

Phillip Island

VICTORIA

Phillip Island has several features of interest for the nature watcher: little penguins, koalas, birds and seals. It is advisable to make your first stop at the information centre, which is 1 km (½ m) onto the island after you cross the bridge from the mainland. This will provide information on all the attractions.

The most famous feature is the Penguin Reserve, a sanctuary for the hundreds of little penguins (or fairy penguins) which have built their burrows in the dunes along the coast. The penguins waddle ashore just after dusk and their quaint appearance and noisy arrival have fascinated people since the 1920s. To protect them, the state government in 1985 adopted the Penguin Protection Plan, which provided the funds for the purchase of all land on the Summerland Peninsula, and for scientific research and proper management of the habitat. The reserve is a non-profit-making organisation, feeding all income back into research and the protection of the little penguins.

Under the plan, elevated boardwalks have been built and floodlights installed. This means you get a good look at these delightful creatures without disturbing their normal routine. Each evening they arrive in the hundreds, surfing in on the ocean waves and filling the night with noise as they squabble over burrows and call to their mates. They seem oblivious to the people watching them, but their numbers are regularly monitored to detect any change.

You should try to arrive a bit before dark to allow yourself time to see through the visitors' centre, which describes the penguin's life cycle and habitat, and to hear the ranger's talk before the penguins arrive. The parade up the beach lasts 45 to 60 minutes. It is very popular and you will need to book ahead during holiday periods.

In addition to the penguin parade, the island has the Koala Conservation Centre; the Wildlife Park, which displays native wildlife; Australia's largest fur seal colony at Seal Rocks; and excellent birdwatching at Swan Lake and Rhyll Inlet.

The island is 140 km (87 m) southeast of Melbourne, through Dandenong and along the South Gippsland and Bass highways.

Serendip Sanctuary

VICTORIA

This is a unique wetlands sanctuary, partly artificially constructed, which provides a safe habitat for the birds of the Western Plains. It was established as a research station in 1959 through a joint venture between the Department of Conservation and Environment and a private organisation. The land had been heavily farmed and only 40 species of birds were left, and most did not breed there. The aims of the research station were to show that wildlife and farming could co-exist, to study wildlife used as game, and to rehabilitate species that had been lost to the region. Trees were planted, lakes and islands were constructed, enclosures were fenced off and stock was kept away from the lake edge. The program was a great success and the regenerated lakeside vegetation attracted ducks, water birds and waterfowl. The regrowth of native bush attracted many other species.

A captive breeding program that began in 1966 has replenished many endangered species, especially the brolga, Australian bustard and magpie goose, which once lived on the Western Plains in large numbers. Now, 140 species of birds are living here and about 60 species are known to be breeding. Interesting walking trails lead through the various habitat enclosures, and bird observation hides allow viewing from close range. From the birdhides you can watch wild birds preening, feeding, incubating eggs and caring for their young. As well, you will see kangaroos, wallabies and emus roaming freely across the property. You should allow a good two hours to see everything. If you take a tour your guide may be either a ranger or a volunteer; anyone interested in assisting is welcome to join the team as a volunteer worker.

The sanctuary is open 10 a.m.–

Echidna

4 p.m. Thursday to Monday and every day during school holidays; it is closed Christmas Day and Good Friday. Free guided tours leave the information centre at 2 p.m.

Situated 60 km (37 m) southwest of Melbourne.

Territory Wildlife Park

NORTHERN TERRITORY

This 400 ha (988 a) park specialises in wildlife found in the Northern Territory, including some introduced species. The idea behind displaying these feral animals — pigs, camels, buffalo, banteng, sambar, rusa deer — is to highlight how much damage they can do to the environment.

Other exhibits include agile wallabies, antilopine wallaroos, red kangaroos, emus and a multitude of glorious Territory birds in walk-through aviaries. A nocturnal house has barn owls, water rats, rock wallabies and the endangered bilby and ghost bat. A walk-through aquarium gives you a chance to look overhead at barramundi, turtles and stingrays — and of course the park has crocodiles. There is an education centre where interpretive talks about the importance of conserving wildlife are given, and an Animal Care Centre where you can see keepers caring for orphaned, injured and newborn animals.

Allow four hours to see the park, which has a 6 km (3¾ m) walking trail as well as shuttle trains. It is open daily, except Christmas Day, from 8.30 a.m.–4 p.m.; the gates close at 6 p.m..

Located 60 km (37 m) south of Darwin.

Pied currawong

Tidbinbilla Nature Reserve

AUSTRALIAN CAPITAL TERRITORY

This reserve of 5500 ha (13 591 a), established in 1939, offers a variety of nature experiences, from seeing animals in large natural settings to bushwalking. Check at the visitors' centre at the entrance for ranger-guided walks, seasonal spotlight tours, maps, audiovisuals and other useful information.

On first entering the park, you walk through large enclosures (from 13 to 26 ha (32 to 64 a)) where native wildlife such as koalas, kangaroos and water birds live in natural environments. Rangers give guided walks on weekends, public holidays and school holidays, and bush birds are fed daily at 2.30 p.m.

After leaving the enclosures you can walk along marked trails through the natural forest and open grasslands. This is an area of native ferns, mosses, moist gullies and tall trees. If you walk quietly you will see and hear many birds, including the satin bowerbird and, if you are lucky, that great mimicker, the lyrebird. Longer walks lead to the wilder areas of the reserve and up onto the mountain ridges where the views are magnificent. The longest walk is to Camel Back Ridge, one of the highest points on the Tidbinbilla Range, with expansive views of Namadgi National Park, the Murrumbidgee River valley and Canberra (allow six hours for the return journey). Shorter walks take you to mountain streams and high areas for good views.

The reserve is open 9 a.m.–6 p.m. daily, with extended hours during summer. It is closed Christmas Day and on days on which there is a total fire ban in force.

Tidbinbilla Nature Reserve Tidbinbilla Road, about 45 minutes southwest of Canberra, following Tourist Drive number 5.

Trowunna Wildlife Park

TASMANIA

This small park has been operating for 15 years, during which time it has nursed back to health hundreds of injured and orphaned animals, returning most of them to the wild. However, some never heal well enough to be able to survive again in the wild and these are kept in the park. Two wedge-tailed eagles which were shot and will never fly again, have an open-topped enclosure with views over the valley that was once their hunting ground, and a magpie that was nursed back to perfect health at the park liked its new home so much that it would not leave after being released — it hops around outside its old cage every meal time.

The park owner, Androo Kelly, said most injuries to wildlife are through human activities: marsh harriers nest in the ground and each season several are ploughed over by farm machinery; brown falcons don't see wire fences when they are in full flight after a running prey and ram into the wires, other animals are hit by cars.

The park has successfully bred koalas, Tasmanian devils, tiger quolls and bettongs. These animals are well adjusted to life within the park and throughout the day the staff give free talks on their habits and allow you to pat and hold some of them.

The activities of the park are being extended to incorporate Aboriginal cultural activities, with local Aboriginal elders coming in daily to give interpretations and tell their stories.

The park is open daily 9 a.m.–5 p.m., except Christmas Day.

Located in the Mersey/Meander Valley, less than an hour's drive from Launceston and Devonport.

BUSHWALKING

No other country offers the variety of walks that can be found in Australia. You can set your soul loose in a measureless desert of red sand, wonder at sheer escarpments that plunge into unexpectedly cool gorges, paddle along an isolated beach, venture into steamy rainforests, trek the ancient wilderness of Tasmania, or ponder life atop a snow-covered mountain peak. Australia is often described as the world's last frontier and it is true that much of its 7.7 million km² (3 million m²) is sparsely populated and has seldom felt the tread of a human foot.

Nearly 6% of the country is protected by national park, forestry or other nature reserve, threaded with walking trails. The range of these trails caters for everyone, from the family on a day's outing to experienced walkers equipped with backpacks and sturdy boots.

Australia's popular bushwalking areas are busiest during school holidays, particularly the long December to January summer break. You may want to avoid the crowds at these times, although this is also when the park rangers in the national parks are at their most active, organising guided walks, spotlighting evenings and informative talks.

Camping is the cheapest way to travel in Australia. Bush camping (no facilities) is usually free, although rangers like you to register with them so they know where people are in the park. Camping areas with tent (and usually caravan) sites and facilities cost about $10 to $20 a night. Commercial camping areas are generally well maintained and some have caravans and cabins for rent, and a kiosk.

It is quite easy to hire camping and walking equipment in Australia. Bushwalking and outdoor shops in cities, and even in towns near major walking areas, have equipment for hire and can provide local information, and maps. Detailed walking maps are produced by government mapping agencies and these can be purchased from their outlets or from National Parks and Wildlife Service offices (see Useful Addresses, page 199).

If you plan to bush camp, protect the environment by using minimal impact techniques, which include:
• camp at existing campsites or on sandy or hard surfaces
• wash in a bowl away from streams and lakes and scatter your water so it is filtered through the soil and does not run off into streams,etc.
• carry your rubbish out of the bush with you, don't bury it
• walk on established tracks
• in open spaces, spread out to minimise damage to the vegetation
• don't walk on soft vegetation and bog, which is easily damaged
• preferably use a fuel stove but if

Sydney nature walk

using a camp fire, collect only dead, fallen wood.

Because Australia is such a dry continent — the driest in the world — bushfires are a major problem and there will be times when fire bans are in place. Always observe these — the massive bushfires which swept through New South Wales in January 1994 devastated vast areas of native bushland and left count-less wildlife dead or badly burnt. Although many native plants need fire to stimulate seeding and regrowth, the intensity of the 1994 fires damaged some plants irreparably and caused horrific loss of wildlife.

Regular burning-off by the authorities controls the fires at a level which can be tolerated by the native bush, and reduces the amount of dried vegetation lying around to feed wild fires. Don't be the person who starts one of these wild fires.

Another wise precaution is to always carry your own water. An adult bushwalker needs 4 to 6 litres (8 to 12 pints) of water a day and you should carry at least this amount. In many areas there is no water at all, and often natural water is not safe to drink without it being boiled first.

Bushwalking in Australia is quite safe. Except for some snakes and spiders and the saltwater crocodile (see National Parks, page 29) there are no dangerous animals to worry about. However, flies swarm over everything, leeches leap from the rainforest floor at the sight of a bare ankle and the little 'bities' — mosquitos, midges, bush ticks — are annoying, although only the bush tick is dangerous if left under the skin for too long. A good insect repellent and basic knowledge on how to remove ticks and leeches will set you right.

Australia's climate is generally mild to hot. More than one third of the continent lies north of the Tropic of Capricorn and is within the tropical zone. South of this, the climate is temperate with seasonal changes becoming more apparent as you travel south into Victoria and Tasmania. The two extremes are the alpine regions in the southeast corner and parts of Tasmania where it snows in winter, and the desert regions in

Blue Mountains National Park, New South Wales

the centre and across to parts of the west coast where it is dangerously hot and dry in summer. The far northern regions experience the summer 'wet' from October to April, a time of torrential rain storms and high humidity which can be uncomfortable, as well as causing flooding and road closures.

The best time of the year to walk varies from one region to another. As a general guide, north of the Tropic of Capricorn is best during autumn, winter and spring when the summer heat and rains have passed. Central South Australia is best from June to September when the temperatures are cooler. New South Wales and Victoria are good at any time of the year although the alpine regions are snow-covered during winter. The southwest corner of Western Australia is suitable year-round but is exceptional during spring when the wildflowers are in full bloom. Tasmania is best in summer, although it has a climate which can produce extremes in any season.

Emu

For local gossip and good information you could buy *Wild,* a popular bushwalkers' magazine available at most newsagents. Among the best books available is a series written by Tyrone T. Thomas (Hill of Content) on walks in Tasmania, New South Wales, Victoria, South Australia and a general guide entitled *20 Best Walks in Australia.*

The following is a guide to walking areas in each state and territory and should be read in conjunction with the chapter on National Parks (see page 29); where bushwalking information has been provided in that chapter it has not been repeated here.

The **Australian Capital Territory** has a good network of walking tracks throughout areas close to Canberra, especially the Namadgi National Park (see page 32). Namadgi is in the northern section of the Australian Alps — the walking trails lead into remote alpine areas with quite steep climbs and an unreliable climate. Carry warm, waterproof clothing and you will enjoy the solitude and panoramic views.

New South Wales is ideal for bushwalking all year round, although if you venture into the mountains of the Great Dividing Range in winter it will be cold and there will be snow on the Snowy Mountains.

Most people think of bushwalking as something that is done outside of cities, and in most cases this is true. However, Sydney is an exception. Its undulating suburbs sweep around a large and very beautiful harbour and along a coast of dramatic cliffs and sandy bays. Large areas of the harbour shores and ocean coastline are designated as native parkland where spectacular walking trails and picnic areas have been established. Birds, lizards, native plants, views and history are all to be found along these walks and if you do not wish to return along the trail, you are still in the city so you can jump on a bus. Libby Buhrich has written a good guide book on walks around Sydney called *Bushwalks and Picnics* (Milner Books).

Surrounding Sydney are three large national parks that are easily reached by car, bicycle or train. Some of the more popular areas become quite crowded, especially at weekends, but all three parks are huge so you can quickly leave the crowds behind and enter a world where the silence is broken only by birdsong and the rustle of leaves.

On the southern border of the city is the Royal National Park, on the north the Ku-ring-gai Chase National Park and to the west the Blue Mountains National Park. The Royal has a sensational coastline and lovely river gorges to explore; Ku-ring-gai has bushland and calm, blue fiords lined with densely treed cliffs. The Blue Mountains — in reality a high sandstone plateau dissected by forested valleys, canyons, waterfalls and sheer cliffs — is one of the most beautiful and accessible walking areas in the state. A popular three-day walk is the Six Foot Track from Katoomba to Jenolan Caves. There are camping sites along the walk and cabins at Binda Flats, which can be booked through the Jenolan Caves Trust.

Most of the state's good bushwalking terrain is in the Great Dividing Range, which runs parallel with the coastline, from the Victorian border to Queensland. Throughout the ranges there are numerous national parks and reserves where you can follow marked walking trails or take off to explore more remote areas. Most parks have rangers and/or a visitors' centre where you can collect maps and other information, or you can write to the state office (see Useful Addresses, page 199).

For experienced walkers, the Budawang Range in the Morton National Park, south of Sydney, is a great favourite. It is remote and challenging and not easily reached by road so it doesn't attract large crowds. Wilderness areas worth exploring are the Castle and Monolith Valley which provides access to Mount Owen.

The Snowy Mountains in the Kosciusko National Park in the southeast of the state is a series of high rolling plains and mountain summits bounded by deep river valleys. Mount Kosciusko is the country's highest peak, 2228 m (7310 ft), and many summits rise above 2000 m (6561 ft), making these the highest mountains in the country. Although not as high and wild as can be found overseas, they are magnificent, with views that go forever in a rolling panorama of summits and valleys. The best time to walk is during spring and summer, when the wildflowers bloom in a profusion of colours and the warm sun brings everything to life. In winter, the alpine areas are snow-covered and become the domain of the cross-country skier.

The rangers at the entrances to the park, and the visitors' centres at Jindabyne and Thredbo Alpine Village can provide maps and information on walking trails. There is also a good selection of guided walks during summer, which will help you understand the geology, flora and fauna of the area. From Thredbo, you can catch the Crackenback chairlift which takes you quickly and easily into the alpine region and allows more time for exploring. The famous 6 km (3½ m) raised walkway to the summit of Mount Kosciusko starts from the top of the chairlift. Accommodation in Jindabyne and Thredbo includes motels, chalets, self-contained apartments and camping areas.

Further inland, the small but spectacular group of volcanic peaks within the Warrumbungle National Park, provides walks of great geological interest and many challenges for rock climbers. Thirty kilometres (18 m) of walking trails have been marked; most are long and steep but the views make the effort worthwhile. The wildlife here is prolific, with hundreds of birds, eastern grey kangaroos, families of emus, wallabies, wallaroos, snakes and many koalas to be seen.

West of the Warrumbungle the state is mostly flat and uninteresting for walkers, except in the national parks where walking trails have been established. The Mungo National Park has three nature walks through the different vegetation communities

Wetlands, Mary River, Northern Territory

that survive this harsh terrain. Walking trails have also been marked throughout the secluded gorges and rugged sandstone hills of the Bynguano Ranges in the Mootwingee National Park, 130 km (81 m) north of Broken Hill.

The **Northern Territory** is a huge landscape of flat, scrubby terrain interspersed with splendid gorges, shimmering waterfalls, sheer escarpments of pink rock and dynamic wetlands. The main areas for bushwalking are the MacDonnell Ranges in the south, and Katherine Gorge, Litchfield National Park and Kakadu National Park in the north. Wherever you go, this is a hot, dry state, so always carry plenty of drinking water, wear a wide-brimmed hat and carry insect repellent to protect against the flies, mosquitos and midges which will have a merry feast of you in wetland areas.

Water lilies, Mary River, Northern Territory

The MacDonnell Ranges has enough gorges and national parks to keep walkers happy for days. This arid, desert range offers amazing walks along sheer cliffs that plunge into gorges with unexpected vegetation and water holes with surprisingly cold water. The colourful landscapes of this region were the inspiration for the works of the famous Aboriginal artist, Albert Namatjira.

Your base for exploring the MacDonnells will be Alice Springs and there are several tour companies here which can help you get to your desired walking area. Most of the national parks and reserves within the ranges have marked walking trails that take you into areas where you can enjoy the isolation of this vast landscape, and bush camping is usually permitted. To venture away from the major parks you will need a reliable four-wheel drive and may need to do some vehicle shuffling to have transport at the end of your walk. The closest gorge to Alice Springs is Simpsons Gap, which is easily reached by car or along the 24 km (15 m) cycle track.

Ormiston Gorge, 132 km (82 m) west of Alice Springs, has a permanent water hole and some good walks, the most popular being the three-hour walk into the Ormiston Pound. If you want to be more adventurous, go to Serpentine Gorge Nature Park which is less developed. If you have a four-wheel drive you can push on past Serpentine Chalet into isolated campsites and do daily walks from there.

The Larapinta Trail is a bold plan

Bushwalking in Kakadu National Park, Northern Territory

by the Conservation Commission of the Northern Territory to build a 220 km (137 m) walking trail in the MacDonnell Ranges. When completed, the trail will have 13 sections with separate information and maps for each section. Most of the trail will be suitable for average trekkers who are prepared to camp out. Some sections will be easy enough for first-time walkers and families. By mid-1994 four sections had been opened: Section 1, which was getting about 8000 walkers a year; Section 2, which has a more remote and challenging aspect; Section 3, which is short but difficult, was built by the local Aboriginal people; and Section 8, which is an easy walk with fantastic panoramic views.

The northern end of the Territory has two seasons: wet (October to April) and dry (May to September). They are quite distinct and will have a major effect on the enjoyment of your visit. The wet is hot and humid and many people find it uncomfortable. However, this is also a time of high drama. The January skies blaze in flash lightning storms, the waterfalls rush over the cliffs, the rivers become raging torrents and the vegetation springs to life. The main problem is access, for many roads are closed and camping can be a soggy affair. By contrast, the dry has slightly cooler temperatures (but remember you are still in the tropics) and little or no rain. Road access is reliable and, as the wetlands shrink, the wildlife has less area to range and is therefore highly concentrated.

The Katherine River has carved a sensational gorge out of the interminable dry plateaus creating a winding passage of sheer, red cliffs and long, slim waterfalls. Along its floor, the river flows quietly in winter and is a raging torrent during the wet. There are many walking trails through the Nitmiluk (Katherine Gorge) National Park which take from half an hour to several days. The most challenging is a five-day walk from the Katherine Gorge main entrance to Edith Falls in the northwestern corner of the park.

A more secluded reserve is the Umbrawarra Gorge Nature Park where the camping is basic and the swimming and walking is good. To reach Umbrawarra, turn off the Stuart Highway just south of Pine Creek and follow the winding gravel road for 25 km (15½ m). Two-wheel-drive vehicles can use this road, but there are many creeks to cross so you may need a four-wheel drive during the wet.

Further north along the Stuart Highway, 100 km (62 m) southwest of Darwin, is the turn-off to Batchelor and Litchfield National Park. This park offers a veritable feast of waterfalls and rock pools, all safe for swimming. After you have feasted your eyes on the magnificent waterfalls, visit Buley Rockhole, where the river tumbles along over many little falls into a series of delightful rock holes. There are camping areas near Wangi, Florence and Tjaynera Falls (Sandy Creek) and at Buley Rockhole. Marked walking trails lead over and around most of the waterfalls. If you plan to bushwalk and bush camp, call in at the Conservation Commission offices at Batchelor or Palmerston for information and maps.

Kakadu National Park is a very special part of Australia, which has been World Heritage listed because of its outstanding natural aspects and its wealth of rock art sites. Most people come here to see the rock art and the thousands of birds which are attracted by the extensive wetland areas, but there are also wide open plains, escarpments, waterfalls, sparkling rivers and rocky outcrops to explore and climb. The population is scant with only one hotel and a few motels and camping areas for visitors, and the township of Jabiru. Two roads lead into Kakadu, one from Darwin and one from Pine Creek and there is a daily coach service from Darwin. Only the main roads are sealed and you will need a four-wheel drive if you plan to leave these.

Many of the marked walking trails can be done in a day. If you plan to bushwalk and camp overnight you will need a permit from the visitors' centre in the park or the National Parks and Wildlife Service in Darwin. Allow 2 to 7 days for a permit to be processed. You will need a lot of fluid in this heat, so fill your water bags from the recommended centres or boil it if using water from streams. And think about crocodiles. Before you leave the visitors' centre check where the big 'salties' live, and you too will live.

Queensland's climate ranges from tropical to subtropical, with a jumble of topographical features — dramatic sandstone gorges, high plateaus, lost beaches, lush rainforests, savannah country and islands lazing in a turquoise ocean. Summertime in the north is hot and humid, but the cooler southern half of the state is suitable for bushwalking all year.

The most popular bushwalking areas are in the Great Dividing Range, which runs along the east coast, and on Hinchinbrook and Fraser islands. Mount Bartle Frere, 50 km (31 m) south of Cairns, is the state's highest mountain and a lush rainforest area. Walking here is challenging because of the difficult terrain, dangerous rivers and high rainfall, but it is highly regarded by experienced walkers.

Carnarvon National Park, 510 km (317 m) inland from Gladstone, is a spectacular area with rich vegetation, ancient sandstone cliffs, Aboriginal rock art, waterfalls, superb views and a stream winding along the gorge floor. Fourteen walking trails range from an easy stroll along the gorge floor with side trips to bluffs and points of interest, to some good scrambles and climbs to the higher regions. If you plan to bush camp, check at the ranger's station near the entrance for maps and information.

Lamington National Park on the Queensland–New South Wales border, is one of the most beautiful and popular walking areas in the state. It is also easily accessible from Brisbane (90 km (56 m)) and the Gold Coast. Two mountain resorts, O'Reilly's Rainforest Guesthouse and Binna Burra Mountain Resort, provide accommodation and promote the natural beauty of the area. They can supply information on the many walks and areas of interest in the park. The popularity of this park means it is well visited, but most people stay on the short walks and easily reached picnic areas so you can find solitude with a bit of keen walking.

The islands, Fraser and Hinchinbrook, are paradise for walkers. Fraser is the largest sand island in the world and is World Heritage listed. Its rainforests, sand dunes and clear lakes are a delight. The rule to not camp near water or wash in lakes and streams is particularly important here, for the water in the unique perched lakes is so pure its quality could easily be destroyed. Hinchinbrook Island is best characterised in the words of wilderness photographer Robert Rankin, who described it in his book *Classic Wild Walks of Australia* (Robert Rankin Publishing, 1989) as: 'one of Australia's most idyllic places for walking, with its rocky headlands and sandy coves, and a backdrop of soaring mountain peaks where giant waterfalls cascade over exposed granite on their steep plunge to the sea.'

South Australia has large areas of desert which are not suitable for walking long distances. This seems to contradict the fact that it also has the country's longest walk, the Heysen Trail.

The Flinders Ranges provide some of the best walking in the state, especially after rain when the vegetation bursts into life and waterfalls plunge, refreshed, into deep, cool gorges. Spring is also lovely with wildflowers carpeting the ground and birds gathering to enjoy the nectar. This is an ancient country where over the aeons earth movement, weather and rivers have shaped and moulded its hills and valleys. The geology in this part of the country is spectacular and is best enjoyed by walking and taking time to speculate over the changes that have occurred. However, it is also hot and dry, so care must be taken in the summer when the temperatures reach 30 to 45°C (86 to 113°F), which can be unpleasant and dangerous for long walks. The best time to walk is in the cooler months from May to October, although at this time you need to be prepared for possible rain and wind. Wherever you go you must carry your own water, heed fire bans and advise the rangers of your plans.

Mount Remarkable National Park, 275 km (171 m) north of Adelaide, is a popular walking area. It is wetter here than further north and there are some beautiful walks with rich vegetation and abundant wildlife.

Another popular area is around Wilpena Pound, a large, natural amphitheatre which has dramatic scenery and stunning views north and northeast over the ranges. If your walk is going to take longer than three hours you are required to fill out a

Eastern grey kangaroos unperturbed by bushwalkers in a national park

A boardwalk protects the alpine vegetation at Jackeys Marsh, Tasmania

bushwalker's log at the information centre, and you will need a permit to camp. Camping permits are available at the Wilpena information centre or from park rangers. The information centre has a pamphlet on marked bush trails that range from one hour to two days, but you will need more detailed maps if you intend to make your own route. The park covers 92 746 ha (229 180 a), so only experienced bushwalkers should take off into the more remote areas.

Further north, about 750 km (466 m) from Adelaide, you come to the Gammon Ranges National Park, which is less used (except during school holidays) because of its distance from Adelaide. The landscape here is as diverse as anywhere in the state, with plateaus, plains, dunes, salt lakes, dry river beds, permanent springs, gorges, pounds and tall mountain ridges providing a great challenge for experienced bushwalkers. The vegetation includes mulga, spinifex, Mitchell grass and river red gums. The Ranger station at Balcanoona can supply information and maps.

Tasmania may be a small island state but it has the most famous wilderness areas in the country. Nearly a third of the state is World Heritage listed for its outstanding natural and cultural attributes. However, do not expect towering mountains — the mountains here are not as high as those on the mainland, but they are robust and dramatic.

Walkers come from around the world to accept the challenge of Tasmania's wild regions, or to take a less risky walk along the marked trails, which are still challenging and spectacular. The isolation of these unpopulated areas creates a great feeling of camaraderie between trekkers who may meet several times at mountain huts and camping areas.

Another feature which makes this the terrain of the dedicated bushwalker is the climate. The most comfortable time is summer and this is when most people do the walks. Only truly dedicated bushwalkers come in winter, when they are likely to encounter bouts of atrocious weather with wind, rain and snow which can completely upset trip timetables. However, the snow produces absolutely beautiful sights and impassioned bushwalkers say these and the crisp and clear air make winter a rewarding time to walk.

Australia's most famous wilderness walk is The Overland Track, an 80 km (50 m) trail within the Cradle Mountain–Lake St Clair National Park. It passes theatrical alpine scenery, lakes, rugged peaks, open moors and forested valleys clothed in a rich garment of forests, shrubs,

heaths, herbs and alpine grasses. Living in this wilderness are birds, wallabies, quolls, possums, Tasmanian devils and snakes, which you should give a wide berth. The track is well signposted and the walking fairly easy, although rain will produce boggy patches. Experienced walkers can take the side trails up the peaks, which the main track circles. There are mountain huts along the way but you must carry a tent and fuel stove for they may be full when you arrive. The walk takes from five to ten days, depending on your fitness and the weather. You need a permit to walk the track and there is a fee.

Other outstanding walks include the wild and spectacular 85 km (53 m) South Coast Track, five to ten days, which can be combined with the Port Davey Track to make a ten to 16-day walk. There is no road to the western end of the South Coast Track so take a charter flight into Cox Bight or Melaleuca. From there you walk east along the coast to Cockle Creek where you meet the road. The walk runs close to the sea and the views are stunning, but rain is frequent. As there are no facilities, you need to carry everything, including a fuel stove as there are camp fire restrictions along the way. The best time to do this walk is in summer when you can dry out and the evenings are longer.

Other good walks include: the Walls of Jerusalem, which can be done in a day but is best done in two; Federation Peak, which is quite difficult; the Western Arthur Range, which has spectacular scenery and mountain lakes; Frenchmans Cap, a three to five-day walk with some long, steep climbs and extensive sections of mud; and the challenging Frankland Range Traverse.

If these walks sound too onerous, there are plenty of shorter walks which also provide drama and beauty. Mount Field National Park has some of the prettiest short walks in the state and is close to Hobart. Cradle Mountain National Park has a host of family walks, one of the best being the two-hour Ballroom Forest walk around the western shore of Lake Dove to a gnarled, old forest of myrtle, sassafras and King Billy pine. I walked here in the winter snow, which was extremely beautiful but a bit chilly; summer would be better for young children. If you have a whole day to spare, you can do the 6-km (3¾ m) (and a bit) circuit of the lake, starting with the Ballroom Forest track and meeting up with the Truganini track, which goes around the eastern shore. The circuit track has duckboarding and hardened sections for easy walking.

Freycinet National Park is popular with walkers because of its milder climate and stunning coastal views. The Hazards Walk takes about four hours and has some of the best coastal views I have ever seen, with the golden arch of Wineglass Bay the most stunning of them all.

The Tasmanian Forestry Commission has a created network of walking trails through its reserves and separate brochures for each region are available from its offices. The Commission allows multiple use of its land so you will see areas which have

been logged and will meet trail bikes and four-wheel drive vehicles if you are on fire trails. Camping is allowed anywhere within the reserves. Some of the best walks in the great southern forests are off Arve Road, south of Hobart, but before you set off into this area stop and spend a bit of time at the interpretative centre at Geeveston which has masses of useful information on the forests.

This is the perfect state for bushwalkers without their own transport — an organisation called Tasmanian Wilderness Transport & Tours runs regular coach services to the out-of-the-way places and will drop off and pick up walkers at the ends of any walking trails. It also runs its own walking tours.

Victoria is a small state with a wide range of terrains for the bushwalker: the magnificent alps, the beautiful Grampians, the windswept scenery of Wilsons Promontory and the Great South West Walk along the coast (see page 107).

The alps extend northeast from near Melbourne to the New South Wales border where they join the Kosciusko National Park. The countryside is rich in panoramic views, rocky outcrops, towering forests, twisted gums, lakes, rivers and wildflowers in spring. The outstanding beauty of this area has been captured in the movies, *The Man From Snowy River* adapted from A.B. 'Banjo' Paterson's famous poem of the same name, and the *Silver Brumby*, the film version of a book written by long-time local, Elyne Mitchell. In fact, if you want a change

A guide explains rock pool fauna, Tasmania

from walking, this is where the hardy mountain horse is bred and there are some great horse rides available.

The ski resorts at Falls Creek, Mount Buller, Dinner Plain and Mount Hotham are open in summer and can supply information on walks in their areas. Bogong National Park is a majestic sweep of alpine meadows and plains perched above deep, forested valleys. You can spend days here making forays up the various peaks, especially Mount Bogong, which is the state's highest mountain.

The Grampians, 260 km (161 m) west of Melbourne, are less imposing than the alps, but they are stunningly beautiful with densely vegetated valleys and heathlands swamped in wildflowers in spring. Aboriginal people have visited this region for generations and most of the state's rock art sites are here. The area is now

a national park, which guarantees protection for its unique vegetation, abundant wildlife and rock art. Some 160 km (99 m) of walking trails have been marked and bush camping is allowed. Alternative accommodation is available at Halls Gap and there is a visitors' information centre on Grampians Road south of Halls Gap.

Wilsons Promontory, 250 km (155 m) southeast of Melbourne, is 49 000 ha (121 082 a) of looming granite outcrops, fern gullies, eucalypt forests, swamps, heathlands, sheltered inlets and coves. It is widely regarded as one of the wildest and most beautiful parts of Australia's long coastline. The walking is varied and interesting, with 20 marked trails ranging from an easy stroll to a four-day trek. There is an excellent information centre at Tidal River with displays, audiovisuals, maps and

Elephant heads, the Kimberley, Western Australia

other information on the Park. Ask here for a book called *Discovering the Prom on Foot*, which describes all the main walks.

A large camping ground is attached to the Park headquarters at Tidal River, however, during Christmas and Easter bookings are essential. Alternatively, there are a number of flats, lodges and units with limited facilities which offer shared accommodation at reasonable prices. A permit is required for overnight hikes and can be obtained from the park information office or by mail to the Ranger-in-charge, Wilsons Promontory National Park, Tidal River via Foster, Vic. 3960 (allow at least a month). Fires are not generally permitted because of the lack of wood, and parts of the Park may be closed to campers in summer because of a lack of water.

Purnululu (Bungle Bungle) National Park, Western Australia

Western Australia is vast — 2.5 million km² (965 255 m²) — and much of it is barren and uninhabited. Its size and remoteness from the rest of the country has created some unique country with challenging walks. The main walking areas can be separated into three zones: the southwest corner, a patch in the middle around the Hamersley Ranges, and the northern Kimberley region. Except for the southwest corner, the terrain is harsh and the climate hot and dry. This is a state where you never venture far without plenty of water, a reliable vehicle and a good bush survival skills.

In the southwest, the Stirling Range rises above the fertile plains in a single chain of peaks 10 km (6 m) wide and 65 km (40 m) long. This is a spectacular country for rough walking and is splendid in spring when the wildflowers are out. The best walking is along the eastern end of the park where there is a good two-day circuit. You can walk in this area at any time of the year although spring offers the added bonus of the wildflowers.

The Nuyts Wilderness Area is in the wildest part of the Walpole–Nornalup National Park and can only be accessed by walkers. Running along the coast, this area provides stunning walks through high rocky hills, deep, forested gorges and a spectacular unspoilt coastline with great sand dunes. Also in the southwest is the Fitzgerald River National Park, which is an internationally recognised Biosphere Reserve under the United Nations

Educational, Scientific and Cultural Organisation (UNESCO) Man and the Biosphere Program.

Accommodation in this southwest corner can be found in any one of the many local towns or at camping areas in the national parks.

Near the middle of the state is gorge and coastal country. The Hamersley Range, the Millstream–Chichester National Park and Cape Range National Park have dramatic gorges that were gouged out long before any human foot made an imprint on the countryside. Cape Range also has beaches and coral reefs to explore. All the parks have marked walking trails ranging from short and easy to long, difficult and recommended only for experienced bushwalkers. But it does not matter which you take, this is an ancient landscape with terrific views and some lovely water holes for swimming. Camping areas are provided in the parks and the best time to visit is winter and spring when the days are cooler and more pleasant for walking.

The Kimberley in the northern section of the state is a vast wilderness with awe-inspiring escarpments, ancient gorges of rugged beauty, semi-arid plains, a spectacular coastline and the mysteriously beautiful Bungle Bungles. But like many a beautiful creature it is not easily controlled — the climate is hot and dry and the distances enormous.

You must plan well before setting out in the Kimberley. Most areas can only be reached by four-wheel drive, helicopter or light aircraft. There are few towns and you need to carry everything with you or arrange for supply drops. If you are an explorer at heart, this region will be a magnet, drawing you back again and again.

Windjana Gorge National Park in the West Kimberley is a 3.5 km (2 m) long gorge formed some 350 million years ago by the Lennard River. On a walk here you will see Aboriginal art, plenty of wildlife, fish, fossils and very few people. Good camping is available in the park.

In the east Kimberley region is the unique Purnululu (Bungle Bungle) National Park, a 350-million-year-old massif of giant beehive-like mounds, gorges and palm-fringed rock pools. Most walks can be done in a day, but it is terribly hot so you should not try to do too much. To do the full Piccaninny Creek and Gorge you should allow two days and advise the ranger living in the park residence near the entrance of your itinerary.

The park has camping areas but no services, food or accommodation, and the road in is for four-wheel-drive vehicles only. It is closed January to March when the rains can be torrential, but even in the dry season the weather can let you down. I was there in the dry season and it rained buckets, forcing the rangers to close all roads and evacuate campers. We were bogged trying to get out but fortunately, two-way radios and the natural friendliness of people travelling in these remote areas, brought help quickly. We were towed out with little difficulty, but I doubt our driver will ever live it down.

A useful guide to walking trails in this state is the Western Australia

Heritage Trails Network. This was a bicentennial project where local communities prepared heritage trails following areas of historic and environmental interest for walkers, drivers and divers. There are 95 trails altogether and a separate brochure has been prepared for each, or you can get the book which lists them all but with limited detail. Brochures can be picked up from local tourist outlets and shire offices or from the Western Australian Heritage Committee.

Long Walking Trails

The following is a list of Australia's major long walks. Each is the culmination of a dream, worked on over many years by bushwalking clubs, enthusiasts and government authorities. Between them they cover virtually every sort of countryside you can image. If you walked them all you could honestly say there was no feature of Australia that you had not seen and no weather you had not experienced. Some are easy, some are arduous. All are long, but they can be done in short segments.

The Heysen Trail
This is Australia's longest walk, crossing 1500 km (932 m) from Cape Jervis at the southern tip of the Fleurieu Peninsula to Parachilna in the Northern Flinders Rangers. Named after Hans Heysen, a highly acclaimed painter who worked in the area, the route has been chosen for its beauty, the variety of the terrain and its many panoramic outlooks.

Starting from Cape Jervis, the trail passes the coastal beaches of the south coast of the Fleurieu Peninsula where seals, sea eagles and albatrosses live. Turning north, it crosses the gum-clad Mount Lofty Ranges, around the famous wine-growing Barossa Valley and past Burra, a historic copper mining town that once saved the state from financial ruin. From here it climbs over hills and into the Flinders Ranges, crossing Mount Remarkable and Mount Brown and on through arid country to the spectacular Wilpena Pound and finally to Parachilna Gorge.

The trail is well marked with red waymarkers and a distinctive red and white logo. Accommodation is provided in numerous huts, hostels, farms, Bed and Breakfasts (B&Bs) or you can camp. It has been designed to be walked in one mammoth trek or in sections of a day or a few days at a time.

The most suitable time to walk the Heysen Trail is during winter when the temperatures are cooler and water is available. It is closed from December to April because of the high fire risk, and sections of it may be closed at other times. You should check with the authorities before setting out.

A book and map are available from the Friends of Heysen Trail, 10 Pitt Street, Adelaide, SA 5000, Tel: (08) 212 6299; Fax: 211 8041. The Friends is a voluntary organisation which welcomes newcomers who would like to help maintain walks and join in on a few social walks.

Bicentennial National Trail

This is an outstanding achievement, linking Cooktown in Far North Queensland with Healesville in Victoria, a distance of 5330 km (3312 m). It is actually longer than the Heysen Trail, but it is not purely a walking trail, being designed for walking, horse, mountain bike, canoe and horse-drawn vehicle. It traces much of Australia's pioneering history following old coach and stock routes, former packhorse trails, brumby tracks, bullock trails, fire trails, country roads and passes through 18 national parks. The extraordinary range of scenery along the way includes the steamy, tropical rainforests of the north, the peaks and gorges of the Great Dividing Range, great rivers, plains, alpine meadows, forested valleys and snow-capped mountains.

To complete the whole trip in one go would take about a year; however, it can be done in sections. It is divided into 12 sections of 400 to 500 km (248 to 310 m), each with its own guidebook and maps. Because it is so long and passes through so many climates, you need to plan your timing very carefully. The northern section from Cooktown to Gunnawarra is best done during the dry season from April to October. The mountainous Kosciusko to Omeo section is closed by snow in winter and, unless you intend to ski, is best tackled from October to April.

Maps and guidebooks are available from the Bicentennial National Trail, GPO Box 2235, Toowoomba, Qld 4350. Tel: (076) 38 3501; Fax: (076) 38 3504.

Wildflowers and panoramas from Kosciusko National Park, New South Wales

The Australian Alps Walking Track

This track winds its way up and down nearly 655 km (407 m) of magnificent mountain country. It started as the Alpine Walking Track but the name was changed in 1994 when it became a tri-state project. It now links the three great alpine parks — the Alpine National Park in Victoria, Kosciusko National Park in New South Wales and the Namadgi National Park in the Australian Capital Territory. It extends from Walhalla, a historic gold mining town two hours east of Melbourne, almost into Canberra.

The walking is interesting and varied, following a combination of walking trails, fire trails and four-wheel-drive tracks. It passes through some very remote high country and is not marked all the way, so anyone attempting it should be an experienced bushwalker proficient in reading a map and compass. Be sure to take warm, waterproof gear because the high country can produce rapid weather changes, with snow at any time.

Australia's alpine areas are quite rounded with high plateaus, rich valleys and blankets of wildflowers in summer. The wildlife includes kangaroos, snakes, dingos and brumbies (wild horses) and many species of birds. A book written by John Siseman called *Alpine Walking Track* (Pindari, 1988) will give you a good idea of what to expect along the way, although the route in the book varies in parts from the official track.

Maps and information for the Victorian section are available from The Department of Conservation & Natural Resources, PO Box 41, East Melbourne, Vic. 3002, Tel: (03) 412 4011, and for the New South Wales and Namadgi National Park sections from Kosciusko National Park, Private Bag, Cooma, NSW 2630, Tel: (064) 56 1700.

Bibbulmun Track
This is a 650 km (404 m) trail which was opened in 1979. It runs between Kalamunda east of Perth, and Walpole, a town on the coast, 423 km (263 m) south of Perth. It is named after the Aboriginal language group which lived here and travelled long distances for tribal meetings and corroborees in this area.

The track passes through bush, forests of jarrah and karri, open farmland, river valleys and country towns, following quiet country roads, forest trails, disused railroads and old logging tracks. As you pass the developed areas you be able to compare the difference between the sections of untouched native vegetation and those where mining, logging and farming have changed the landscape forever. You should allow about four weeks to do the whole walk. The best time is spring or summer when wildflowers spread like a beautiful Persian rug over the heathlands and forest floors.

The Bibbulmun Track is one of the Heritage Trails compiled by the Western Australian Heritage Committee.

Hume and Hovell Walking Track
This track stretches for 370 km (230 m) between Yass and Woomargama in the southeast corner of New South Wales, closely following the route taken by the explorers Hamilton Hume and William Hovell in 1824. It leads you on a historic journey through the beautiful Southern Highlands, over alpine regions, past lakes and through forests, national parks and private land. Along the way you encounter much that is man-made, but there are also forests and lakes where birds sing as you pass and the wildflowers bloom in spring and early summer.

The Hume and Hovell Walking Track was developed by the Department of Conservation and Land Management and a map-kit and guide book are available from district offices, or from head office at 23–33 Bridge Street, Sydney, NSW 2000, Tel: (02) 228 6111. If you would like to join a group, the Department runs two or three guided walks a year with tents and food supplied.

The Great North Walk

This is a city to city walk of 250 km (155 m) from Sydney to Newcastle. It is amazing to realise that there are enough bush tracks to create a single walking trail linking one big city with another. The walk runs between Governor Macquarie's Obelisk in downtown Sydney to Bicentennial Park in Newcastle. In between these two points it passes the Sydney Harbour, Hawkesbury River, Brisbane Water National Park, Lake Macquarie and the Newcastle coastline.

In Sydney, it starts with city streets, passes through the charming suburb of Hunters Hill, then follows river valleys where the dense bush conceals most of the surrounding urban development. As it leaves the city, it follows bush tracks, fire trails, country roads, river banks and beaches. The amazing range of environments it passes through includes forests, rolling pastures, lonely bush tracks, country villages, lakes and finally the ocean.

You should allow about two weeks to do the whole walk and you can join it along link tracks from Parramatta and the Hunter Valley. Campsites are provided along the route and occasionally the walk passes close enough to small towns for a night in comfortable country accommodation.

One of the originators of the track, Garry McDougall, has co-written an excellent guide book

called, quite simply, *The Great North Walk* (Kangaroo Press). A discovery kit with maps is sold through map supply outlets and the Department of Conservation and Land Management.

Great South West Walk

This is a 250 km (155 m) circular trail starting and finishing at the steps of the Portland Tourist Office, 362 km (225 m) west of Melbourne. It begins along ocean cliff tops and beaches then turns inland to follow quiet country roads through stringybark forests, past the Surry and Fitzroy Rivers and on to open marshlands where frogs, kangaroos and emus live. For a short leg it follows the limestone cliffs of the Glenelg River into South Australia then back to Nelson — this is about halfway. After Nelson, the trail follows the sweep of Discovery Bay with is wild, sandy beaches and natural dunes, then it climbs to the cliffs of Descartes Bay. The final sections follow the crescent of Bridgewater Bay, along part of the Sea Cliff Nature Walk in Cape Nelson State Park and home through trees and heathlands.

The walk has 16 campsites and can be completed comfortably in 12 days. The best times are from October to early December, and March to early June. As some of the campsites are popular, you may need to book before setting out.

Information is available from the Department of Conservation, Forests and Lands, PO Box 471, Portland, Vic. 3305, Tel: (055) 23 3232.

Bird-watching

Australia's bird population is one of the richest in the world, with nearly 800 species, of which about half are endemic. The continent, extending as it does from the tropics to cool temperate regions, has a diversity of habitats, with areas of wetlands, mangroves, rainforests, sclerophyll forests, woodlands, grasslands, heathlands, scrublands and deserts. All it lacks are very high mountains, and in some areas the wetlands are limited by low rainfall.

Woodlands

The greatest number of Australian bird species (more than 300) live in woodlands, where the ground cover comprises low shrubs, ferns, herbs and grasses. A variety of woodlands, ranging from tropical to arid, extend in a band slightly inland of the east coast, across the top of the continent and in a patch in the southwest. Good bird-watching occurs in all these areas and there are numerous national parks and forest reserves which provide camping areas, marked walking trails and sometimes bird lists.

Australia's capital, Canberra, with its leafy suburbs and surrounding wooded areas, is home to more than 130 species of birds and a further 50 species migrate to the area from Alaska and Japan each year. The beautiful eastern rosella and the red-

Feeding birds, O'Reilly's Rainforest Guesthouse, Queensland

Crimson Rosella

rumped parrot provide flashes of colour around Parliament House (where colour is normally confined to the language of the dark-suited politicians). Australia's largest bird, the flightless emu, and its smallest, the weebill, are both found here.

Just south of Canberra, the **Namadgi National Park** has grassy valleys and woodlands. You will see wedge-tailed eagles and Australian kestrels hovering over the grassy areas, while pacific black ducks live in the pools of Naas Creek, and fairy-wrens live where there is thick understorey vegetation. Other birds you should see include gang-gang cockatoos, crimson rosellas, pied and grey currawongs, white-throated treecreepers, yellow-faced and white-napped honeyeaters, grey fantails, striated thornbills and, if you are lucky, the olive whistler.

Wetlands

The wetlands that spread across parts of the **Top End** of the Northern Territory provide some of the country's most spectacular concentrations of waterbirds and are a haven for magpie geese, brolgas and jabirus, which were once widespread in Australia. During summer, when it rains extensively, the floodplains, swamps and rivers fill to overflowing and the birds spread out over wide areas. This is not the best time to see large concentrations of birds — wait until the dry winter months when they are clustered around the few remaining water holes. When the bushfires flare from May to July, you will see many birds of prey hovering and feasting on the reptiles and insects fleeing the fires.

Fogg Dam is the closest wetlands area to Darwin, 70 km (43 m) southeast along the Arnhem Highway. The dam was built for rice growers but this venture failed and it is now designated as a wildlife wetlands; waterlilies, birds, crocodiles and snakes abound. By driving or walking across the raised causeway through the centre of the dam you can observe the plants and wildlife on either side.

From the carpark there is a 3.6 km (2.2 m) marked walking trail through pockets of monsoon rainforest where you may see the rare and beautiful rainbow pitta. The pit toilets here are interesting because they are solar powered to keep the air fresh and the nightlights working. An excellent visitors' centre is located on the Arnhem Highway, just past the turn-off to the dam and it is worthwhile to visit this first, then backtrack to the dam.

Further along the highway (two hours from Darwin), turn left into Point Stuart Road and on to the Rock Hole Boat ramp for a tour on **Mary River** (check times with Wildman River Wilderness Lodge). The river is home to many species of birds, fresh and saltwater crocodiles, fruit bats, snakes and thick beds of waterlilies which flower profusely in April. On an evening cruise I saw a huge saltwater crocodile, two freshwater crocodiles, a water snake, hundreds of bats hanging about in the trees, and flocks of birds. But the most beautiful sight was that of a tall, elegant jabiru, stalking the shallows with the setting sun

highlighting its glossy, blue neck feathers and long orange legs.

There are two places to stay along Point Stuart Road — Wildman River Wilderness Lodge and Point Stuart Wilderness Lodge. Both provide good basic accommodation. Point Stuart was an abattoir but was closed when the buffalo herds were all but eradicated to halt the spread of disease. Accommodation is in renovated staff houses and bunk rooms and there is a camping area and swimming pool. The management provides boat cruises for small groups on a quiet part of Mary River, has books on the local flora and fauna, and has mapped a walking trail through rainforest where you could see the file snake, a popular food for Aboriginal people.

Further along Arnhem Highway you enter **Kakadu National Park** which is World Heritage listed and renowned for its wetlands birdlife. About one-third of all Australian bird species live here: magpie geese, pelicans, ibis, ducks, jabiru, brolgas, radjah shelduck, rufous night herons, kingfishers, comb-crested jacanas, spoonbills, egrets — the list goes on. You will see many of these birds at waterways alongside the road, although keen birdwatchers and photographers should not miss the Yellow Water Cruise, which drifts past areas thick with waterlilies and is home to thousands of waterbirds.

Kakadu has a reasonable choice of accommodation, including camping areas, three budget motel/hostel/ camping complexes, a Youth Hostel and the Gagudju Crocodile Hotel, which is shaped like a crocodile (you enter through its gaping mouth). Jabiru has the usual range of small-town facilities and an airport, and the nearby visitors' centre has displays, slide shows, videos and information about the park.

The **Burdekin–Townsville Wetlands** in Queensland is one of the most extensive coastal wetlands in the country. At the Townsville Town Common, an environmental park on the northwestern outskirts of the city, birds gather throughout the year. The greatest concentration is during the dry winter months (June to August), when thousands of birds have to leave the shrinking inland waterways. This is a good place to see the large, stately brolga and if you are lucky you may see a pair of brolgas dancing. Brolgas perform the dance facing each other with an elegant display of bows, bobs and leaps with wings half open and shaking.

Further north, the **Cairns City Esplanade** foreshore is an excellent place to see migratory waders, and you will have none of the problems associated with access to most tidal flats. At high tide the water comes almost to the Esplanade wall; as the tide recedes a wide band of mud flats is exposed, providing excellent pickings for a host of waders: graceful egrets, herons, spoonbills, ibis, pelicans, numerous small waders and, of course, the ubiquitous sea gull. The international migrants arrive for summer during late August and leave between March and May. Pelicans are in greatest numbers between June and December.

An important waterbird and wader region in the south is the **Coorong National Park**, a long, narrow, coastal waterway southeast of Adelaide. Coorong Lagoon stretches for about 100 km (62 m), protected from the pounding waves of the Southern Ocean and chilling winds by the tall, well-vegetated, sand dunes of Younghusband Peninsula. The Peninsula is home to numerous birds, including the superb fairy-wren, pied oystercatcher, hooded plover, crested tern and emu. In summer, the lagoon is visited by the red-necked stint, which comes all the way from Siberia, via Japan.

Some islands in the lagoon are off-limits to humans to allow the birds to breed in peace and safety. Pelicans, cormorants, egrets, herons, ibis, spoonbills, black swans, Cape Barren geese, terns and numerous other water and land birds live and breed here. Many migratory species arrive around November and leave in early April. Some 250 000 birds are estimated to gather during the breeding season and most are easily seen from the shore. In fact, some flocks are so dense you can mistake them for a dark cloud shadow until they take off, then they fill the sky. If you would like an experienced bird guide in this area, contact retired ranger and keen bird-watcher and photographer Herman Bakker at Meningie.

There are several places you can launch a boat, but be careful because the water is shallow and can become quite choppy. Camping is

Magpie Goose, Kakadu National Park, Northern Territory

Brolga

Galahs mate for life

allowed along most shores and most small towns in the region have motels and camping areas. Contact the rangers at the National Parks and Wildlife Service office at Meningie for bird lists, information and details of park fees.

A little north of the Coorong and 17 km (10.5 m) south of Naracoorte, is **Bool Lagoon**, a valuable freshwater lagoon system recognised by the United Nations as a wetland of international importance. More than 140 species of birds visit this wetland, including ibis, brolgas, Cape Barren geese and magpie geese. Rangers from the park office give a 90-minute guided walk along Tea-tree Board-walk four times a day, and dawn and dusk tours by arrangement.

Croajingolong National Park and the surrounding waterways along the eastern coastal region of Victoria provide a diversity of forests, lakes, rivers and coastline. Some 250 species of bird have been sighted, including the rare ground (swamp) parrot, southern emu-wren, chestnut-rumped hylacola, calamanthus, tawny-crowned honeyeater and the beautiful firetail. Accommodation is available in local towns or at Gypsy Point Lodge.

Tropical Areas of Far North Queensland

The **Atherton Tablelands** west of Cairns has ancient rainforests and wilderness areas visited only by keen bushwalkers. The birdlife here is prolific and often unique, making this a popular bird-watching area.

Cape York Peninsula has a profuse birdlife with some 230 species recorded, 13 of which are endemic. The best time of year for bird-watching is October to March when migratory birds from New Guinea and elsewhere are in residence. However, this is a relatively undeveloped region with most roads north of Cooktown unsealed and likely to be closed during this wet period. You need to travel well-prepared and with a reliable four-wheel drive, or you can fly to Pajinka Wilderness Lodge at the northern end of the Peninsula. During the rest of the year, the roads are more reliable and you will still see abundant wildlife.

Australian Birds

The great variety of birds in Australia makes bird-watching particularly rewarding, especially when you see in the wild a bird that is so often seen only in a cage. Parrots, budgerigars and cockatoos appear much more colourful when they are wild and free and chasing each other through native bushland. Even the dull coloured emu looks more regal when stalking across an open plain. The following are my observations of the interesting, tuneful and occasionally funny types of birds you will find on a journey through Australia.

Honeyeaters make up the largest family of Australian birds — 65 species — and they are found in every corner of the continent.

Among the best singing birds in Australia are the butcherbird,

Australia's only stork, the jabiru, Mary River, Northern Territory

Australian magpie, songlark, honeyeater, whistler and the grey shrike-thrush. The eastern whipbird has a very distinctive voice, which starts with a soft whistle and builds to a sharp crescendo, which sounds like a whipcrack. This sharp whipcrack is a familiar sound to all who have spent time in the wet forests and heaths along the east coast. Bellbirds are another local favourite; their song is the pure ping of a perfect note.

Australia has 52 species of parrot, more than any other country except Brazil. Their noisy, colourful presence gives radiance to the countryside over most of the continent. The pretty little lorikeet is found in most coastal regions and colourful rosellas are found in patches around the mainland coast and Tasmania. The grand king parrot lives along the east coast, especially in timbered mountain regions and forests.

The rare princess parrot is seen only in drier, inland areas, usually near waterways. Another inland dweller is the chirpy little budgerigar, the best known of all cage birds. This small parrot lives wild and free throughout inland Australia and I was amazed to see a huge flock near where I was camped beside a bore, north of Mount Isa. I heard them first — because they are very noisy — chattering like children at play. They were a spectacular sight — there were hundreds in the flock and they swirled and dived in rapid formation creating astonishing flashes of colour against the blue sky.

Some birds have unique characteristics which have endeared them to Australians who have put them into song and legend. The most famous is the laughing kookaburra which starts its song with a quiet chuckle, building up to

114

Rosella

a raucous human-sounding laugh. There is no sound more guaranteed to stir an Australian away from home than this audacious song. The kookaburra is widely distributed, living along the east coast, across into South Australia, in the south-west, and Tasmania.

As for clowns, there are few better than the beautiful pink and grey galah. Their circus acts include skilful aerial acrobatics, high-wire tricks like dangling upside down on power lines, balancing acts, such as hanging by the beak from the top of a pole, and they are also great mimics. They usually mate for life and a tree filled with galahs looks like a Christmas tree with all the decorations in pairs. Galahs live throughout Australia, except for narrow strips along the east coast of Cape York Peninsula and the southwest coast and parts of Tasmania.

The sulphur-crested cockatoo is a popular pet and can be taught to talk, it appears to be amused by humans and enjoys attention. In the wild it lives in timbered country along the northern, eastern and southeastern coastlines, in Tasmania, on some offshore islands, including Kangaroo Island, and it has been introduced to the Perth area. It is very beautiful with a clean, white body washed in parts with yellow. Unfortunately, its song is not as attractive as its appearance and many campers know what it is to be woken by the strident call of cockatoos in the early hours of the morning. Its handsome cousin, the red-tailed black cockatoo, is more widely distributed. This lovely bird is found across most of the northern half of the continent, down the west coast and in patches of South Australia.

The lyrebird is famous for its ability to mimic other birds; it is said it can also mimic animals and other noises. The male has a long tail of filigree-like feathers — the two outer

Kookaburra

feathers shaped like the musical instrument, the lyre — which it displays spectacularly to attract a female. It lives in coastal forests between Brisbane and Melbourne and in parts of Tasmania. It is shy and difficult to find in the wild.

The willie wagtail is seen throughout Australia, riding on the back of farm animals and digging for worms, insects and spiders. Most Australians are familiar with its characteristic 'wiggle', its sleek black feathers and its white eyebrows and belly.

The emu, which is on the Australian coat of arms, is a large, flightless bird just a little smaller than the African ostrich. Its naturally curious nature has made it easy prey to man, firstly to the Aboriginal people for food and later to the Europeans, who considered it a nuisance on their farmlands. It has survived though, and can be seen in most parts of the continent with the exception of urban areas, parts of the east coast and Tasmania.

Bird-watching Clubs and Organisations

The **Bird Observers Club of Australia** has its headquarters and shop in Melbourne, with 15 branches and 50 club representatives around the country. The club does not prepare individual itineraries but organises many outings for members. The club's monthly magazine, the *Bird Observer*, is filled with interesting articles and information on club activities.

The **Royal Australasian Ornithologists Union (RAOU)** is a non-profit organisation of keen bird-watchers. It has been operating for 90 years and has undertaken many studies of Australian birds. The RAOU also works with land owners and managers, conservation agencies and governments on the rehabilitation of natural habitats that have been lost through farming or other human intervention.

The RAOU does not organise tours but willingly accepts volunteers for its bird conservation projects. It has four observatories, which provide a fixed location for detailed studies of birds in the wild and a fascinating place for amateur and keen birder-watchers to visit. As they are basically self-funding, all income from tours and accommodation is welcome.

Broome Bird Observatory is located at Roebuck Bay, 19 km (12 m) from Broome in Western Australia. The climate is arid–tropical and the habitats include intertidal flats and beaches, pindan woodland, open plains, mangroves and salt marshes. It is regarded as one of the six most important sites for migratory shorebirds in the world. Bird-watching is excellent throughout the year, but especially from September to April when many thousands of migratory waders arrive.

Observatory staff give guided walks, courses suitable for people with little knowledge of birds, and invite visitors to join other studies. The area is also popular for photography and bushwalking.

Accommodation is in camping grounds, a self-contained chalet which sleeps five, or in rooms with shared facilities. Overnight guests will be picked up from Broome; call (091) 93 5600.

Eyre Bird Observatory is on the coastal edge of the Nullarbor Plain, 1250 km (777 m) east of Perth and 1522 km (946 m) west of Adelaide; the nearest town is Cocklebiddy (48 km (30 m) away). It is set in dense mallee country and is an excellent place to look for dry-country birds. Studies have been made of the malleefowl, red-capped plover, southern scrub-robin and white-browed scrub-wren. Visitors can join in any of the current bird studies, or take a course in mammals, reptiles, plants, history, art or photography. The observatory is within walking distance of the beach and within the Nuytsland Nature Reserve ((090) 39 3450).

Accommodation is in an old stone building built in 1897 as the Eyre Telegraph Station and restored in 1977; camping is not allowed. Access from Cocklebiddy is possible by two-wheel-drive vehicle to the Lookout, about 12 kms (7½ m) from the observatory; from here it is restricted to four-wheel-drive vehicles and takes about 45 minutes. By prior arrangement a warden will pick-up at Cocklebiddy or the Lookout and there is a transfer fee.

Rotamah Island is on the shores of Lake Victoria, a short walk from Ninety Mile Beach, east of Melbourne. Vegetation is coastal woodland and heathland swamps, which attracts large numbers of ducks, swans, pelicans and other waterbirds. The observatory has a variety of short courses including bird-watching, insects, flora, fungi, wildlife painting and sketching. Visitors are welcome to participate in current bird studies.

Accommodation is basic and you will need your own sleeping bag and pillow case. If arriving from the north you can arrange boat transport from Paynesville. If coming through Loch Sport, phone the observatory ((051) 56 6398) from there, and a warden will meet you at Trapper Point, 35 minutes from Loch Sport.

Barren Grounds Bird Observatory is, despite the name, part of a large and beautiful nature reserve that boasts a spectacular display of wildflowers in spring. It is located on the road between Jamberoo and Robertson on the New South Wales south coast, an easy day trip from Sydney, Canberra or Wollongong. Habitats range from coastal heathlands through to rainforest. Many honeyeaters are seen during the day but the main attractions are the ground parrot and the eastern bristlebird — both best seen at twilight or dawn. You can guide yourself along the marked trails, or enrol in one of a variety of courses, which include photography and bird-watching.

Bunkhouse style accommodation is available in a stone hut with a shower but no hot water (you need your own sleeping bag). Book with the warden ((042) 36 0195) if staying overnight and require a cooked meal.

Australian Wildflowers

Australia's flora has developed over the centuries in isolation from the rest of the world and in extremes of climate. As a result, it is very diverse, with species and characteristics unique to Australia and of great interest to botanists. An estimated 25 000 native plant species are known to grow here, but Europeans only arrived in Australia a little more than 200 years ago and new species are being found every year.

While the botanists fossick for the rare and unknown, most people are happy just to drive into the country in spring to see the wildflowers that line the roads and spread in joyful patches of colour across the countryside. Blooms usually start to appear with the onset of warm weather — about August to September — and go through into early summer. The alpine regions bloom a little later, waiting for the warmer summer months of January and February.

In arid and semi-arid regions the wildflowers wait until it rains before they burst into life. The displays are spectacular, and a fascinating aspect

Alpine wildflowers, Thredbo, New South Wales

Cup gums

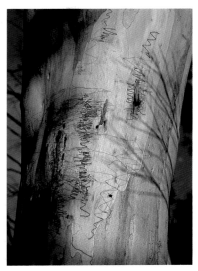

Scribbly gum

of desert plants is that so many will lie dormant for years, waiting for a good downpour or a substantial fire before they start the flowering, seeding and regrowth cycle.

Australia has a few unusual plants and some extremely pretty ones. The Pandani heath found in Tasmania, grows to 12 m (39 ft), and is the tallest heath in the world. Tasmania also has a tree which is estimated to be 4000 years old, making it the oldest living thing on earth. And there are rainforests which have evolved from species living on the ancient continent, Gondwana.

Australia's most famous tree is the gum (eucalypt) of which there are about 450 distinct varieties plus numerous related species and hybrids. Gums range in size from the huge 90 m (295 ft) mountain ash to stunted arid-zone types. The

smaller, dry country trees usually have the best flowers. The jarrah is one of the world's hardiest and most durable woods.

The country's other well-known tree type is the wattle (genus acacia) of which there are about 900 species in Australia. The golden blossoms of the wattle are stunning and splash the countryside with brilliant colour in spring. Wattles are akin to the mimosa genus of Northern America and Europe.

On a worldwide scale, the sandstone country of coastal New South Wales has more varieties of plants than the British Isles, and the wildflowers in the southwest corner of the country provide one of the most varied and largest displays in the world.

The families Proteaceae, Myrtaceae and Mimosaceae are very

much part of Australia's horticultural kaleidoscope, along with the orchid family which has more than 600 species. The Proteaceae family, which includes the waratah, grevillea and banksia, has some 1500 species throughout Australia, of which more than half are indigenous. They are found in most regions but particularly in the southwest where some 500 species have been identified.

The widely distributed Myrtaceae family, with more than 1000 species, includes the eucalypt, which is found in virtually every corner of Australia. Only in rainforests or arid regions may it be missing or sparse. The Myrtaceae is the largest family of flowering plants in Australia, ranging in size from tiny shrubs to mighty trees. Within this family are the well-known ironbark, crimson bottlebrush, swamp paperbark and tea-tree.

The acacia from the Mimosaceae family is often the only woody vegetation to be found in the semi-arid and arid interior. Anyone who has travelled these areas will be familiar with gidgee, mulga, brigalow and myall. Also in this family is the Australian Golden Wattle, the national floral emblem.

Western Australia

Western Australia is the undisputed wildflower centre of Australia, with its southwest corner regarded as one of the finest wildflower regions of the world. Isolated for thousands of years by ocean on the west and desert on the east, the flora has developed its own persona. Of the state's more than 10 000 plant species about 75% are endemic to the area. Most of the wildflowers bloom in spring, starting in July north of Perth to about Carnarvon, and lasting to the end of the year in the cooler southwest corner. The prime time is August, September and October, which is when the wildflower shows are held and hundreds of people arrive just to walk and feast their eyes on the splendour nature has provided.

What makes Western Australia's wildflowers so exciting is their countless numbers and the different environments in which they live. In the south, forests of towering jarrah and marri trees are alive with colour when the spring blooms appear on the lower-growing yellow wattle, white pimelias, blue lesbenaultia, mauve pepper-and-salt and blue-eyed reed. Along the coast at West Cape Howe, near Albany, the coastal heath is coloured with banksias, dryandras, hakeas and plants from the Myrtaceae family.

In January and February, the blooms of the swamp bottlebrush turn the swamps of the Scott National Park, near Augusta, scarlet. The golden kangaroo paw also flowers in summer on the sandy coastal plains — the red and green kangaroo paw is Western Australia's floral emblem.

It is impossible to name all the places to see wildflowers in spring in the southwest. Oakley Dam, near Dwellingup, has displays of blue squill, white bunny orchids and tiny star in winter and early spring; golden dryandras and sea urchin hakeas in spring; and yellow and pink verticordias, red bottlebrush, white beard-heaths and orange lemon-scented darwinia in summer.

All the national parks are ablaze with colour at this time and have good walking trails for access to the wildflower areas. Along the south coast, Cape Le Grand National Park has undulating heath-covered sandplain with swamps and freshwater pools; Stokes National Park has coastal heath, scrub and low forest; Ravensthorpe Ranges has rare flora from eucalypts to orchids; and further inland is the Fitzgerald River National Park, one of the state's two biosphere reserves. Here wildflowers include royal hakea, pincushion hakea, four-winged mallee, scarlet banksia, and qualup bell.

Stirling Range National Park has 1000 m (3281 ft) high ranges, which produce a slightly different climate to the surrounding district, and 1500 species of flowering plants, of which 60 are endemic. Of interest are the ten species of darwinia, or mountain bell, (nine endemic to the ranges, including the pendulous Cranbrook Bell). Orchids grow in the wandoo woodland south of the caravan park. The park is 75 km (46 m) north of Albany and the best months for wildflowers are September to November. The town of Cranbrook has a wildflower display featuring orchids, banksias and darwinia in September–October.

The southern township of Ongerup has a large wildflower show in September–October with the local flora botanically named and seeds for sale. Other shows are at Nannup, which has a week of wildflower and nature walks in September, and Augusta, which stages its annual Spring Orchid Show in September.

North of Perth there are so many places to see wildflowers it is difficult to select only a few. The area around Coomallo Creek, near Badgingarra, 205 km (127 m) north of Perth, is often described as having the most beautiful wildflowers in the state. Some of the 200 varieties include black and yellow kangaroo paws, blue smokebush, painted and scarlet featherflowers, scholtzias and the local Coomallo banksia. The renowned 'Wildflower Way' extends from Wubin (272 km (169 m) northeast of Perth) to Mullewa (450 km (279 m) north of Perth), a distance of 178 km (110 m). You will want to stop many times along this road, for native foxgloves and everlastings carpet the ground beneath brilliant yellow wattles. Adding to all this splendour are the hundreds of birds that are attracted by the nectar. The flowers bloom after rain but as a guide, the best months are August, September and October. The Mullewa Wildflower Show that runs during August and September displays more than 200 species native to the region.

At Kalbarri National Park the Murchison River has cut a deep gorge through rolling sandplains, and 300 flowering plants give a spectacular display from August. The park is 590 km (366 m) north of Perth and accommodation and tours are available at Kalbarri.

Close to Perth (120 km (74 m) north), the Moore River National Park is a spectacular wildflower reserve which has displays all year round. It is especially good in December when the shoulder-high, golden Christmas morrison blooms. Bindoon, 80 km (50 m) north of Perth, holds an annual Wildflower Weekend in September, with a massed wildflower display, arts and crafts and other activities.

In Perth, the 400 ha (988 a) Kings Park and Botanic Garden has an excellent display of Australian wildflowers in spring. It also stages Australia's largest native plant display and wildflower exhibition annually in October. Indoor and outdoor areas are used for this massive festival, which includes scientific, educational and trade exhibits as well as guided walks.

Numerous organisations run wildflower tours out of Perth during wildflower season. The longest established is **Westrail Travel,** which has been running coach tours with a botanical guide on board for more than 40 years. Westrail is at the City Rail Station in Wellington Street and has a range of tours lasting from three days/two nights to eight days/seven nights. **Falcon Tours** also has wildflower tours in season (see Tour Operators, page 171), and **Footprints Expeditions** has weekend wildflower walks in season and wildflower identification courses with a botanist (see Bushwalking, page 87).

Contact the Western Australian Tourist Centre for information on other tour operators and ask for its excellent brochure called 'Wildflower Discovery'.

Victoria

Victoria is promoted as the 'Garden State' and is spectacular during spring and summer when wildflowers bloom profusely. It has about 2500 recorded species of native wildflowers, shrubs and trees and a long flowering season from August to March.

The Grampians National Park offers one of the best displays in the country and attracts botanists and naturalists from all over the world. Some 900 flowering plants are found here, including wattles, orchids,

Wattle — Australia's floral emblem

white smoke bush, tea-trees, guinea flowers, pink heaths, blue lilies, pincushions, purple mint bushes, boronias and scarlet grevilleas. The park is located 260 km (161 m) west of Melbourne and the best time to visit is from August to November. There is plenty of accommodation in neighbouring towns.

Within an easy drive of Melbourne is the Brisbane Ranges National Park, which has spectacular wildflower displays in spring, the nectar attracting hundreds of birds. Wilsons Promontory, 250 km (155 m) southeast of Melbourne, is one of the most southerly points of the Australian mainland and contains tall forests, fern gullies and coastal heathlands which flower in spring.

Take time to visit Lilly-pilly Gully, a patch of temperate rainforest where the lilly-pilly tree displays its shiny, dark green leaves and white or purplish berries.

Victoria's alpine regions bloom in spring and summer and there is a good network of walking trails leading to the wildflower areas. The Alpine National Park has more than 1100 native plant species, 12 of which are unique to this area, and its best displays are during summer. Mount Buffalo National Park's wildflowers are at their best from November to March, and the Bogong High Plains near Falls Creek are best just after the snow has melted in October and November.

If you would like to see the

Orange grevillea

Banksia

wildflowers with a guide, contact **Bogong Jack Adventures** at Oxley (see Tour Operators, page 171). Bogong runs wildflower and heritage tours (also Mount Kosciusko wildflower tours) during January and February, taking small groups and staying in local lodges. A local field naturalist escorts all tours and the walking is easy.

For wildflower displays of the semi-arid parts of Victoria, visit the Little Desert National Park where the countryside becomes a mass of pink, red, yellow and white flowers during spring. The park is 365 km (227 m) northwest of Melbourne in a relatively sparsely populated area but accommodation is available at Nhill or the Little Desert Lodge (see Tour Operators, page 171). A wildflower exhibition is held at Little Desert Lodge during the first week of October.

New South Wales

New South Wales is a state of contrasts. From its wet coastal regions to the alpine areas to the dry interior, it has a wide range of soil types and climates which produce a diversity of wildflowers. Most wildflowers bloom in spring, although they appear later in the alpine regions and perhaps will not appear at all in the arid regions unless there has been rain.

Close to Sydney, the heathlands of the Ku-ring-gai, Royal and Bouddi national parks give superb wildflower displays in spring and the Blue Mountains National Park shows off its banksias, waratahs, grevilleas and pea bushes. The waratah, the state's floral emblem, is a beautiful ornamental shrub and its big, red flower head fills the bush with colour.

The arid and semi-arid inland areas are sparsely vegetated and only bloom after good rain. However, the Warrumbungle National Park, 490 km (304 m) northwest of Sydney and on the edge of the western plains, is an oasis of flora and fauna with hundreds of wildflowers blooming in spring. The park is located where east meets west and its diversity of landform and microclimate produces plant species from the moist east coast, as well as the dry western plains. Wildflowers include wattles, peas and heaths, which are usually associated with coastal areas.

It is an interesting exercise to drive west from the coast south of Sydney and study the vegetation as you go; you will pass through a microcosm of Australian plant life. Along the coast there are plants which can survive sandy soils and salt spray. As you drive inland you come to tall forests of eucalypts, then a steep escarpment which captures the clouds and produces cool temperature rainforest with ferns underfoot. At the top of the escarpment the plateau of dry, poor soil reduces the vegetation to open woodland and stunted eucalypts.

Continuing inland you come to the base of the Snowy Mountains, where the valleys and lower regions support ferns and dense vegetation. This changes quickly as you start to climb up the mountainside. Taking the chairlift from Thredbo you can watch the trees and shrubs twist and shrivel, shrinking closer the ground where they can find shelter from the harsh climate. Mountain plum pine, tree violet, mountain baeckea, yellow kunzea and alpine oxylobium all reduce in size as they climb up the mountain.

At the top of the chairlift you reach treeless alpine country. The plants living here survive part of their life under snow, which makes their springtime display all the more remarkable. Some 200 plant species live on the alpine plateau, many of which are found nowhere else in the world. The floral display lasts all summer with some blooms lasting into autumn; the peak time is late January to early February.

From the top of the chairlift, there is a 6 km (4 m) raised, mesh walkway to the summit of Mount Kosciusko. This marvellous walkway lets light filter through so the plants underneath can grow healthy and strong, and allows for the normal flow of water. The first part of the walk is through sphagnum bog which has dense low growth, perfumed herbs and beautiful bright flowers such as billy-buttons, silky daisies, bluebells, hoary sunrays, purple eyebright and Kosciusko pineapple grass, which is endemic to the region. If you look into the clear pools of water you will see little tadpoles swimming. The walk takes about two-and-a-half hours. It is not a difficult walk, but has a gradual uphill grade — the return journey is quicker. As you follow the walkway you will notice a worn path where

the vegetation has been badly damaged by walkers before the raised walkway was installed. The vegetation had also been damaged by the trampling and grazing of sheep and cattle and the burning back by leaseholders, none of which is now permitted within the park.

The choice of accommodation in the region is extensive, including tourist units in the township of Jindabyne, mountain lodges, camping along the leafy banks of the icy Thredbo River and ski lodges at Thredbo Alpine Village. Thredbo Village has a comprehensive summer program of guided mountain walks, cycling, golf, tennis, horse riding and occasional evening activities.

Australia's largest botanical garden specialising in native flora is the Mount Annan Botanic Garden at Narellan, 57 km (35 m) southwest of Sydney. The garden, which opened in 1988, covers 400 ha (988 a) of rolling hills and man-made lakes. Establishing the garden is a mammoth task. Already, hundreds of Australian natives have been planted here but it will be years before the planting is complete and the plants have reached maturity.

You can drive or cycle around Mount Annan, or take the free guided bus tour. The garden is designed in a series of themed gardens, which include the Bottlebrush Garden, Wattle Garden and Arboretum, Banksia Garden, Eucalypt Arboretum and the Fig Arboretum. Of particular interest, is the 4.5 ha (11 a) Terrace Garden, which is arranged in family groups

Tea-tree

One-sided bottlebrush

following the evolutionary progress of plants from the most primitive to the more advanced.

The park is open daily, except Good Friday and Christmas Day, and has lovely picnic areas with gas barbecues, a visitors' centre, bookshop and kiosk.

Australian Capital Territory

The Australian National Botanic Gardens, covering 90 ha (222 a) on the lower slopes of Black Mountain, specialises in native plants. Its collection of more than 6000 native species includes many plants gathered on field trips around the country. Walks lead through the gardens where special features include the Rainforest Gully, Eucalypt Lawn and the Rockery. The gardens, located on Clunies Ross Street in Acton, are open daily except Christmas Day, and contain a visitors' centre, bookshop and kiosk.

Although Canberra's annual spring festival, Floriade, does not specialise in wildflowers, it is so

Lemon-scented myrtle

Billy buttons protected by raised walkway

spectacular I feel it should be mentioned. The city literally festoons itself with flowers which blaze with colour during the day and are floodlit at night. The best of the private gardens are open to the public, all major buildings have special floral displays and Commonwealth Park, on the northern shore of Lake Burley Griffin, is the setting for entertainment, arts and crafts and more flowers. The festival is held from mid-September to mid-October.

Northern Territory

The best source of information on the plants of central Australia is the Olive Pink Reserve on the east bank of the Todd River in Alice Springs. The 16 ha (39 a) reserve specialises in plants living within a 250 mm (10 in) rainfall zone and is the only arid zone botanic garden in Australia.

It contains more than 1700 labelled plants and a visitors' centre and is open daily, except Good Friday and Christmas Day.

The state's floral emblem, the Sturt's desert rose, is a pretty hibiscus-style flower of delicate mauve with a red centre. It is a desert shrub but is not often seen in the wild; you are more likely to see it in people's gardens, flowering during the hot months from spring to early autumn.

Hoary sunrays

If good rains have fallen, the seemingly barren desert can suddenly be knee-deep in wildflowers. Many of the flowers here are ephemerals, and members of the daisy and pea families, which have adapted to the arid conditions, extremes of temperature, winds and long dry spells. Some seeds lie dormant for years until there is sufficient rain to stimulate germination and take the plant through its phase of flowering and seed production. Although brilliant after rain, if the season has been dry there will be little here to excite you. The gorges in the MacDonnell Ranges near Alice Springs have good displays of daisies in winter and early spring if there has been sufficient rain. By October it is too hot and they will have shrivelled away. Most plants in the northern end of the state flower and fruit during the dry season (May to September) so their seeds are dropped to be nourished by the rains of the wet. However, you will see some wildflowers most of the year. When the Darwin currajong (the city's floral emblem) and the kapok bush flower the locals know the dry is coming. The vast wetlands of the region are covered in dense lily bushes which start to flower in April, and the paperbark trees blossom in October, attracting fruit bats. The wildflowers in Katherine Gorge National Park bloom in late summer–early autumn.

Queensland

To many wildflower aficionados, the Girraween National Park near Warwick is the best wildflower region along the eastern seaboard. Its rugged landscape of granite peaks, balancing rocks and moist valleys nurtures a wide variety of plants. When the wattles are out the hillsides are bathed in yellow and the heaths flower profusely from July to October.

Queensland's climate ranges from wet tropical to subtropical along the coast and is dry inland. The wet rainforests in the north at Daintree and Bartle Frere are relics of the ancient forests of Gondwana and are of extreme biological significance containing a host of unusual plants, many of which are endemic. The jungle of vegetation includes huge buttressed trees, strangler figs, palms, mosses, ferns, vines, some interesting fungi which glows in the dark, and magnificent staghorns, elkhorns and bird's nest ferns that cling to host tree trunks. Rainforests support some lovely orchids and the varieties you are most likely to see in Queensland include the spider, orange blossom, king (or rock lily), ravine, moth and bearded orchids. The Cooktown orchid, which can be white, light pink, blue or deep pinky purple, is native to northern Queensland and is the state's floral emblem.

In the southeast, the plateaus along the coast and the higher regions of the Great Dividing Range become a mosaic of colour in spring. An easily reached coastal heathland is the Noosa National Park, which has a great diversity of wildflowers. Inland from Surfers Paradise, low, shrubby and often aromatic heath communities grow around the cliff tops in Lamington National Park and bloom in spring. The rest of the park is covered in subtropical rainforest, open forest and woodland.

South Australia

Good wildflower displays are found during spring in many parts of the state, especially the southern Flinders Ranges, along coastal heathlands and on Kangaroo Island. Inland areas are arid and really only bloom after a good downpour.

Kangaroo Island has more than 700 native plant species, 150 introduced species and 60 varieties of orchids, including the green-hooded, spider, and donkey orchids. Wildflowers can be found most of the year but are at their best from August to November. Heaths, scarlet bottlebrush, mallee, mauve Melaleuca, yellow rice flowers, banksias and the purple fringe lily are but a few. Sugar gums, blue gums, swamp gums and river red gums grow along rivers and in spring the golden wattle is in full colour. Kangaroo Island can be reached by air from Adelaide, or by ferry from Cape Jervis and Port Adelaide. It has an active tourist industry and offers a wide choice of tours and accommodation.

The Mount Remarkable National Park at the southern end of the Flinders Ranges is a wetter area than further north and has a rich vegetation with masses of wildflowers in spring. A hibiscus may seem out of place in this cool climate, but the pretty lilac hibiscus is native to the state and blooms in spring, along with the fringed myrtle, needle-bush, dog wattle and the cassinia daisy bush. Accommodation is available at nearby Melrose and Wilmington, or you can camp in the park.

It is remarkable that plants can survive the immense, low-lying areas of salt plains and arid desert which make up the Lake Eyre basin in the north of the state, but some have. The hardy saltbush, bluebush, mulga, spinifex and pittosporums (wild apricot) survive here, and the coolabah and river red gum grow where there is water. But it is after rain that the area really explodes with colour. Great patches of colourful daisies, billy buttons, wild geraniums, poached-egg daisies, pink daisies, purple and brown vetches, and grasses appear as though from nowhere for a short burst of life.

Tasmania

The island state of Tasmania has many endemic plant species, some having close relatives in South America and New Zealand. It is Australia's stronghold of the descendants of the flora of the ancient continent Gondwana, with pencil pines more than 1000 years old and stands of huon pines up to 2000 years old. The wet, temperate rainforests here are home to ancient myrtle beeches, sassafras, native laurel and celery-top pine. The gullies are luxuriant with ferns, mosses and lichen.

In the higher regions the trees give way to wonderful alpine moorlands

Cushion plant

which become a mass of ground-hugging, flowering plants in spring and summer. The famous walks that crisscross the alpine national parks are lovely at this time of the year. In the north you can drive up the Great Western Tiers near Deloraine to Jackeys Marsh where there is a boardwalk crossing a bog of ancient pencil pines, flowering tea-tree and heaths. At Cradle Mountain–Lake St Clair National Park the visitors' centre can supply information on a choice of excellent alpine walks.

The coastal heathlands of Freycinet and Mount William national parks also have brilliant wildflower displays throughout spring and into summer. And if you are in Hobart, take a quick run up Mount Wellington, 1271 m (4170 ft) above the city. This windswept, rocky plateau is densely covered in flowering alpine vegetation during spring and summer and the views are spectacular.

Alpine heathlands, Jackeys Marsh, Tasmania

CYCLING

There are few more pleasant ways to see a country than on a bicycle: the pace is not too fast, the effort not too strenuous (depending the terrain!), bicycles do not use our diminishing fossil fuels and they do not pollute the air.

The modern bicycle is extremely sophisticated, the touring bike and the tougher mountain bike having been developed to the nth degree to provide serviceability and comfort. Equipped with a good cycle and a selection of maps, cyclists are spreading out all over Australia, cruising the country roads and bouncing along old logging roads and fire trails where once only walkers and four-wheel drive enthusiasts travelled.

Mountain-bike cycling

Australia's size and diversity makes it a fascinating and beautiful country to cycle around. It is approximately the size of the United States minus Alaska, but has a population of less than 18 million. With such a small population over such a large area you can hum along country roads and forest trails in glorious isolation for days.

The size and different climatic zones, however, mean you need to give a bit of thought to where you will go and at what time of the year. The mountain ranges through New South Wales and Victoria offer cool, crisp cycling during summer and glorious colours through spring and autumn, but can be icy and snow-covered in winter. The spectacular Great Ocean Road along Victoria's coast is best in spring and summer when the winds off the Southern Ocean have less bite. The southwest corner of Western Australia is magic in spring when its famous wild-flowers are in full bloom. The island of Tasmania, with its World Heritage listed wilderness areas and charming historic towns has a changeable climate, but is best in summer when the weather is at its warmest. The northern areas across Queensland, the Northern Territory and Western Australia are best during the cooler, drier winter months from May to September. The central desert regions are almost always hot and dry and the only time to cycle here is during winter.

The Australian scenery is a smorgasbord of delights. The coast roads of New South Wales and Victoria offer breathtaking views and safe beaches for a cooling swim; the wine-growing regions of South Australia, Victoria and New South Wales offer many gratifying 'fuel' stops; the central desert has soil almost as red as its spectacular sunsets, and the ancient tropical rainforests of Queensland are to be taken slowly and treasured. The Great Dividing Range offers challenging rides alternating between hard uphill drudge and daring down-hill dashes. History and wilderness lie side by side in Tasmania and the Northern Territory is a test of stamina.

The revival of interest in cycling in recent years has put an estimated six million people onto two wheels and this has compelled governments, retailers and cycle clubs to provide better cycle tracks, better bikes and more touring options. New South Wales and Victoria are the most populated states and have a comprehensive road network, which puts them at the forefront for cycling enthusiasts. The road rules for bicycles are the same as those for motorised vehicles, and helmets are compulsory in all states. The only other rule you need to remember is the rule of common sense: Australia is a big, hot country with a powerful sun, so always carry plenty of drinking water and protect yourself from the sun and wind with sunscreen and protective clothing.

Transporting bicycles from place to place is not difficult. On most trains you can purchase a separate ticket and your bike travels in the guard's van without disassembly. On coaches, the front wheel and sometimes the pedals need to be removed, however, some coach companies refuse to take bikes and others may be reluctant to do so during school holidays. By air, bicycles will need to be made as thin and compact as possible or boxed (boxes are available at most bike shops). As prices and restrictions are changeable, you should check with the relevant carrier close to your time of travel.

As for books on cycling, there are many. A few which have been written after personal experience and therefore provide good reliable information are: *Bicycle Touring in Australia* by Leigh Hemmings (Simon & Schuster, 1991), *Cycling the Bush — 100 Rides in New South Wales*, and *Cycling the Bush — 100 Rides in Tasmania* by Sven Klinge (Hill of Content, 1991; 1993); *Bicycle Tours of Southeastern Australia* and *Pedalling Around Southern Queensland* by Julia Thorn (Kangaroo Press, 1989; 1991), and *Bicycling Tasmania* by Ian Terry and Rob Bedham (Nugara Guides, 1991). The bi-monthly magazine, *Australian Cyclist*, published by the Bicycle Federation of Australia, is the Australian cyclists' bible and is full of useful information.

For the cyclist who wants to go it alone, the best place to start is with the principal cycling club in each state and territory (see page 202). Each club will give you information on cycling in its region and probably a list of regional clubs and activities.

For those who prefer to travel with a group there are quite a few tour options available. Most cycle companies concentrate on one region, and they have been listed according to the state or territory in which they operate. This is by no means all of the bicycle tour operators in Australia, but it is a good selection.

Australian Capital Territory

Canberra has a 130 km (81 m) network of cycle tracks which is heavily used by commuters as well as tourists (collect a cycle ways map from the Canberra Visitors' Centre). In the centre of the city there is a lovely lake encircled by a 22 km (13½ m) cycle track which takes about two hours to pedal around. It passes through lovely parks with trees and pretty picnic spots. You can hire a bike from Mr Spokes Bike Hire at Barrine Drive, Acton Park, on the north side of Lake Burley Griffin.

New South Wales

Before going anywhere in New South Wales you should visit the Bicycle Institute of New South Wales shop at Level 2, 209 Castlereagh Street, Sydney. It has a large selection of touring books, maps and other helpful information. Particularly useful is a specially prepared information package for touring in New South Wales, which has been

Cycling on the beach at Cape Tribulation, Far North Queensland

compiled by bikers. Another of its publications, *Cycling Around Sydney*, lists 33 rides ranging from 15 to 145 km (9 to 90 m) in length and all are linked with public transport.

Sydney is a cyclist's paradise having numerous parks and reserves, glorious harbour and ocean roads and large national parks on three borders. The great advantage of the three national parks is that they can all be reached by train. Ku-ring-gai Chase National Park on the northern boundary of the city and the Royal National Park on the southern

boundary are both coastal plateaus with breathtaking water views. The terrain is relatively easy until you drop down to the water's edge, which leaves you with a hard push back up again. The famous Blue Mountains National Park offers all types of terrain from easy — around the charming mountain villages — to extremely difficult down steep fire trails and escarpments to the valleys below.

Wollemi National Park, the state's largest wilderness area, 100 km (62 m) northwest of Sydney, has magnificent

roads in the park. You can even cycle almost to the top of Mount Kosciusko — take the road to Charlotte Pass and carry on along the well-formed access road which is closed to vehicular traffic but not to cycles. You will have to leave your cycle just below the base of the summit and walk the last bit. Another option is to get a friend to drive you up the road to Perisher so you can cycle the mostly downhill run to Jindabyne from there. There are numerous trails within the park and you can get maps from local shops or from the rangers. The best time to cycle is during summer; in winter many trails are closed by snow.

Paddy Pallin is an outdoor adventure company located 2 km (1¼ m) west of Jindabyne opposite the Thredbo Road turn-off. It has good mountain bikes and helmets for hire and maps of the cycle trails in the park. It also runs an easy half-day guided tour on private land and has longer options available.

canyons, cliffs and forests to explore, as well as ruins at Newnes and glow-worms in the old railway tunnel.

Kosciusko National Park in the Snowy Mountains, 450 km (279 m) south of Sydney, offers skiing in winter and a fabulous choice of trails for walking, cycling and horse riding in summer. Pioneer has a daily coach service to the resort town of Jindabyne, leaving Sydney at 10 a.m. and Canberra at 3 p.m. The cycling here ranges from easy along the country roads, to thrilling along the numerous fire trails and access

Good budget tours are offered by the **Youth Hostels Association of NSW Inc**. It has a one-day tour along the abandoned railway line to the glow-worm tunnel in Wollemi National Park, with a night at the Blue Mountains–Katoomba hostel. This is a total package with bike hire, helmet, guide, lunch and accommodation all included. Other YHA options include: a day bush-walking with a second day cycling in the Snowy Mountains, or a day abseiling and a day cycling in

Morton National Park. The organisation's *Hostel Travel* magazine has all current tour options listed.

Sydney-based **Morrell Adventure Travel** offers a selection of guided cycle tours throughout the state and has mountain bikes for hire. Tours options include: a half-day cycle around the beaches of Sydney; a day in the Blue Mountains; three days in the Southern Highlands, and three to seven days exploring the magnificent Kosciusko National Park. Accommodation on the longer trips is by camping and there is a support vehicle to carry your gear — and you if your legs give out. John Morrell has been involved in adventure travel for 12 years and leads the tours himself, or employs guides with good knowledge and people skills.

Northern Territory

Cycling in the Northern Territory is not recommended during the full heat of the summer months (October to April). It is mostly open, semi-arid and arid country with shadeless roads and long distances between small towns and water supplies. Be prepared to carry plenty of water and always wear clothing that will protect you from the sun as well as the mosquitoes and midges which thrive near the wetlands.

The Territory may pose a bit of a challenge for cyclists but it is worth the effort because it has some of the country's most magnificent desert and wetland scenery.

In the north, Kakadu, Litchfield and Katherine Gorge national parks are oases of exceptional beauty. They will reward you with views of magnificent escarpments, birds, waterfalls and luxuriant gorges with clear, cool water for swimming. But be prepared to cycle long, hot highways to reach them. From Darwin it is 100 km (62 m) to Litchfield National Park, 253 km (157 m) to Kakadu and 354 km (220 m) to Katherine. As an alternative you could catch a coach to the nearest stop and cycle from there.

Travelling south from Katherine, the next area of real interest is Alice Springs and the MacDonnell Ranges, a hot and mostly boring 1100-km (683 m) ride along the Stuart Highway. The MacDonnells have lovely cooling gorges with an unexpected amount of vegetation and wildlife but the gorges are a long distance from each other and you need to be fit and experienced to cycle here.

Before setting out on a major trip into the MacDonnell Ranges it may be a good idea to hire a bicycle (if you don't have your own) at Alice Springs and take the 24 km (15 m) sealed cycle track to Simpsons Gap, the nearest of the gorges. The track passes arid country, creek flats and low hills, but the grade is easy and suitable for all ages. Simpsons Gap is well worth seeing and the trip will give you a chance to experience the terrain and desert temperatures.

After Alice Springs, it is another 441 km (274 m) south along the Stuart Highway with a turn-off on to the Lasseter Highway, to reach Ayers

Rock Resort. Here you have a range of accommodation from camping to a 5-star hotel, and this can be your base for cycling around Uluru (Ayers Rock) and Kata Tjuta (the Olgas).

The MacDonnell Ranges and Ayers Rock areas are in the Red Centre of Australia, an area of timeless red deserts, scrubby vegetation and occasional gorges of awesome magnificence. It is not easy country to cycle through and I suggest you read Leigh Hemmings' description of touring the Red Centre in his book *Bicycle Touring in Australia* before you set out. It will either turn you off the idea, or whet your appetite for the adventure of a lifetime.

Queensland

Cairns, in Far North Queensland, staged the Grundig Mountain Bike World Cup in 1994. This was the first time this event had been held in the southern hemisphere and was a great boost for cycling in the region. The first round of the Australian Downhill Championships was held at the same time.

Queensland is a tropical and subtropical state, with rainforests, a glorious coastline backed by a forested mountain range, many off-shore islands, far-stretching western plains and the laid-back lifestyle hot weather fosters. Fabulous terrain for cycling, but remember most of the state is in the tropics so it is hot, steamy and very often raining. The best time to cycle the northern half of the state is from May to September when the climate is at its driest and the temperatures are cooler. The only disadvantage is that this is also the peak holiday season, so there will be a lot of traffic on the roads and accommodation could be heavily booked.

A lovely scenic ride is the coast road from Cairns to Cape Tribulation, about 104 km (64 m). Follow Cook Road past Mossman and take the Daintree River ferry (which operates from 6 a.m. to midnight daily, except Christmas Day and Good Friday). From here the road winds along low coastal plains and through rainforest-clad hills. The ocean is safe for swimming except from October to May when the stingers (box jellyfish) are in the water. However, do not swim in any coastal rivers or estuaries where the dangerous saltwater crocodile lives. There are several lodges, camping areas and basic backpacker accommodation along the road.

From Cape Tribulation the road is unsealed and very steep in parts, however, if you are fit, it is sparsely populated and has beautiful beaches all the way to Bloomfield km (22 m).

Dan's Tours offers a full-day Cairns to Cape Tribulation cycle tour with 21-speed mountain bikes and a backup vehicle for the return journey. Dan Foley, a Cairns-born cycle enthusiast, has other day- and half-day tours available, as well as a weekend tour of the Bloomfield area. One of the rides Dan has made famous is the historical bump track, a hair-raising ride down an old goldminers' trail through ancient rainforest from the top of the mountain range to Port Douglas. This can be done as a half-day ride, or as a full-day incorporating other tracks and including lunch.

The Atherton Tableland above Cairns is another beautiful area to cycle (you can save yourself the very steep climb from Cairns by taking the historic and scenic train ride to Kuranda). Before leaving Kuranda you should visit the Australian Butterfly Sanctuary, one of the largest butterfly aviaries in the world. The Tablelands is a very pretty area with townships, hilly farmland, volcanic crater lakes and ancient rainforests of giant trees, waterfalls and abundant birdlife. The area is quite high — Mount Bartle Frere is 1612 m (5289 ft) above sea level — so it is cooler than the coast and is often shrouded in cloud.

Accommodation and camping areas are plentiful in the townships and resort areas on the plateau. You could stay at Chambers Rainforest Holiday Apartments, where you can hire bikes and John Chambers will show you the best places to cycle.

Cairns-based **Raging Thunder,** is a large commercial company which organises a variety of soft adventures including ballooning, sea kayaking, whitewater rafting, snorkelling on the reef, horse riding and cycling. It has half- and full-day cycle tours downhill through the hinterland behind Cairns, as well as longer adventure packages which incorporate a little of each of the activities.

At the southeastern end of the state is the Gold Coast, Australia's premier beach resort. You can hire cycles in Surfers Paradise, but the 50 km (31 m) stretch of golden beach is so heavily developed that you need to head west into the hinterland to touch nature. It requires a bit of effort to cycle up into the hinterland but once there, the subtropical rainforests, escarpments, crystal-clear streams, wildlife and panoramic views make it all worthwhile. You can camp in the national parks in the hinterland or select from a choice of local accommodation.

South Australia

The graceful city of Adelaide has many parklands and gardens with excellent bicycle tracks and Linear Park is being developed to provide a bicycle and pedestrian path system from the Adelaide Hills to the sea.

The Mawson Trail is a very challenging 800 km (497 m) cycle trail running from Adelaide to the outback town of Blinman. It has been

Tammar wallaby

Cycling through the bush

prepared by Recreation SA in association with local bike clubs and follows country roads, fire trails, station access tracks and unused road reserves. It passes through the Adelaide Hills, the Barossa Valley winegrowing region, pastoral land, country towns, and finishes in the spectacular Flinders Ranges (the last 70 km (43 m) within the ranges has still to be completed). There are some steep uphill sections but it is generally a magnificent trail, crossing some of the most scenic parts of the state. It is recommended that you use a mountain bike although a touring bike can make it with care on the rough parts.

A distinctive logo marks the Mawson Trail. Most sections have been planned as a day's cycle between towns where accommodation or camping areas are available; only in the far north has this not been possible. Detailed maps of each trail section (about $10 each) are available from the Office for Recreation, Sport and Racing Resource Centre.

Another trail planned for South Australia is the Riesling Trail which will accommodate cyclists, walkers, horse riders and wheelchairs. It will be 80 km (50 m) long, running along fairly level ground through the Clare and Gilbert valleys between Spalding and Riverton. It was only in early stages of development at the time of publication but is expected to be completed during 1996.

Kangaroo Island is a haven for wildlife and flora and has some good cycling along coastal roads with sandy bays and wild cliffs, and through national parks. Koalas have bred so successfully here that they are eating their way through their favourite eucalypt trees and supplies are becoming exhausted. Other wildlife includes platypuses, sea lions, kangaroos, Cape Barren geese, tammar wallabies, brush-tailed possums, echidnas and beautiful native birds. In spring, the ground is a mass of wildflowers. Accommodation is plentiful in the small towns, on farms or in camping areas, but the cycling is not for the unfit. Most of the island's 145 km (90 m) of roads are unsealed and often rutted with body-shaking

corrugations. You need a sturdy mountain bike and if you haven't got one you can hire one from Jackies Toy Box in Kingscote on a daily or longer basis. The best time to cycle is late summer or winter when rain has flattened the corrugations a bit and the summer tourist buses are not on the road revitalising them.

You can cycle all year in South Australia but it is best to avoid the very hot months of January, February and March, especially in the Flinders Ranges.

The Bicycle Institute of South Australia Inc has been operating for 20 years and has maps for sale and a library for members. It suggests you contact the following groups for recreational rides, camps and get-togethers: Adelaide Mountain Bike Club, PO Box 3127, Grenfell Street, Adelaide, SA 5000; Cycling for Pleasure Group, 15 Grant Avenue, Rose Park, SA 5067; SA Touring Cyclists Assoc, 1 Sturt Street, Adelaide, SA 5000.

Freewheelin Cycles in Adelaide hires out bicycles, runs cycle tours and will organise special itineraries for groups. Its tours range from a day discovering Adelaide to seven days cycling through the Flinders Ranges or Kangaroo Island. Ian Seymour has been running the company for three years and has equipped it with 30 mountain bikes, trailers to transport them and a mini bus. He is an experienced operator having organised tours for international travellers, school groups, fitness groups and individuals.

Tasmania

One of the most popular ways of seeing Tasmania is by bicycle. Its rolling farmlands, forests, wilderness areas, historic towns, numerous accommodation houses and great fresh food make for excellent touring. The island is well geared for tourism and along with all its historic accommodation, hotels and motels it also has a good network of backpacker hostels and youth hotels.

You would be wise to get 'cycle-fit' before tackling Tasmania as it is a roller-coaster ride for much of the way. Also be prepared for a change-able climate. Summer is the best time for cycling but even then it can turn cold enough for you to need a warm jumper and you must carry wet weather clothing.

A popular, all-encompassing ride is to do a loop of Launceston–Bicheno–Hobart–Strahan–Burnie–Launceston — about 1100 km (683 m). This would take a couple of weeks but you would need longer if you wanted to do side trips into the forests and World Heritage wilderness areas.

An excellent service for both walkers and cyclists is Tasmanian Wilderness Transport and Tours which specialises in pick-ups and drop-offs at out-of-the-way places. This is perfect for quickly getting to specific areas; you can collect timetables at most tourist outlets around the state.

Brake Out offers a choice of easy to moderate cycling tours of the state with accommodation in motels,

country pubs, host farms and holiday units. All guides are fully conversant with Tasmania's natural history and geography and national parks are visited for a walk with nature. Tours range from a half-day to a challenging eight-day 'Sun, Sea, Sand and Cycle' tour from Launceston across the Weldborough Pass, down the coast through tiny fishing villages to Freycinet Peninsula, and ending in Hobart. If none of the regular tours suit you, Brake Out will plan a special itinerary for a group of four or more.

Should a burst of madness overtake you in Hobart, join Brake Out's half-day, downhill run from the summit of Mount Wellington, 1271 m (4170 ft) above the city. You start in the moorlands at the top of the mountain where the vegetation is ground-hugging alpine shrubs and whiz all the way down, passing tall trees and ever increasingly denser vegetation until you are back in the city.

Tasmania Expeditions offers a good choice of cycle and mixed activity tours in Tasmania (see Tour Operators, page 171).

Victoria

Victorians like to cycle and it is easy to see why. Melbourne is mostly flat with hundreds of kilometres of lovely trails through parks and along the tree-lined banks of the city's famous Yarra River. The *Melbourne Bikeways Book*, published by Bicycle Victoria, is an excellent guide; call in at Bicycle Victoria's office at 19 O'Connell Street, North Melbourne for the book and while there you can make use of its reference library, buy maps and discuss touring ideas. You can cycle any time of the year in Victoria but it gets very cold in winter in the mountain regions and along the coastal roads.

If it is wildly beautiful cycling you want, take the Great Ocean Road, probably the most spectacular coastal ride in Australia, offering shipwrecks, sheer cliffs torn by crashing seas, idyllic beaches with white sand, pretty resort towns, old forests, unique limestone formations, the famous Twelve Apostles and history. If starting from Melbourne, take the train to Geelong to avoid the traffic on the main highway between these two cities. A charming stop would be the historic township of Port Fairy. After this it is westward all the way to South Australia, a distance of 430 km (267 m) from Geelong.

For a quieter, country journey you could head into the rich farmlands north of Melbourne. Here sparsely populated roads crisscross the countryside and it is so quiet you can hear the birds singing in the trees. Choose a route that takes you past Healesville, which has one of the finest native wildlife sanctuaries in Australia, and Kinglake National Park with its forested spurs, fern gullies and pleasant camping area.

Northwest of Melbourne is the state's famous goldfields country where spirits were broken and fortunes made. Gold was found in the little town of Clunes in 1851 and many other places after that. The population exploded as miners of

many nationalities arrived with hope in their hearts and dirt under their nails. Those boom and bust days are long gone, but the towns from Ballarat north to Bendigo are splendid with the extravagances of the successful miners who built ornate Victorian homes with fine gardens, and lined the streets with trees.

Keep cycling north from Bendigo and you will come to Echuca, a riverfront town of pubs, paddle-steamers and riotous fame in the early days of settlement. From here you can follow Australia's largest river, the Murray, west along flat, even country, camping beneath river red gums or finding lodgings in the country towns.

Victoria's high country in the northeast is renowned for its rolling mountains, alpine vegetation, springtime wildflowers, crisp air and spectacular views, to say nothing of the thrilling downhill cycle runs. This is get-away-from-it-all country. Here you can camp with nothing more than the stars and the wildlife to keep you company, or you can find accommodation in one of the many ski resorts or small towns. Wangaratta-based **Bogong Jack Adventures** has a good choice of one-day and longer cycles of this region, extending up into Echuca and the Barmah wetlands (see Tour Operators, page 171).

Western Australia

An excellent network of bicycle trails in Perth leads you past the sweeps and curves of the Swan River, along ocean beaches and through the

Most roads on Kangaroo Island are unsealed

centrally located Kings Park with its fabulous natural bushland and great views of the city.

The northern half of this state is huge, hot, lightly populated and mostly inhospitable for cyclists. But if you like a challenge, it is powerful countryside with spectacular escarpments and great swimming in richly vegetated gorges. However, there are long distances between gorges, towns and areas of beauty. Cycling here is only suitable in winter when the temperatures are cooler and the heavy summer downpours have passed.

Rottnest Island 20 km (12 m) off the coast from Perth, is a glorious place to ride a bike — there are few motor vehicles, the roads are all paved and the terrain is undulating. The only real difficulty is the afternoon wind in summer, which is a bit difficult to push against unless you have timed your ride to have it behind you, in which case the ride is a breeze. Bikes can be hired 200 m (220 yd) from the main arrival jetty and don't worry about missing out — there are 2000 high-quality mountain bikes for hire.

The southwest corner of Western Australia is glorious for cyclists. It has spectacular wildflowers in spring, excellent wineries around Margaret River, and in some areas the countryside is so heavily timbered with giant karri and jarrah trees that you pass through tunnels of branches and leaves. The coastline has sculptured sand dunes, rocky outcrops and sandy beaches. Spring is the best time for cycling although you will need wet weather gear as this is the damp time of the year. Parts of the southwest are hilly but there are no mountains to break your spirit and there is an abundance of accommodation in hostels, farms, lodges, country pubs and camping areas.

If you want to get into the southwestern area quickly, or just want to do a one-way cycle, you can transport your bike by rail to Albany on the south coast, about 400 km (248 m) from Perth.

Stirling Cycle Tours runs five-day camping and cycling trips through the southwest and will prepare special itineraries for groups of ten or more. Owners Val and Tim Saggers know the bush well and will explain how the Aboriginal people used it for food and medicine. Val uses mostly home-grown produce in her cooking and Tim is an enthusiastic amateur botanist and stargazer. They are strong believers in conservation and are actively involved in regeneration. Stirling also runs weekend trips to nature spots near Perth with accommodation in cabins or on farms.

For the really keen mountain biker with plenty of energy to spare, **Remote Outback Cycle Tours** has three remote, outback trips, which can be linked to make one great expedition encompassing the great desert and gorge areas of Western Australia and the Northern Territory. The first leg of the journey starts in Perth and travels via the famous goldfield towns of Kalgoorlie and Coolgardie, across the Great Victoria

Cycling country roads in New South Wales

Desert to the Aboriginal community of Warburton and finally the Petermann Ranges and Uluru (Ayers Rock). It takes 10 days and along the way you will meet Aboriginal people and learn about their culture. The second leg (five days) goes from Uluru to Alice Springs via the dramatic Kings Canyon and Palm Valley. The third and longest leg (14 days) goes from Darwin to Broome, with time spent at Kakadu National Park, the Bungle Bungle National Park and along the ruggedly beautiful Gibb River Road to Broome.

This is not for the faint-hearted — you often ride up to 120 km (74 m) a day and, although starkly beautiful, this is hot, dry terrain. A support vehicle carries all the gear and the bicycles on some long stretches of road between areas of interest. Tours run from April to September and are limited to 12 people with a minimum age of 16 years. For something a little

less strenuous, try the company's two-day Pinnacles Adventure with sand-surfing, windsurfing, abseiling, swimming, caving and cycling.

An extensive list of heritage trails which network the whole state has been prepared by the Western Australian Heritage Committee. Although mostly for walking or driving, they could provide some interesting alternatives to keen cyclists (see Useful Addresses, page 199).

Great Australian Bicycle Rides

These are organised events where you can meet other cyclists in a social atmosphere. They are not so much to do with nature as they are with cycling for pleasure, but I have included them because they offer a great Australian cycling experience. They are friendly, healthy, heaps of fun and a occasionally a tad competitive.

Bicycle Victoria's **Great Victorian Bike Ride** is the grand-daddy of them all. It was first run in 1984 as part of the sesquicentennial celebrations in Victoria. That event attracted 2100 cyclists but the ride now draws up to 5000 riders. This moving mass of colour and pedal power winds its way from the Blue Mountains in New South Wales, through wheat country, along great rivers and over mountains to Melbourne. It takes 16 days and is held in early December. If 16 days is too long you can take the eight- or nine-day options.

Bicycle Victoria has perfected the organisation of this ride and has it running like a Swiss timepiece. A huge team of volunteers plan the trip, provide all the food, carry the luggage and set up camp with toilets, hot showers and a field kitchen at each stop. All you need to provide is your own tent, bicycle and sleeping gear. To make life even more comfortable, there are medical facilities, massage clinics, bike repair workshops, movies, live bands, theatre and information via a radio station and a daily newspaper.

Every year Bicycle Victoria, which is a non-profit membership organisation, organises other rides with the same high-quality services. The following seven rides are a sample, but dates and routes can change. Only the Great Victoria and the Great Melbourne Bike Rides, and the Easterbike are regular annual events.

The Great Melbourne Bike Ride is an easy, one-day, carnival ride around the streets of Melbourne, held in March each year. To say it is popular is an understatement — it attracts about 15 000 riders. People ride as families, work groups or individuals, stopping at cafes along the way and finding streets they never knew existed.

Easterbike is for everyone. A base camp is set up at one of Victoria's country towns and from here bike rides and activities for all ages and energy levels are organised each day. Held over four days at Easter, it attracts about 1000 people.

Around the Bay in a Day is another famous one-day ride organised by Bicycle Victoria, although at 210 km (130 m) it is not for the faint-hearted or the unfit. If you cannot do it on your own, you can make up a team and do it as a relay. It is held in October each year.

The Great Ocean Road Bike Ride follows this stunning coastal road (mentioned earlier) of dramatic scenery and delightful fishing villages. The ride takes eight days, with distances ranging from 28 km (17 m) to 87 km (54 m) a day and one rest day. It is held in April and is limited to 500 participants.

Moving out of the state, Bicycle Victoria takes its organisational abilities north, south and across the Tasman to organise the **Great Queensland Bike Ride,** the **Great Tasmania Bike Ride** and the **Great New Zealand Bike Ride.** These three rides take you through a variety of terrains with some memorable views — tropical rainforests, sugar cane and sparkling white beaches in Queensland; historic towns, waterfalls and highlands in Tasmania; and glaciers, snow-fed lakes, snow-capped mountains and fertile plains in New Zealand.

The longest is the 18-day New Zealand ride which is held in February and can be done in eight- or ten-day options. The Queensland ride is held in August–September and takes eight days or can be done as a four-day option. The Tasmanian ride is held in January and takes seven days.

The Big New South Wales Bike Ride is a nine-day ride of about 500 km (310 m) through country towns and marvellous countryside. The route changes each year and it is so popular that the organiser, the Bicycle Institute of New South Wales, has had to place a limit of 1800 cyclists. Each day the ride arrives in a new country town and the residents really lay out the red carpet; it is big business for these small towns to receive so many visitors in one night. Nightly entertainment includes the Big Brasserie, sporting events, treasure hunts, talent quests, bush dances, a casino and local entertainment. A daily newspaper, the *Cycling Courier*, keeps everyone up to date with the news and satellite telephones allow you to keep touch with those back home. Accommodation is in a tent camp with hot showers, portable toilets, a general store, bike repairs, a medical centre, massage and much more.

Distances range from 45 to 85 km (28 to 53 m) a day and there are several routes each day so you can choose the one best suited to your fitness level. The ride starts on the first Saturday in March.

The Big Sydney Bike Ride is a day for the whole family. It is a relatively easy 65 km (40 m) ride around Sydney suburbs, along a different route each year. The average turnout is 2000 but the Bicycle Institute of New South Wales is hoping it will become bigger. It is always held on the last Sunday in May.

The Kellogg's Sustain Cycling Challenge is a day of fun and fitness with different distances pitched at riders of different levels. Its emphasis is on fitness and it offers good competition for riders who want to test themselves against others. You can choose from two different routes: a testing 100 km (62 m) route geared to the serious racer, or the 50 km (31 m) route for the less serious. Thus you can fly and be timed, or go slow and enjoy the scenery. It is held in August–September.

DIVING

—

ustralia is the largest island in the world, bounded by a coast-line of more than 36 000 km (22 369 m), 47 000 km (29 204 m) if you include its many islands. Most of the population lives in urban centres along the east coast, leaving thousands of kilometres of unspoilt beaches, quiet bays and rocky shelves around the coast. Water tempera-tures range from warm to tropical in the north and temperate to cold in the south.

As can be expected with such a long coastline the diving is fantastic and extremely varied. There are thousands of shipwrecks, coral reefs, caves, swim throughs, sand plains, drop-offs, forests of seaweed and kelp, and a diverse marine life ranging from the tiniest flash of colour to giant whale sharks.

Australia's most famous diving area is the Great Barrier Reef which extends in colourful abundance for 2300 km (1429 m) along the

Shore diving, Sydney, New South Wales

Heron Island, the Great Barrier Reef, Queensland

coast. But there is much more. Mount Gambier in South Australia has world renowned freshwater sink holes, Tasmania has jungles of kelp, Western Australia has dugongs and whale sharks living safely in huge marine parks, Darwin has wrecks galore, and the cool southern waters offer a diverse marine life.

So, where to start? Almost anywhere. High-quality, professional dive shops operate in virtually all cities and resort towns around the coast, as well as on some islands. They offer training courses with internationally recognised ratings, air, hire equipment and guided shore and boat dives. You must produce a certification card for air fills and gear hire in Australia. Some dive shops also provide ancillary equipment such as diver propulsion vehicles and underwater cameras.

The dive scene in Australia is friendly and generally speaking, easy going. Most dive shops run regular shore and boat dives for members and for visitors, and many produce a chatty newsletter for their members. Charter boats with experienced crew are available for longer trips, especially in Queensland where the tropical climate and the reef are perfect for extended dive trips.

Clown fish, the Great Barrier Reef

Most underwater flora, fauna and shipwrecks are protected, and must not be damaged or removed. Numerous marine reserves have been established around the coast and, although you can dive almost anywhere, it is wise to check with the local authorities or dive shop to find where it is safe and whether you require a permit. It is also wise to ask about any 'nasties' in the water. The dangerous saltwater crocodile likes warm water and lives near the coast in estuaries and rivers across the north of the continent. The box jellyfish also lives in the sea and coastal creeks of the warm northern regions and are in their greatest numbers from October to May. One box jellyfish can inflict severe stings which have been known to kill. Fully protective clothing is your best defence and it helps to carry copious quantities of vinegar to pour over stings.

If diving seems a bit scary, try snorkelling. Next to sitting in a glass-bottomed boat, this is the easiest way to view coral reefs and marine life. All you need is a snorkel, flippers and the ability to swim. No serious training is required and most dive shops and cruise boats have snorkelling equipment for hire. However, beware the power of the Australian sun. It burns very quickly and when snorkelling your shoulders and arms are exposed for long periods of time. As they say in Australia: 'slip, slop, slap' (slip on a shirt, slop on some waterproof sunscreen lotion and slap on a hat).

New South Wales

In the north of the state, charming Byron Bay offers good diving around Julian Rocks near the lighthouse where the water is still warm enough for tropical and subtropical fish. Travelling south, the warm waters fade out at about Coffs Harbour where the Solitary Islands offer good diving. South West Rocks at the entrance to the Macleay River has some large ocean caves, in particular Fish Rock Cave, which attracts divers from around the world. Forster has sponge gardens and offshore reefs, and Seal Rocks has abundant fish life.

Sydney has one of the world's largest, natural deep-water harbours. Ocean-going ships, cute green and yellow ferries and hordes of private craft give life above water, but there is also plenty to see underwater. Most shore diving is done from Little Manly Beach on the north side, or Camp Cove or Lady Jane Beach on the south side. Night diving when the crustaceans go walking and you can approach fish sleeping in crevices is also popular.

Sydney's ocean beaches are also suitable for shore diving. Drive to any coastal car park on a weekend and you are sure to see groups pulling on wet suits and planning their day. The coastline has good rocky reefs, sponges, corals and masses of fish. Numerous wrecks can be reached in a relatively easy 6 m (19 ft) of water, or a deep dive to 75 m (246 ft) or more. Although the water is cold in winter, this is when it is clearest and best for diving.

Fun Dive Frolics offers regular shore and boat dives in and around Sydney Harbour, equipment hire, charters, Scuba School International (SSI) courses to instructor level, and International Association of Nitrox and Technical Dives (IANTD) courses to Trimix instructor level. It is a busy dive centre which sends its regulars a breezy newsletter with divers' gossip and a monthly calendar of events, of social nights, early morning dives and weekends away. Fun Dive introduced 'mixed gas' (a technique that automatically tailors the balance between nitrogen and oxygen at different depths) into Australia in 1991.

Dive Centre Manly is just minutes from the magnificent Manly Beach and a pleasant ferry ride from downtown Sydney. It offers a range of dives from shore or boat and a special shark dive in the Manly Oceanworld shark tank. It is a Professional Association of Diving Instructors (PADI) 5-Star Instructor Training Facility with special courses for advanced divers, night and wreck dives, underwater photography and underwater naturalists. Korean-, Japanese- and Danish-speaking instructors are available. The centre has equipment for hire and will charter its 7 m (23 ft) Shark Cat to private groups. Members receive a regular newsletter listing forthcoming trips and general gossip.

South of Sydney is picturesque Jervis Bay with an underwater world of huge boulders, caves, tunnels and reef sponge gardens. The bay has a prolific fish life that changes with the seasons. During winter large schools of fish arrive with many pelagic species and the huge Australian cuttlefish. In late winter the harmless Port Jackson sharks enter the bay. In spring the shellfish are laying their eggs. Dolphins are plentiful and friendly, and whales are often seen on their migration north in early winter.

Further south, off the coast at Bermagui, is Montague Island where you can swim with seals. About 600 Australian fur seals live here and the mothers and pups often swim with divers. Montague Island also has large areas of shallow reef and deep drop-offs.

Lord Howe Island, 700 km (435 m) east of Sydney, has steep volcanic cliffs, strangely shaped caves, a labyrinth of arches and tunnels, and soft corals. Its lagoons and reefs offer excellent diving and snorkelling and the marine life is a mingling of species from the cool southern waters and the tropical northern waters. A dive shop on the island has gear for hire and offers PADI beginner courses and snorkelling courses.

Northern Territory

Darwin Harbour has more than 30 wrecks left over from a turbulent history of air raids during the Second World War and cyclones, especially Cyclone Tracy in 1974. For history enthusiasts, the oldest wreck is the steamship *Brisbane*. In recent years, a few artificial reefs have been laid and these, along with the natural coral reefs in the area, attract an great variety of marine life. The reefs are

Underwater, the Great Barrier Reef

mostly of soft corals and sponges, which are brightly coloured and make for great night diving.

Darwin's waters have a few lurking dangers of which you must be wary. One is the big tidal flow, which limits visibility from 3 to 5 m (10 to 16 ft) most of the time, 8 m (26 ft) on a good day. The spring tides are the worst, rising and falling some 7 m (23 ft) and badly clouding the waters. During spring, local divers stay home or head inland to the freshwater sites. Good inland sites can be found at Berry Springs, 30 minutes from Darwin, and Edith Falls and Mataranka near Katherine. Other dangers include the saltwater crocodile, which will attack if you enter its territory, the box jellyfish, stinging hydroids and stonefish. The box jellyfish is most prevalent from

October to May and during this time divers must wear fully protective clothing. It is a wise precaution to have a talk with a local dive shop before entering the waters in this region.

The best and safest way to enjoy diving in the Northern Territory is to go with someone who knows the area. **Coral Divers** is a well-established local company. It offers wreck and reef dives, hire equipment and National Association of Underwater Instructors (NAUI) dive courses. Two research trips for experienced open-water divers include counting the marine life on artificial reefs and a weekend course every September led by a marine biologist. It also takes groups into the freshwater dive sites. **Fannie Bay Dive Centre** also offers dive

Beginners receive instructions onboard a diveboat

excursions to the wrecks and coral reefs.

Queensland

Without doubt some of the Australia's most spectacular diving is in the warm waters washing the Great Barrier Reef. This magnificent World Heritage listed reef extends along the coast from the tip of Cape York to just north of Fraser Island, encompassing 2900 individual reefs and 600 islands. The reef is one of the world's treasures and is monitored and protected by the Great Barrier Reef Marine Park Authority at Townsville (see Useful Addresses, page 199). Check with the Authority for areas where you may dive and to obtain permits. The reef is described in more detail in the chapter on World Heritage Areas (page 13).

For divers and snorkellers the reef is a paradise with endless underwater miles of hard and soft living coral, giant clams, multitudes of colourful tropical fish, stingrays, manta rays, turtles and other fascinating sights. At the famous Cod Hole, experienced divers can meet giant potato cod fish that will take food from your hand and let you stroke them.

Diving and snorkelling tours, from half-day to extended trips, are available all along the Queensland coast, especially at Port Douglas, Cairns, Townsville, the Whitsunday Islands, and the Capricorn Bunker group of islands (Heron, Lady Elliott and Musgrave).

Port Douglas Dive Centre offers

PADI dive courses and snorkelling and dive tours for groups of up to ten people. It offers hand-held scuba diving for beginners and underwater scooter hire for something a bit different. On day trips to the reef an informative talk on the reef is given during lunch. Extended dive trips are also available.

Quicksilver Diving Services runs daily dive trips from Cairns and Port Douglas to its permanent mooring at Agincourt Reef on the outer edge of the Great Barrier Reef, and snorkelling trips to the Low Isles on the inner reef. Quicksilver uses large, fast catamarans that give a comfortable ride. Marine biologists on board give an informative talk and slide show, highlighting the beauty of the reef and explaining how to preserve this wonder. All dive-masters and the marine biologists are qualified to interpret the reef whether you are diving, snorkelling, beach walking or taking a ride in the semi-submersible vessel. Quicksilver's dive school offers PADI dive lessons and multilingual instructors are available.

Marlin Coast Divers, based at Palm Cove Travelodge Resort, 25 minutes north of Cairns, takes small groups on day trips to Upolu and Oyster reefs. Beginners can take an introductory dive on the reef, or, if time permits, have a free pool lesson before going out. The company has a 15 m (50 ft) luxury ketch, and a talk is given on the Reef and its inhabitants. Snorkelling and PADI dive lessons are available.

Cairns is the major centre for Far North Queensland and at its wharf you will find a good choice of dive charters, ranging from huge catamarans to smaller, more personalised dive boats. **TUSA Dive** offers personalised day trips to the reef in one of its two fast dive boats. Groups are kept small, with a maximum of 25, and instruction is available, although most people who choose TUSA are certified divers. Diving and snorkelling equipment is carried and a video is shot throughout the day; you see the video on the home journey and can buy a copy which will be converted to your home system. Night dives are offered during summer and the boats are available for charter.

Ocean Spirit Cruises provides the opportunity to sail to the reef on a large, luxurious catamaran. Once moored, dive tenders take experienced divers to a variety of sites and inexperienced divers can take an introductory dive or can snorkel. PADI dive courses are available, with two days in the pool followed by two more on the reef.

Pro Dive offers PADI courses as well as daily and extended trips to the Reef. It has two 21 m (69 ft) dive boats with diving equipment and underwater cameras for hire. Its day trips are suitable for all levels including hand-held dives for beginners. The 'Dive to Adventure' three-day/two-night trip offers up to 11 dives, including two night dives. And a special three-day/three-night expedition to the Cod Hole north of Lizard Island departs Cairns twice weekly.

Taka II Dive Adventures runs a

four-day dive trip to Cod Hole twice a week and a five-day Cod Hole/ Coral Sea combination twice a month from Cairns. Taka II is owned and operated by the Cairns Underwater Camera Centre and the two companies combine their resources to provide a unique two-day underwater photography trip with instruction and camera equipment for hire.

Heron Island, a tiny coral cay at the southern end of the Great Barrier Reef, is renowned for its spectacular diving, birds and turtles. The reef around the island, and nearby Wistari Reef, have spectacular coral bombies, crevices, lagoons, drop-offs and abundant tropical fish. People have been diving here for so long that the fish are quite used to humans bubbling around among them. In November, Heron Island hosts a dive festival with guest speakers and diving throughout the day. The festival started more than 30 years ago when the emphasis was on spearing fish, however, it is now limited to leisure divers and underwater photographers. The island has a dive shop with gear for hire and professional staff (see Accommodation, page 188).

Lady Elliot Island is a 42 ha (104 a) island at the southern end of the Great Barrier Reef. It offers excellent reef diving, has a dive shop with gear for hire and professional staff offering PADI dive courses. Special dive packages which include air fares to the island, shared tent or cabin accommodation and shore and boat dives with experienced guides are offered throughout the year.

The Reef Eco Centre has been established on the island as an educational facility to give visitors an understanding of the reef and how to care for it.

At Hervey Bay, **Diver's Mecca** offers NAUI dive lessons for beginners and takes dive trips to Roy Rufus Artificial Reef, one of the largest artificial reefs in the southern hemisphere. Its pile of sunken ships and old car bodies has become home and hideaway to hundreds of fish which are quite tame. The bay is protected by Fraser Island so the water is generally calm. The depth averages 15 to 18 m (49 to 59 ft) and the best time to dive is during winter when the water is at its clearest.

South Australia

The gorgeous, leafy sea dragon is one of the popular attractions here, along with the seals, dolphins and crayfish that can be found in abundance around some of the islands. There are 130 islands off the coast, many wrecks, rich vegetation, limestone caves and abundant marine life. The best time for diving is summer, November to May.

Just south of Adelaide there are two marine reserves: Port Noarlunga Reef and Onkaparinga Estuary, and Aldinga Reef. The Noarlunga Reef is at the end of a charming, old jetty, which is always lined with people fishing. The reef is home to more than 200 species of marine plants and animals, including more than 50 species of fish. A great attraction for divers is the 800 m (875 yd) long

Port Noarlunga Marine Reserve, South Australia

marine trail, which is marked with 12 plaques describing the reef ecosystem and all that lives within it. The shoreward side of the trail is relatively shallow and suitable for beginner divers and snorkellers. You should be more experienced to dive or snorkel in the outside section. You need a boat to visit the Aldinga reserve, which has a great drop-off and caves falling away from a limestone plateau.

The Adelaide suburb of Glenelg, a tram ride from the centre of the city, offers good diving from the shore, with some wreck dives. Further south of Adelaide on the Fleurieu Peninsula, Port Willunga and Victor Harbour have artificial reefs, wrecks, caverns, crevasses and overhangs. Diving around the foot of the Yorke Peninsula offers dramatic scenery and cliffs but there is a bad ocean swell. However, with a bit of local

knowledge you can always dive on the side away from the worst of the swell. Port Lincoln is famous (or infamous) for its monstrous white pointer sharks. A macabre adventure that is becoming increasingly popular, is to be lowered into the water in a cage while the boat crew spreads food to attract the sharks.

In the southeast of the state you have Robe, a charming fishing village, and the famous sink holes of Mount Gambier. Robe has clear water and fantastic diving, however, there can be ocean surges so check with local divers. Mount Gambier's best known sink hole is Piccaninnie Ponds which descends more than 60 m (197 ft) into the earth. It features a forest of tall strands of algae which supports yabbies, eels, turtles, trout and some sea fish. As most of the sinkholes are on private land you need the owner's permission to dive there, and a permit system exists to ensure that divers have the necessary experience and equipment standards. Mount Gambier is 486 km (302 m) southeast of Adelaide and, if not familiar with the area, you could ask a dive shop to organise a tour and the necessary permits.

Southern Diving Centre at Christies Beach, next to Port Noarlunga, is fully equipped to provide dive charters and PADI training to instructor level. Beginners get their first experience in a solar-heated, 9 m (29 ft) deep, indoor training tank with viewing windows. Owner David Brooksby will take boat charters to any waters in South Australia and can arrange permits to visit wrecks or the sinkholes at Mount Gambier.

Kangaroo Island, the third-largest of Australia's islands, is a short ferry ride from Cape Jervis. It offers the thrill of diving with resident sea lions, dolphins and fur seals, along with 230 species of fish and more than 50 wrecks. Wrecks such as the *Fanny M* near Kingscote are safe and easily reached, but others, such as the *Loch Vennachar* are more treacherous and dangerous during big swells.

Adventureland Diving has been running dive charters on Kangaroo Island for 13 years. Based at Penneshaw, Adventureland offers dive charters, snorkelling excursions, diving lessons and a variety of other activities, such as canoeing and abseiling. For qualified divers it offers weekend diving holidays from November to March with accom-modation, meals, equipment, pick-up from the ferry, land transport and boat dives. For inexperienced divers, it provides a three-day adventure with accommodation, hire equipment, meals, land transport and lessons.

Kelp forests, Bicheno, Tasmania

Tasmania

Tasmania has 5400 km (3355 m) of coastline with a diverse marine life and giant kelp forests. Its waters are fairly cool — as low as 12°C (54°F) in winter, with a top of 18°C (64°F) in summer. Bicheno on the east coast, is rated highly as a temperate dive area and offers some of the island's most picturesque diving. The waters here have kelp forests, sponge gardens, caves, crayfish, dolphins, anemones and other marine life. Winter is the best time for diving, when visibility reaches 30 m (98 ft) and more. It is also the time when humpback whales call into Bicheno bay during their annual migration.

Bicheno Dive Centre provides, air, instruction, daily boat and shore dives and snorkelling. It has a 7 m (23 ft) Shark Cat Explorer, and a coach to pick up and deliver from Launceston and Hobart airports and the ferry terminal at Devonport. The centre has its own lodge accommodation, or you can stay at a motel or camping area nearby. Once a sealers' and whalers' base, Bicheno is now a pretty beachside town with good beaches, fascinating rock pools and busy crayfish and abalone industries.

Other good diving areas in Tasmania include Sorell, east of Hobart, where there are giant kelp forests and great caves, and Wynyard on the northwest coast which has access to the 100-year-old wreck of the *Southern Cross*. There are an estimated 400 shipwrecks around the coast with good wreck diving around Flinders and King islands. Marine reserves have been estab-lished at Governor Island at Bicheno, Maria Island, and Ninepin Point and Tinderbox in the D'Entrecasteaux Channel. Tinder-box, just south of Hobart, has a 100 m (328 ft) underwater nature trail marked by eight information blocks explaining the underwater ecosystem. The shallow water trail is suitable for snorkellers.

Victoria

The Victorian coast offers good wreck dives and underwater photography. Wilsons Promontory juts out into Bass Strait and is a popular bushwalking, fishing, picnicking and diving area. The diving here offers colourful fish, drop-offs, canyons, swim throughs, huge boulders, wrecks, sponges and corals and is excellent for photography. The Prom is 225 km (140 m) southeast of Melbourne, and there is accom-modation and camping areas at the township of Tidal River. However, you will need a boat to reach the good dive sites. **Bluewater Tours** at Port Welshpool near Wilsons Promontory has an 8.5 m (28 ft) Shark Cat and runs diving charters for groups of up to eight people.

At Port Phillip Bay you can dive from piers among hundreds of fish and seals, explore wrecks and rock bombies, or drift dive. In many parts of the bay the fish have become so used to humans they will come close for food. There are also some scuttled submarines below 27 m (88 ft), for experienced divers.

The **Geelong Dive and Outdoor Centre** offers a range of outdoor activities, including rock climbing, abseiling, whitewater rafting, cross-country skiing, parachuting, scuba diving and snorkelling. It conducts NAUI dive courses and has a 7 m (23 ft), twin-hull craft for dive boat charters from Queenscliff. For beginners, the centre offers a one-day adventure which includes a theory lesson, a practice dive in the pool and a dive from the boat. For certified divers it offers advanced diving in the Bay and beyond.

Western Australia

This state has a 12 500 km (7767 m) coastline with numerous wrecks, pristine coral reefs, huge caves and an amazing variety of marine life.

About 1200 km (746 m) north of Perth is Ningaloo Marine Park, a 5000 km (1930 m) coral reef. Ningaloo is the closest coral reef to the west coast, stretching from a mere 100 m (328 ft) offshore to nearly 7 km (4 m) at its furthest point. More than 180 species of coral and 460 species of reef-dwelling and pelagic fish live here. This is one of the few places you can swim with the massive but harmless whale shark, which can grow to an amazing 40 000 kg (88 185 lb) in weight and 18 m (59 ft) in length. It swims slowly, just under the surface, making it easy for snorkellers as well as scuba divers to reach. The humpback whale visits the reef from July to October. Both Exmouth and Coral Bay have dive shops with equipment for hire and

charter boat operators who go onto Ningaloo Reef. The visitors' centre at Milyering, in the Cape Range National Park which borders the northern shoreline of the marine park, can supply you with information on this important marine environment.

Coraldive at Coral Bay offers a choice of dive–snorkel trips, as well as PADI dive courses. One option is to beach dive or snorkel in a small lagoon, which has hard, soft and some Gorgonacea corals, turtles, sharks and fish. Another option is to boat dive inside the reef, where the depth ranges from 8 to 12 m (26 to 39 ft) and there is a varied fish life with mixed hard corals. To go outside the reef, where the large pelagics and Gorgonacea corals are, Coraldive waits for still days when there is no swell. Under these conditions escorted dives go from 20 to 35 m (65 to 115 ft).

Rowley Shoals, about 170 nautical miles off the coast of Broome, is one of the few areas of shelf atolls in the world that are still in pristine condition. It comprises three atolls, two above water level, over an area of about 7 km (4 m) long by 4 km (2½ m) wide. The shoals are virtually in the middle of nowhere and take about 10 hours to reach by boat from Broome. Charter companies in Broome will take divers out for several days, anchoring in the sheltered waters around the shoals where the diving is excellent.

Rottnest Island, less than an hour's boat ride from Perth, is surrounded by reefs, massive caves, a

TUSA dive boat, Cairns, Queensland

stunning array of fish, and wrecks at Transit Reef. You can see the wrecks and reefs from a glass-bottomed boat, or you can snorkel along the Heritage Wrecks Trail. There is a regular ferry service to Rottnest Island from both Perth and Fremantle and the information centre on the island will provide a map for the Heritage Wrecks Trail.

As you travel south along the coast from Perth you come to many interesting diving areas. Shoalwater Islands Marine Park, 47 km (29 m) south of Perth, has seagrass beds, limestone reefs, sandy sea floors and islands inhabited by little penguins and sea lions. Busselton, 229 km (142 m) south of Perth, has excellent diving from its 3.2-km (2-m) long, restored jetty and good boat diving. This is the southernmost area you will find coral bombies along the west coast.

Dive Boss Charters offers diving and snorkelling trips and SSI dive courses out of Dunsborough Bay Village Resort near Busselton. Trips range from one day to two weeks, with options of night dives around Busselton jetty and deep scallop-bed dives to 35 m (115 ft). Dives are held regularly from December to April and, weather permitting, during October, November and May.

About 80 km (50 m) south of Busselton is Hamelin Bay, where 11 wrecks lie as a grim reminder of the treacherous nature of this part of the coast. The Western Australian Heritage Trails Network (see Useful Addresses, page 199) has an underwater 'Wreck Trail', which passes five wrecks within 1 square km (⅓ square m). You need to be an experienced diver or snorkeller to attempt this trail.

COAST WATCHING

Whales, sea lions, little penguins and all the other ocean creatures that come to our shores provide a small window into a world we know so little about. What they do out there in the wide oceans is filmed by a few specialists, but basically it is still a mystery. We have to take what pleasure we can from watching them when they are on or near our shores, and Australia is lucky in that so many come here to mate and give birth.

Whales

Whales belong to the order of mammals called cetaceans, which returned to the water more than 50 million years ago. Cetaceans are not fish but air-breathing, warm-blooded mammals that give live birth and nurse their young. Ancient history is full of evidence of the awe and sometimes fear these gentle mammals engender. The Minoan, Greek and Roman civilisations admired the dolphin and used its image as decoration on walls and pottery. Large whales, however, were a danger to ships and were greatly feared by sailors. Today, the greatest fear is that they will become extinct through over-hunting.

Whaling was one of the first industries in Australia and for many years one of the most profitable. But declining whale numbers and the worldwide outcry over their killing eventually succeeded in closing the industry completely. In 1980 the government legislated to protect all whales, dolphins and porpoises in Australian waters. Then, in 1981, the importation of all whale-based products was banned.

Whale watching, Hervey Bay, Queensland

161

THE HUMPBACK WHALE

The humpback which visits Australian waters is the fifth largest species of whale. It is a blackish colour with white under the throat and flippers, which makes it easy to see and wonderful to photograph. It is very playful and extremely acrobatic, making energetic underwater rolls and leaps out of the water, which end in amazing backward somersaults. It is also curious, often swimming up to boats with its eyes just out of the water, as though peeping at them from the safety of its ocean.

About 1200 humpbacks migrate from their summer feeding grounds in the cold waters of the Antarctic to the warmer waters around Australia to breed and give birth. They reach our shores and travel north along both the east and west coasts around June each year and leave again from October to November. As they travel they stay close to land, sometimes calling in to shallow bays to rest.

People watching from the shore have reported seeing whales from August to early October near Heron Island, and Point Lookout on Stradbroke Island, near Brisbane. Further south, in northern New South Wales, whales often come to within 100 m (109 yd) of the shore at Cape Byron during June and July.

At various points along the coast, cruise boats go out on whale-watching tours and guidelines have been established to prevent too many boats going too close to the whales at any one time and distressing them. This may mean your skipper will not go as close as you would like, but this is the whales' territory and we must respect this. Another aspect of whale-watching that sometimes disappoints people is that there may be none to see. Unfortunately, this is the way of wildlife viewing and there is nothing that can be done about it. The day I went out I saw only a few minke whales, some dolphins and the huge triangle-shaped tail of an upside down humpback which apparently hangs like this quite often. Yet a friend of mine on another trip came home with photos to die for.

One of the best areas to see the humpback is in the relatively calm, shallow waters of Hervey Bay, between Fraser Island and the Queensland coast. No-one is sure why they stop here on their way back to Antarctica, although there are many theories: that they pass on the wrong side of Fraser Island and become trapped in Hervey Bay for a while; that they stop to rest after giving birth and mating for several months without food, or that they come into the bay to give the calves time to develop a protective layer of blubber before they reach the cold Antarctic waters.

Whale-watch boat charters from Hervey Bay township range from a fast catamaran which takes you out and back in a couple of hours, to a slower cruise boat which provides lunch and can take a whole day. The best months to view whales are during August and September and often into October. I have listed a few cruise boat charters below and the Hervey Bay Visitors' Centre can supply more. One of the original charter companies out of Hervey Bay is **Whale Watch Safari**. This company has a stable, 17 m (55 ft) Hydrofield tri-hulled vessel, fitted with an underwater microphone so you can hear the whales sing. An educational commentary is given on the whales and free tea and coffee is available all day. Tours run from the end of July to the end of October, leaving at 8.30 a.m. daily and return-ing after everyone has seen enough.

From Bundaberg, **Lady Musgrave Barrier Reef Cruises** has whale-watching tours from August to October. The cruises leave from Port Bundaberg jetty, 20 minutes from Bundaberg, and coach pick-up can be arranged from Bundaberg, Bargara Beach and Mon Repos. Scientists from the Pacific Whale Foundation are present on all cruises and provide a commentary on the whales and their habits.

TraveLearn Australia has whale-watching tours headed by Dr Bob Morris, an experienced oceanographer who has been engaged in whale and dolphin research for more than 15 years. It offers whale-watching tours in Hervey Bay from mid-August to mid-October, and whale- and dolphin-watching from Stradbroke Island during October (see Tour Operators, page 171).

At Eden in southern New South Wales, **Cat Balou Cruises** runs its 12 m (39 ft) catamaran out to watch the whales on their migration back to the Antarctic during October and November. The morning trip takes about five hours, during which time a commentary is given on the whales and the history of whaling in the area. Cat Balou has a hydrophone so you can hear the whales singing. Light refreshments are served but guests are welcome to bring their own food and drink. Occasionally, southern right whales are seen between June and August.

On the west coast, cruise boats run daily out of Perth and Fremantle to watch the whales as they travel south back to the Antarctic. The following two companies operate along the west coast and the Western Australia Tourism Commission (see Useful Addresses, page 199) can provide more names.

Underwater World, a marineland/museum 20 minutes north of downtown Perth has whale-watching safaris with a research naturalist on board to give an expert commentary. Regular tours are run during the weekends and by private charter on weekdays from September to November. The cost of the tour includes entry to this very good marineland.

Coraldive, a diving and charter company based at Coral Bay, runs whale-watching tours from July to October around Ningaloo Marine Park, about 1200 km (745 m) north of Perth. Ningaloo is a large reef with an abundance of corals and fish and the whale-watching trips include time for diving or snorkelling.

Little penguins, Kangaroo Island, South Australia

THE SOUTHERN RIGHT WHALE

The southern right whale swims slowly and sluggishly, making it easy to catch, and yields good quantities of oil and whalebone (which was once used for corsets). This is why the early whalers dubbed it the 'right' whale to catch. Sadly, it was hunted almost to extinction.

The southern rights migrate from their summer feeding grounds in Antarctic waters to the warmer Australian waters in winter (July to October) to mate, give birth and raise their young. They play very close to shore, often within 40 m (43 yd), making them easy to see from land. These whales breed very slowly — about one calf every three years — so it has taken many years for their numbers to grow; about 4000 are thought to come into Australian waters every winter.

The best places to see these whales in South Australia are from the cliff tops in the Great Australian Bight, Encounter Bay near Victor Harbour, and Vivonne Bay on Kangaroo Island. They are also seen in bays along the south coast of Western Australia, especially near Albany, at Storm Bay in Tasmania, and sometimes near the former sealing and whaling port of Warrnambool off Victoria's 'Shipwreck Coast'. You may also see the southern right whale in Port Phillip Bay near Melbourne and occasionally up the east coast as far north as Eden.

Albany Sailing Academy The

increase in the number of southern right whales visiting the bays and harbours of Albany has led to an increase in the number of boat charters. Jack Baxter of the Albany Sailing Academy is now combining sailing with whale-watching from July to September. His yacht, the *Sidewalk Cafe*, leaves the town jetty at 9 a.m. each morning and returns about midday.

Nullarbor Adventure Tours, led by Gary White, has southern right whale-watching tours to the Great Australian Bight from late May to October. As well as viewing and photographing the whales, the tour includes a visit to a few of Gary's other favourite places, such as the state's famous inland caves and the historic Fowlers Bay, with its white sand dunes and rustic jetty.

Nullarbor runs two- and three-day tours leaving from Ceduna, a country town 792 km (492 m) northwest of Adelaide. Motel accommodation is provided on the two-day tour and camping on the three-day trip. At other times of the year the company offers nature and caving tours around the Nullarbor Plains region.

Dolphins

Dolphins live in the waters all around Australia and are a common sight riding the bow waves of boats near the coast. The Irrawaddy dolphin lives only in the northern waters, but the common and bottle-nosed dolphins are found virtually everywhere.

They often come into bays where humans are swimming, seemingly because they enjoy contact with humans. Monkey Mia at Shark Bay, 900 km (559 m) north of Perth, has become world famous for its bottle-nose dolphins that come right into the shallow water and swim around people's legs. Guidelines have been established here to protect them from harm and overfeeding. A guide from the Monkey Mia Dolphin Resort monitors the amount of food they receive and gives a talk on their habits.

At Tangalooma Resort on Queensland's Moreton Island, dolphins have been encouraged to come close to shore for a small supper each evening. Care is taken to give them only a small amount of food so

Sea lions, Kangaroo Island, South Australia

they do not become dependent on this supply. You can feed them yourself under strict guidelines that have been established to ensure the well-being of the dolphins.

Dolphin Watch Cruises has been running morning, lunch and dinner cruises since 1982 at beautiful Jervis Bay on the New South Wales south coast. There are so many dolphins here that you are virtually assured of seeing them, and the skipper gives a good commentary on the history of the area and the dolphins. The company also runs evening cruises to Bowen Island from October to March to watch the little penguins come ashore. Cruise times change so check first.

Eco-Escapes runs weekend and five-day camping trips on Corrie Island just north of Sydney, and dolphin-watching is one of the special activities (see Tour Operators, page 171).

Melbourne's Port Philip Bay is home to a variety of marine life including dolphins, Australian fur seals and seabirds such as the albatross, skua and penguin.

Polperro Dolphin Swims runs charters out to where the dolphins play in the bay and you can jump in the water and swim with them. All gear is supplied including wet suit, mask and snorkel. A dolphin researcher is on board to explain the dolphin's habits and the cruise also visits Pope's Eye Marine Reserve where Australasian gannets and Australian fur seals live. Polperro has morning, afternoon and lunch cruises and will pick you up from Melbourne and Frankston.

Dugongs

This large, gentle creature is the world's only herbivorous marine mammal. It is a grey-brown, air-breathing mammal which can grow up to 3 m (10 ft) in length and weigh up to 4000 kg (4½ tons). Because of its size and shape it is often mistaken for a whale.

On the west coast, Shark Bay has one of the largest populations of dugongs in world, estimated at 10 000. They graze on the vast beds of seagrass that grow there. A catamaran takes sightseers out from the Shark Bay resort when they are feeding close to shore — usually early summer — and charter boats can be hired by large groups.

On the east coast, they live in Moreton Bay near Brisbane and on the eastern side of Cape York in Far North Queensland, especially at Princess Charlotte Bay.

Seals and Sea Lions

Seals were greatly prized for their skins by the early settlers and hunting reduced their numbers to dangerously low levels. Fortunately a few colonies survived and are now protected by law.

The country's largest colony of Australian fur seals is at Seal Rocks on Phillip Island, 120 km (74 m) southeast of Melbourne. An estimated 5000 to 6000 fur seals gather there at the peak of the breeding season, which starts in October with the arrival of the males.

The males come ashore aggressive and ready to fight over the females. These battles can be vicious and long-lasting and are quite impressive to watch. You can see the seals through telescopes at Nobbies Kiosk on the island or take a two-hour ferry tour from the jetty at Cowes. Phillip Island has an interesting wildlife population and your first stop should be the visitors' information centre near the bridge after you cross onto island (see Wildlife Parks and Sanctuaries, page 76).

Seal Bay Conservation Park on Kangaroo Island in South Australia is the best place to see Australian sea lions at close range. The park encompasses a wide sandy beach and dune area where the sea lions can safely spend their days nursing their young, enjoying the sun and frolicking in the waves. They do not seem to mind humans coming quite close to them, although there are sensible restrictions on how close you may go. The young sea lions spend their day romping and playing and flopping over on top of each other then dropping off to sleep after amazingly short bursts of energy. They pay scant attention to the humans on the beach. The big bulls also ignore humans, unless there is a female ready to mate, then they gather up their bulk to a frightening height, bare their teeth and rattle a warning deep in their throats.

To protect the sea lions, access to the bay is restricted and you can only go onto the beach with a ranger or an approved tour guide. Rangers run regular guided tours throughout the day and you can check tour times at the Tourist Information Centre in Dauncey Street, Kingscote, or the signpost off the South Coast Road, which leads to the bay. There is a carpark and ranger's hut on the hill above the beach and a fee charged for the tour.

Kangaroo Island is also the home of a colony of New Zealand fur seals which lie around the rocks at Admirals Arch looking like big, wet, black slugs. A boardwalk and viewing platform was built because the seals were becoming distressed by the human visitors and this has been successful; the seals are more relaxed and can still be observed at close range. Admirals Arch is a spectacular natural bridge over rocks and crashing waves, which makes this trip doubly worthwhile.

Other seal colonies in South Australia are at Point Avoid in Coffin Bay National Park near Port Lincoln — swimming here is not recommended as the seals attract monstrous white pointer sharks — and at Dangerous Reef, about 40 minutes by high-speed boat from Port Lincoln, where there is a marine viewing platform on the reef.

A colony of about 600 Australian fur seals lives on Montague Island, 9 km (5½ m) from Narooma on the New South Wales south coast. The island was declared a nature reserve in April 1990 to protect the wildlife, and it is listed as a historical site to protect the old lighthouse and other buildings. The New South Wales Parks and Wildlife Service manages the island and allows two cruises to the island a day: a daytime cruise to visit the lighthouse and an evening cruise to see the little penguins as they come ashore to return to their burrows. Both tours cruise past the seal colony allowing plenty of time for observation and for photographs to be taken. The greatest number of seals can be seen from August to December. Bookings for the cruises can be made at the Narooma Visitors' Centre.

Along the West Australian coast you can see Australian sea lions and little penguins at Shoalwater Islands Marine Park, less than an hour's drive south of Perth. This is a popular tourist area with good picnic and barbecue facilities. Boat tours of the marine park leave from Mersey Point to view the sea lions on Seal Island, and a ferry leaves from Mersey Point for Penguin Island.

Penguins

One of the best-known places in the world to watch the little penguins come ashore each evening is Phillip Island, 120 km (74 m) southeast of Melbourne. This fascinating penguin parade has attracted thousands of people since the 1920s (see Wildlife Parks and Sanctuaries, page 76). However, purist nature-watchers may prefer to avoid the crowds and take a rug to a quieter coastal spot. Penguins come ashore all along the southern shores of Australia, from the south-west corner to the southern parts of Queensland, but you will need some local knowledge about where to position yourself; check with the local tourist office or national parks rangers first.

At Kangaroo Island in South Australia, the National Parks and Wildlife Service runs guided tours each evening from Penneshaw and Kingscote. You can also contact any of the local tour operators, such as Kangaroo Island Wilderness Tours, which will take a personalised tour on demand.

In Tasmania, **Bicheno Penguin and Adventure Tours** takes evening tours to a nearby penguin rookery. The company will pick you up at your accommodation and provide torches and a guide but no flash photography is allowed as this disturbs the penguins.

Montague Island (see seals and sea lions on page 166), is the second-largest penguin breeding area in Australia with about 10 000 nesting pairs. You can expect to see a large number of penguins throughout the year, with the exception of March–April when they are moulting. The island is also the breeding ground for crested terns, silver gulls and three different species of shearwaters.

Shearwaters

The shearwater, or muttonbird, is a migratory bird that arrives on Australian shores from the Arctic in millions from September onwards. It may lack the colour of other Australian birds but it is a brilliant flier — its name comes from its graceful gliding flight and its ability to sweep from water level to high in the sky.

Its migration pattern is remarkable, although it is not fully

A baby shearwater peeps out from its burrow

understood. Every April shearwaters fly from Australia to the Arctic region, a journey of about 15 000 km (9320 m), returning again in September to breed. It is believed they do not go ashore during these migrations and many die along the way of causes not fully understood, although starvation is believed to be one of them. To understand its migration better and to ensure the birds survival, Japan and Australia have a joint protection program whereby each country monitors the birds numbers when they are in their region.

Although there are millions of shearwaters, they, like all other creatures of the wild, have their predators. Soil erosion and farm animals destroy their habitats, snakes eat their eggs, and feral cats take defenceless chicks out of burrows. Large numbers die during migration and by gill-net fishing fleets in the North Pacific. Humans are also predators. We harvest the bird for its down, oil and as food. In Tasmania, the harvest season is restricted to the month of April and there are limits to prevent over-harvesting. Even so, an estimated 300 000 chicks are taken each year.

With a little knowledge of the whereabouts of shearwater colonies you can go to the coast about half an hour after dark and watch the parents return to shore. The colonies are usually located on headlands and islands — the short-tailed shearwater around the southeastern coast of Australia, including Phillip Island and Tasmania; the wedge-tailed shearwater in the tropical regions of Queensland, the Northern Territory, Western Australia, and New South Wales down to Montague Island. However, do not use a torch and keep quiet so they are not disturbed by your presence.

Tasmania is the main breeding ground in the world for the short-tailed shearwater. It has an estimated 11 million burrows, compared with one million each in Victoria and South Australia and 30 000 in New South Wales.

The muttonbirds' mating and breeding pattern is so well established that observers can virtually tell you on what day each event will happen. First comes the arrival of the birds in September–October. They find their mates and set up a burrow. In November they go out to sea for about three weeks and return at the end of the month to lay a single white egg. The parents take turns at sitting on the egg for 54 days. The chick hatches in the second half of January; both parents then spend the day at sea and return to feed the chick each evening.

With breeding and feeding over the adult birds leave Australia in early April. After the parents have left, the chick receives no food and quickly loses its baby fat and grows its flight feathers for the long journey ahead. Amazingly it has very little practise at flying before it starts its 15 000 km (9320 m) journey, without parental guidance, to the Arctic.

Viewing tours in Tasmania are offered at four colonies: Clifton Beach, 30 minutes' drive south of Hobart; Bruny Island Neck in the south; Stanley Nut in the far northwest; and Ocean Beach at Strahan on the west coast. The best viewing time is from October to the end of February and the local tourist office can advise you of tour times.

Another breeding ground is Heron Island, a tiny coral cay at the southern end of the Great Barrier Reef. An estimated 30 000 wedge-tailed shearwaters come here every year and honeycomb the island floor with their burrows. The island has a resort and wildlife research station and guides will explain how important it is not to walk off the marked tracks as the burrows are very shallow and you could easily crush a chick.

As well as the muttonbirds, Heron Island is home to some 100 000 black noddy terns, herons and rails. In season, up to 200 000 birds can be nesting on the island; the noise is deafening and the air-drops dangerous, but the photographic opportunities are fantastic.

Tour Operators

Choosing a list of tour operators who conduct their trips in an environmentally sensitive way was a difficult task. So many companies these days promote themselves as 'ecotour' operators — but what does this mean? To me, it means more than just going into the bush and setting up camp. Good ecotour operators know and love the environment. They have taken the trouble to learn about the flora and fauna and interdependence within ecosystems, and the geology and human culture of an area. They enjoy telling their fellow travellers what they know, and showing them how to move through the countryside without damaging the environment.

Some tour operators are specialists in one field, which may be birds, botany, marine life or Aboriginal history. Others follow passive adventure pursuits such as bushwalking, cycling, diving and kayaking. I think a good ecotour operator also carries a library on the natural and cultural history of the areas passed through because, after all, no-one knows everything.

Some people talk about ecotourism and educational tourism as separate identities. To some extent they are, but more often than not they blend. I believe ecotourism and educational tourism walk hand-in-hand.

Knowledge is a vital tool for the survival of our environment and some research companies and groups are inviting people to join a research program. Thus you could spend your holiday working alongside experts and doing some very unusual things, and when you return home you will have more than a bundle of photographs. You will have memories of wonderment and compassion; you will remember the sensation of holding a wild creature while it was being tagged, the emotions that welled up when the chicks being studied made their first attempts to fly, the cool dampness of the soil around a tree being planted, and the evenings spent discussing the day's progress and its effect on the future.

Some tour companies do small, helpful surveys as they move along. They may keep a list of plants seen along the way, count birds or report sudden changes in wildlife numbers. Many companies run special trips for school children and give talks on the environment to community groups.

Minimal impact on both the cultural and natural environment is the key to ecologically sustainable travel. It means practising the philosophy of minimal impact bush travel mentioned in the chapter on Bushwalking (see page 87). I have listed only companies that offer tours with at least one overnight stop. Shorter tours than this are easily researched and booked once you are in the area.

General

AMESZ TOURS

Hanz Amesz has been running four-wheel-drive camping tours into some of the most remote parts of Australia for more than 20 years. Some groups are now large, using coaches with up to 25 people. However, there are still smaller group tours. Amesz is possibly the only company travelling the historic Canning Stock Route. Its 19-day safari departs every August with a maximum of 14 people. Only experienced outback drivers should attempt this journey.

The Canning Stock Route was completed in 1910 and provided a route to drive cattle from the Kimberleys to the markets at the goldfields and in Perth. It passes through the Great Sandy and Gibson deserts and wells were sunk about 20 km (12 m) apart. Many of these wells have collapsed and the water is polluted, only Well 26, located at about the middle of the route, is reliable because it was restored to celebrate the 75th anniversary of Alfred Canning's great effort. The total distance travelled on this tour is more than 2000 km (1242 m).

Amesz also offers a 21-day safari starting in Perth and travelling through the isolated regions of the Great Victorian Desert, Oodnadatta Track, Lake Eyre, the Birdsville Track, Sturts Desert, Cooper Creek, the Coongie Lakes system and the Flinders Rangers, finishing in Adelaide.

All vehicles carry books on local flora, fauna and human history. The price of the two tours mentioned ranges from $118 to $139 a day. There is a cook on every tour.

AUSTRALIAN ALPS WILDERNESS TOURS

These small, four-wheel-drive tours take you into the wilds of the Australian Alps from Mount Kosciusko in New South Wales to the high country in Victoria, without necessitating a lot of walking, and accommodation is in mountain lodges or chalets. Owner Garry Smith has spent his life in the high country and either he or another experienced high country guide leads the tours. The tours operate only during October to May and cost about $150 a day,

Anbangbang wetlands, Kakadu, Northern Territory

inclusive of meals. The maximum group size is six people and tours average from three to five days.

AUSTRALIAN AND NEW ZEALAND SCIENTIFIC EXPLORATION SOCIETY

ANZSES is a non-profit society formed in 1977 by a group of explorers, scientists and adventurers. It gathers scientific information which is fed back to research and educational institutions, museums and the National Parks and Wildlife Services. Its youth (17–25 years) expeditions are held in December–January and it has a women-only expedition in September–October and one for all ages during the year.

All expedition leaders are scientists and environmentalists and there is an emphasis on not damaging the environment being studied. Volunteers are trained in low-impact camping. Recent expeditions include studying the southern right whale in the Great Australian Bight and the arid-zone flora and fauna of South Australia. The cost varies from $65 to $100 a day.

AUSTRALIAN TRUST FOR CONSERVATION VOLUNTEERS

This is a non-profit, community-based organisation which works towards ecological conservation and education. Volunteers work in teams with the field staff on projects such as assisting local groups and landholders in management plans and protection of endangered species.

The most popular program for young people is the six-week Echidna Program where volunteers average a week at each place. It offers travel, variety and costs only $17.50 inclusive.

AUSTRALIS PTY LTD

Australis is a Melbourne-based company owned and run by academics qualified in botany, zoology and physiotherapy. These tours delve deep into the damage being done to the environment and how it can be corrected.

Australis runs regular tours, and designs tours with expert leaders for special interest groups. Its regular tours range in length from a half-day Koala Watch out of Melbourne to a six-day tour of western Victoria. Australis specialises in designing and guiding tours; all travel arrangements are handled by licensed travel agents.

The Koala Watch costs $56 and the longer tours range from $128 to $176 per day, including meals.

BOGONG JACK ADVENTURES

Bogong Jack has been showing people Victoria's wine and high country since 1981. Emphasis is on active outdoor pursuits with travel by bicycle, canoe, walking, cross-country skiing or a combination of any two or more. Accommodation is usually camping, although cabins, host farms, lodges and guesthouses are used.

The cost varies — day tours range from $30 to $55, overnight tours average $120 a day.

Bogong Jack keeps its groups small and its guides are chosen for their knowledge of local history and attractions.

COATE'S WILDLIFE TOURS

Coate's offers a range of natural history tours through Western Australia. Owners Jan and Rob Brandli engage guides who have a knowledge of a specific subject: birds, wildflowers, fungi, photography and Aboriginal culture. The number of people on natural history tours is limited to 16 and they cost about $100 a day depending on whether camping or using other accommodation. Coate's will also prepare individual charters.

DAVIDSON'S ARNHEMLAND SAFARIS

Max Davidson, a former buffalo hunter, has a set up a comfortable safari camp and leads tours into the Mount Borradaile area in Aboriginal-owned Arnhem Land (visitor numbers are limited by a permit system). Full accommodation costs from $300 a day and you need to add to this the cost of a light aircraft flight from Darwin or Jabiru. If driving in, you need a four-wheel-drive vehicle. Davidson's camp is 350 km (217 m) from Darwin or 100 km (62 m) from Jabiru.

DENISE GOODFELLOW

A respected authority on the geology, wildlife and Aboriginal culture of the Northern Territory, Denise Goodfellow has lived here for 20 years and was a founding member of the Ecotourism Association of Australia. Through her deep love of nature and close association with the Aboriginal people, she provides tours that are a bit different to the usual tours offered.

She does not have a list of planned trips, preferring to prepare an itinerary to suit each group and the season. She recommends geology and ecology tours any time of the year; butterfly, herb and wildflower tours from March to May; reptile and mammal tours March to June and October to December; and bird-watching October to December or March to May. Bush tucker tours are best from October to December and February to May. Her tours cost about $150 a day depending on the number of participants.

DESERT TRACKS

Formed six years ago, Desert Tracks was initially run as a joint venture between Diana James and Nganyinytja, a Pitjatjantjara woman. It is now wholly owned by Aboriginal people and run as a cross-cultural education ecotour. Diana James coordinates the tour from Ayers Rock Resort and Nganyinytja runs a bush college teaching Aboriginal law and lifestyle.

They average one seven-day tour a month from March to November with about 20 people on each tour. Each seven-day tour spends three to five nights' camping just south of the Northern Territory–South Australian border and the other nights near Uluru (Ayers Rock) where you learn its significance to the Aboriginal people. It costs about $1825 per person. Shorter tours are available.

DISCOVERY ECOTOURS

Formed in 1987 (as Desert Discovery), this partnership of Penny Van Oosterzee and Noel Preece is one of the leaders in high-quality ecotour holidays. Both partners are ardent naturalists, well known for their speeches, writings and generous support of ecological research. When you go on holiday with them you could be travelling with a scientist funded by the company, or you may meet one along the way and spend a few days helping out. Some tours meet Aboriginal communities to learn about their traditions and culture.

These are comfortable tours and accommodation is in the best available motel or hotel or at a safari camp. All cooking is done by experienced chefs. Tours average $250 a day.

The choice of tours includes a seven-day expedition into Kakadu, Arnhem Land and the Cobourg Peninsula; a 14-day land/sea trip of Shark Bay and Kalbarri National Park, and a cruise around the Great Barrier Reef and Indonesian islands. Special tours for groups of up to 12 people can be arranged.

EARTHWATCH AUSTRALIA

Part of the $1000 to $3000 you pay to spend 10 days on an Earthwatch project covers transport, food, accommodation and training, and the rest goes towards running the research expedition.

Earthwatch is a private, non-profit organisation founded in the USA in 1971. The Australian branch opened in 1980. Members receive the *Earthwatch* magazine, which lists about 150 research projects around the world. Volunteers do not need any experience, but must be aged 16 years or older.

ECO-ESCAPES

This company provides walking, canoeing and cycling trips north of Sydney, usually for a weekend. The walks follow level bush tracks at Myall Lakes, or steeper tracks at Barrington Tops. Canoeing is on the tranquil Myall Lakes. Cycling is downhill at Barrington Tops or through historic towns in the Hunter

Valley. Accommodation is in a base camp or lodge. The emphasis is on enjoying the natural environment and gaining a better understanding of its needs.

Groups are limited to 12 people and tours cost about $100 a day for adults and budget tours are offered.

ECOTREK

Ecotrek specialises in bushwalking and canoeing camping trips in South Australia, Victoria and New South Wales. Owner Peter Kellett is an historian who took up outdoor education 18 years ago and started Ecotrek 12 years ago. All tours have well-trained guides and books on the local flora and fauna and land management plans.

Most tours are from three to nine days and graded easy to moderate.

Prices vary considerably but average $81 to $100 a day.

FALCON TOURS

This small touring company based in Perth, specialises in bird-watching and wildflower tours in Western Australia with some longer trips into the birding areas of South Australia, Northern Territory and Queensland. Simon Nevill is a keen wildlife photographer and occasionally organises photographic tours.

Tours range from a weekend with accommodation in timber cottages, to a 14-day camping tour of the wildflowers and wildlife of the southwest. Groups are never larger than 20 people and tours cost about $80 a day when camping.

GAWLER RANGES WILDERNESS SAFARIS

This is a wilderness holiday with the locals of South Australia — and who knows the countryside better than a local! Five farmers who have lived in the area adjacent to the Gawler Ranges all their lives set up this company to provide tours over their land. It is an ancient part of the country with abundant wildlife and spectacular wildflowers in spring.

On the three- and four-day safaris into the Gawler Ranges there is a base camp with shower and toilet facilities and you make day trips in a clover-leaf pattern which enables you to see as much variety of landform as possible. The guides know this land well and will explain the habits of the wildlife, natural and cultural history, seasonal effects on vegetation and how Australians live out here. The five-day tour includes the above, and two days exploring the west coast from Point Lincoln to Point Labatt. All tours leave from Wudinna, 578 km (359 m) northwest of Adelaide, or Port Lincoln and cost $150 a day.

Each day is taken at a leisurely pace to allow time to enjoy and talk about the environment. Meals are cooked over an open campfire and everyone has a go at cooking bush damper. All the partners are conscious of the need to preserve the environment and all waste is separated and carried out, even other people's rubbish is collected along the way.

GO BUSH SAFARIS

This company is run by John Sinclair, one of Australia's best-known conservationists, who fought to save Fraser Island from sand mining.

These tours study wildlife, plants, the effects of land uses on the environment, and Aboriginal culture. All trips involve camping because John believes that only by living in the bush can you smell it, hear it and really get to know it.

Go Bush visits many World Heritage listed areas, the Torres Strait, the Kimberley, Snowy Mountains and occasionally overseas. Tours average one to two weeks and cost about $100 a day.

GREEN & GOLD ADVENTURE TOURS

Stefan Mitich, an ardent bushie and nature lover, takes small groups (maximum 10) on four-wheel-drive camping safaris through Far North Queensland.

His five-day circle tour from Cairns heads north along the Peninsula Developmental Road past Palmer River and Laura to the magnificent natureland of Lakefield National Park. Then back via the coast road through Cooktown, Bloomfield and Cape Tribulation. It involves camping and costs $450. Special tours for five or more people can be organised.

interNATIONAL PARKTOURS

This company, started in 1975 by Tony and Connie Groom, specialises in walking in national parks and nature reserves, hence its unusual name. Their interests are natural history, photography, ornithology and the environment.

Tours average one to two weeks and involve walking with camping or other accommodation. Prices vary but expect to pay $100 a day for camping, and $50 to $80 a day extra if using commercial accommodation.

Aboriginal children at a Corroboree (gathering)

JANKANGYINA TOURS

Bill Harney grew up near Alice Springs learning the stories of his Aboriginal people and the ways of the white man. This mixed cultural upbringing adds an extra dimension to his tours into his ancestral land, Wardaman country (an hour west of Katherine). For two days you follow him through the bush, visiting numerous rock art sites, listening to his stories and learning how the Aboriginal people used plants for food and medicine.

The tours leave twice weekly and cost about $230 per adult for the two-day trip.

LANDSCOPE EXPEDITIONS

Landscope is a quarterly wildlife and conservation magazine which organises expeditions in association with the UWA Extension at the University of Western Australia and research staff from the Department of Conservation and Land Manage-

ment. The research looks into issues that affect the future of the environment of Western Australia.

Tours depart from various West Australian towns and cost from $117 to $249 a day. All income received flows directly back into study and research projects.

LITTLE DESERT TOURS AND LODGE

The story of Whimpey Reichelt's struggle to get the lodge and tours up and running is recorded in a booklet called *One Man's Dream*, available at the lodge. The tours go into the Western Victorian desert for half- to full-day trips with lunch supplied and provide a wonderful insight into the way in which desert plants and animals survive. The tours are priced from $20 to $35.

Most people come here with a group, although families and individual travellers are just as welcome. Accommodation is in motel or bunk rooms.

MANYALLALUK TOURS

Manyallaluk is a former cattle station in the Northern Territory where you can live with the Jawoyn and associated Aboriginal people.

There are daily tours from Katherine, or you can drive the 110 km (68 m) from Katherine and stay in the Manyallaluk camping area. The Aboriginal people will teach you about their culture, show you how to find bush tucker and medicines and will demonstrate their arts and crafts.

If you are adventurous and reasonably fit, you could join their four-day walk from Manyallaluk across the Arnhem Land escarpment and down to the Katherine River over quite rough terrain. The trek operates from April to October and costs a little less than $100 a day.

MUDMAPS PTY LTD

MudMaps specialises in short nature and soft adventure tours into Namadgi National Park and the alpine regions near Canberra. The guides spot wild-life and explain how different environments nurture different birds and animals.

MudMaps prefers to organise tours to suit individual group needs rather than program regular trips. Groups can be from two to 12 people and all travel is in four-wheel-drive vehicles and by walking. Accommodation is in mountain huts, camping, lodges or hotels. Expect to pay about $100 a day.

NANGAR WILDERNESS EXPEDITIONS AND NATURAL HISTORY FIELD TRIPS

Botanist and explorer Dr Arthur Weston has been leading walking tours into some of the most magnificent and untouched areas of Australia since 1977. On these trips you go exploring to find rare and unusual plants and wildlife, and you learn about the region's natural history. Dr Weston practises minimal impact travel.

Groups are kept small (never more than 16). There are two types of tours offered: weekend walks (not always led by Arthur Weston) near Perth, and longer expeditions into Kakadu, East Kimberley, Far North Queensland, Tasmania and the forests and caves of southwestern Australia. The weekend tours average $40 per day; the longer trips $67 a day.

ODYSSEY SAFARIS PTY LTD

With Odyssey you travel into remote and wild parts of the Top End, the Gulf of Carpentaria and the Kimberley region by four-wheel-drive vehicle. These are up-market tours and cost about $240 a day camping, more if accommodated. Odyssey specialises in private charters with tour itineraries tailored to suit the group and staff to do all the leg work.

Odyssey is one of the few tour operators with permission to enter Aboriginal-owned Arnhem Land.

OSPREY WILDLIFE EXPEDITIONS

Osprey is a pioneer of natural history and cross-culture tours established by Adelaide-based Iain Greenwood. All regular tours are led by Iain or an experienced naturalist, and experts are called in for private tours for special interest groups.

Coastal tours include Kangaroo Island, Coorong, off-shore islands and whale-watching at the Great Australian Bight. Inland tours go to the Flinders Ranges, central deserts, Kakadu and Far North Queensland. Cross-cultural tours involve Aboriginal communities around the Coorong and the Flinders Ranges.

Prices range from $132 a day for inland tours to $365 a day for whale-watching with motel accommodation.

SAVANNAH GUIDES

This organisation was established to provide excellence in guiding with an emphasis on interpretation, public education and the promotion of ecologically sustainable tourism. It operates only in the savannah region of the Gulf of Carpentaria.

I have included the Savannah Guides because they are specialists in the natural and human history of their chosen area, and are well worth seeking out if you are travelling through this region. At the time of publication there were 13 fully accredited guides working at six stations: Undara Volcanic National Park (lava tubes), Tallaroo (hot springs), Lawn Hill National Park, Hell's Gate, Borroloola (river activities) and Cape Crawford.

SOUTHERN SEA VENTURES

Southern Sea Ventures offers five- and seven-day paddles around the idyllic Hinchinbrook and Family islands off the Queensland coast from May to October at a cost of about $135 a day. The guides are professionals who know the area. You do not need kayaking experience but should be fit enough to paddle every day. The company provides stable two-person kayaks and all safety and camping gear.

SPINDRIFT INTERNATIONAL GUIDING

Geologist and environmentalist Max Cowell runs weekend and extended sea kayaking trips around south-east Victoria, Flinders Island and

occasionally other states. He keeps the arrangements flexible to suit the participants and provides information on heritage and environment. Some trips combine activities such as bush-walking, horse riding and fishing.

Costs vary from $75 for a day trip, to $85 for self-catered camping trips, to $130 per day for fully catered tours with accommodation.

TASMANIAN EXPEDITIONS

This is an experienced adventure company which has been offering walking, cycling and whitewater rafting since 1989. Groups are kept small and special tours can be organised for six or more.

Tours range from an easy one-and-a-half day walk in Cradle Mountain National Park, to longer walks and cycle trips which require a moderate level of fitness, to hiking and rafting the wilds, suitable only for fit people. Accommodation can be camping, cabins or motels. Prices vary but average $112 a day.

Most tours operate October to April; the three-day Cradle Mountain walk operates during winter.

TRAVELEARN AUSTRALIA

TraveLearn is a licensed travel agent which runs educational tours on behalf of the Universities of Queensland and Central Queensland. The guides are academics or naturalists who are specialists in their field, but they are also chosen for their ability to communicate with non-academics.

Tours explore the rainforests and coral reefs of Queensland, the Kimberley region, the Red Centre and Kakadu. Tour lengths vary but average one week and cost about $180 a day.

Accommodation includes lodges, motels, camping and cabins on the cruises.

TREZISE BUSH GUIDES

Percy Trezise has worked with Aboriginal elders, archaeologists and anthropologists exploring and recording the Quinkan rock art since the late 1950s. Trezise's work led to the establishment of the Quinkan Reserve, which was handed back to the Aboriginal people in 1992.

The rock art is protected by this reserve and two other wilderness reserves — Jowalbinna and Deighton River — established by the Trezise family. Matt and Steve Trezise lead tours into this spectacular countryside of rainforests, escarpments, crystal-clear streams, birds and rock art sites.

Day tours from the camps cost $50 per person with special rates for families. The reserves can be reached by four-wheel drive, or by private aircraft to Jowalbinna. A camping area is provided for a small fee or you can stay at the company's bush camp for about $55 a day, including meals.

UMORRDUK ABORIGINAL SAFARIS

Arnhem Land covers 94 000 km² (36 294 m²) of rugged escarpment country and is owned by the Aboriginal people. You need a permit and a four-wheel drive to enter the area. Umorrduk was established in 1989 by the Aboriginal people in a joint venture with Australian Wilderness Expeditions. A permanent, 16-bed tent camp was set up at Imilgil and guides lead day trips from here.

Day tours run throughout the year but overnight tours operate only from May to December. Tours cost more than $200 for a day visit and more than $300 a day if staying overnight, plus airfare from Darwin.

WEST COAST ADVENTURE HOLIDAYS

This family-owned company has been operating tours since 1975. Alan and Kim Breeden keep groups small and will prepare special itineraries for private groups. The tours are designed so you see and learn about the wildlife, wildflowers, Aboriginal sites and geology of the area.

The company has two bases, one at Exmouth for tours of the centre and north of the state, and the other at Busselton for tours of the southwest and southern coastal areas. However, most long safaris can be joined at Perth. Transport is in four-wheel-drive safari buses which take up to 14 people, and accommodation is in cabins, country homesteads, motels, chalets or by camping. The price averages $110 a day.

WILD QUEST

There are many tour companies operating out of Darwin and this is one of the best in the moderate price bracket.

A three-day Kakadu tour with lodge accommodation and basic meals costs about $100 a day. Travel is by four-wheel drive with groups no larger than 12 people. Because Kakadu is so large a lot of time is spent in the vehicle travelling from one place to another, so you need three days to see the main attractions. Owner Peter Roper has planned this tour so you see rock art and wetlands and have time for a swim.

WORLD EXPEDITIONS

This was one of the first adventure companies in the world to protect the environment through which it was travelling. Its guides are chosen for their love of nature and adventure and enforce the company philosophy of minimal impact travel.

Most trips are quite active and involve trekking, cycling, kayaking, rafting, sailing or a combination of each. For example, the 11-day rafting trip down the Franklin River requires fitness and courage, but, the Coral Trekker sailing trip around the Whitsunday Islands is very relaxed.

Accommodation is mostly camping, although sometimes cabins and country pubs or motels are used. Where possible, a support vehicle carries the heavy gear and is a back-up if you need a rest. Tours cost about $126 a day.

Bushwalking

ALPINE NATURE RAMBLES

This company is based in Falls Creek on the edge of the Bogong High Plains. Owner Jill Dawson has an infectious enthusiasm for the region and each tour is packed with discussions about the soil, plants, insects, history and the interrelationship of one to another. She gained her knowledge of the region over 26 years as a visitor and for the past 14 years as a resident. She has half-day walks on weekends from November to April when the wildflowers are out, and will arrange other times and camping trips for groups of ten or more.

COUNTRY WALKS

Country Walks is owned by Ian Hutchison, who takes groups of six or more on one- and two-night walks along the historic Six Foot Track in the Blue Mountains, west of Sydney. The 45 km (28 m) track was constructed in 1884 as a bridle trail. It is popular with walkers because it offers a spectacular but moderate walk through rainforests and along undulating valleys from Katoomba to the Jenolan Caves. Ian has a support vehicle to carry the food and camping gear.

CRACLAIR TOURS

Most of the tours are graded moderate and there is a ratio of one guide to three guests so your food and equipment is carried for you. The emphasis is on enjoying the scenery and moving at a pace that suits the group.

Craclair has trips along the Overland Track (eight to ten days), the Walls of Jerusalem (five days), Frenchmans Cap (seven days) and Mount Ossa (five days). Other options include the four-day 'Around Cradle Mountain' and the 'Gentle Adventure', an eight-day tour visiting several parts of Western Tasmania.

Regular tours run from November to May, but special tours for groups of two or more can be arranged at any time of the year.

CRADLE HUTS PTY LTD AND FREYCINET EXPERIENCE PTY LTD

These companies offer up-market walking tours. They are renowned for their attention to detail and the quality of their accommodation which has been built to the highest environmental standards.

Cradle Huts runs a six-day/five-night walk of the Overland Track with accommodation in its own huts. Freycinet Experience offers a five-day/four-night walk in the Freycinet National Park with accommodation in a lodge at Friendly Beaches and in permanent camps at Cook's Beach and Bluestone Bay. Both tours include a rest day and start and finish at Launceston. All food, fuel, etc. arrives by helicopter or other transport.

ECHIDNA WALKABOUTS

Echidna Walkabouts specialises in day walks into the Brisbane Ranges and the You Yangs from Melbourne, with some longer treks during summer. The longer treks include two days in the Brisbane Ranges with accommodation in a bunk house, or six days in East Gippsland with camping in national parks. Echidna was started in mid-1993 by Roger Smith and Janine Duffy and they have studied the history, flora and fauna of the areas.

EXPLORANGES

Exploranges' speciality is to transport small groups to areas where they can set up a base camp and explore the surrounding area each day. Robyn and Graham Guy have been leading tours for 13 years and are experienced bushwalkers and keen ornithologists with skills in nursing, botany and mechanics.

All tours start and end in Adelaide. Regular tours go to base camps in the Flinders and Gawler ranges and Kangaroo Island. More far-reaching tours go to Western Australia, Carnarvon Gorge and the beaches of Queensland and Victoria. Tour times are planned to suit the seasons and range from eight to 24 days.

FOOTPRINTS EXPEDITIONS

This company offers weekend bushwalks around southwest Western Australia, and extended tours into the wilderness regions of Western Australia, Kakadu and Tasmania. The weekend trips are leisurely. Special wildflower identification and Aboriginal guided tours also offered. The tours into the Karijini National Park in the Hamersley Ranges are spent with the local Aboriginal people.

All the trips in the northern regions are held in winter and Tasmania is walked in summer. All tours involve backpacking and camping, so a reasonable level of fitness is necessary.

FOREST WALKS AND ECOTOURS

Rosemary Norwood and Sean Cadman offer one- to three-day walks into the wilderness areas of the Great Western Tiers and the Central Plateau of central northern Tasmania, with the option of caving and fishing. You need good supportive shoes and a reasonable level of fitness. Packages range from camping with guides carrying the heavy gear, to walking by day and staying in budget accommodation at night, to an expensive package with accommodation in a historic home.

GREAT AUSTRALIAN WALKS

This company is based in Sydney and runs tours in the Blue Mountains, along the Great North Walk, Barrington Tops and Kosciusko National Park. Walks are usually three to four days' long and support vehicles carry the camping gear. Staff set up camp and cook meals.

Owner Garry McDougall leads some of the walks or enlists a local person with good local knowledge.

HAPPY WALKER ADVENTURE TOURS

These tours visit parts of Victoria in the summer and other parts of the country the rest of the year. Jenny Flood and Jope Bodegraven lead all tours. Tours to the Victorian alpine regions are in summer, and to the Grampians and desert parks in spring when the wildflowers are blooming. Coastal walks are in February. Others include Western Australia, Kakadu, Kimberley, the Red Centre, Flinders Ranges Tasmania and New South Wales. All tours involve setting up a base camp and taking day walks.

JUNGLE TOURS AND TREKKING AUSTRALIA

This is a low-impact bushwalking company formed in early 1994 when Hans Van Veluwen of Take a Walk on the Wild Side and Raffi Shlomi of Jungle Tours joined forces. It is one of the few to have a permit to enter the rainforests from Mulgrave River Valley south of Cairns to Lake Morris on the Tableland. All walks involve carrying a pack and sleeping in hammocks. The two-day walk is suitable for any age, but you must be fairly fit for the long walks.

OPEN ROAD RENTALS WA

This company walks the Bibbulmun Track twice a year, in autumn and spring. Peter and Fay Lynch have been running this walk since 1977

and have established a network of attractions and local people give talks on their region. The total walk takes 31 days, but it is divided into four stages and you can join any one of these. A support vehicle carries all the heavy gear and camping equipment.

WALKS ON THE WILD SIDE

Rosemary Norwood owns this company in association with the Wilderness Society of Tasmania. It offers four- to seven-day walks in Tasmania with an emphasis on education and understanding the environment. Accommodation is in cabins or camping (carrying your own food and equipment). A 12-day ecotour of the ancient forests, history and heritage of Tasmania is available for special interest groups.

WILD ESCAPES

Wild Escapes is based in Sydney and runs one- to three-day walks in the Blue Mountains National Park and the Kanangra Boyd National Park, as well as whitewater rafting, abseiling and four-wheel drive adventures. Some walks are led by the owner, Bob Charlesworth, a longtime bushwalker and educator; others by guides chosen for their personality and a knowledge of local flora, fauna and geology. Some of the walks are accommodated and some are set up at a base tent camp. Special itineraries for groups can be organised.

WILLIS'S WALKABOUTS

This is an adventurous walking company that traverses some of the most remote and starkly beautiful areas of the north, the centre and the west. Russell Willis established the

Banded stilts, Coorong National Park, South Australia

company in 1986. His program changes each year, but he usually walks in Kakadu National Park, Nitmiluk (Katherine Gorge) National Park, the MacDonnell Ranges and the Kimberley area. These are serious bushwalking trips where you carry your own pack, so you need to be fairly fit. There are also off-season walks so you can experience places like Kakadu in the 'wet', when the vegetation is at it lushest and the waterfalls are in full flow.

Walks range from five to 34 days. Most begin and end in Darwin and there is an option to do only part of the trail on some trips.

Birdwatching

CASSOWARY HOUSE

Casowary House at Kuranda, inland from Cairns, is a small lodge catering specifically for bird-watchers. It is located 305 m (1000 ft) up the forested coastal hills, close to a variety of habitats. You can expect to see up to 180 species within a 60 km (37 m) radius of the house, including representatives of most of Australia's 16 endemic bird families and more than 35 species which are not seen elsewhere. Mid-altitude forest birds, the shy birds of paradise and cassowaries often visit the grounds.

Owners are John and Rita Squire. John, a biologist and experienced ornithologist, leads all tours. Guests receive a bird list and the library is well stocked with bird books.

CHAMBERS RAINFOREST HOLIDAY APARTMENTS

The apartments are near Lake Eacham on the Atherton Tablelands and are owned by John Chambers, who has lived in the area for more than 20 years. The birds you are likely to see from the apartments include catbirds, Lewin honeyeaters, grey-headed robins, kookaburras, crimson rosellas, king parrots and Victoria rifle birds. You might also hear the calls of the boobook and lesser sooty owls, orange-footed jungle fowls and, in spring, the rasping mating call of rifle birds. Guests receive a list of birds and rainforest animals seen in the area. Accommodation is in self-contained apartments encircled with rainforest.

EMU TOURS

This company was started in 1986 by ornithologist Richard Jordan. He includes RAOU bird observatories in many of his trips and leads most tours himself, or employs guides who are experienced birders. Most tours are on the east coast, with some longer trips into South Australia, Western Australia, Tasmania and overseas. Special itineraries can be planned for individual groups.

Regular tours range from a weekend jaunt to a 14-day trek. Transport is by 20-seat bus and accommodation is in tents or local accommodation that offers something a bit different — a tour called 'Pubs and Parrots' used outback pubs, shearers' quarters and farmhouses for accommodation.

FALCON TOURS

(See page 175).

GIPSY POINT LODGE

This small guesthouse bordering Croajingolong National Park specialises in bird-watching with day trips, a five-day bird-watching package and a program of Bird Weeks. Group sizes are limited to 12 people and are paced to suit the various needs of each group. All outings are led by experienced, local bird-watchers or field naturalists and the Bird Weeks are conducted by prominent birders. The lodge's bird list has 225 species, and staff say

birders on the package will see about 80 species during the first day and up to 130 over a week.

INLAND BIRD TOURS

Philip Maher specialises in finding rare and elusive birds and will prepare tight schedules for people with limited time. Regular tours of two to six days are run from Deniliquin, New South Wales. The plains-wanderer is the star attraction on these tours and the best time is October to January.

Philip also organises longer tours (usually camping) to the Northern Territory, Tasmania, northern Western Australia, Far North Queensland and the Strzelecki Track. He is flexible and will plan special itineraries around a birder's 'hit list'.

KIMBERLEY BIRDWATCHING

This company offers a choice of tours of the famous wader bird areas around Broome and into the remote Kimberley region. All tours are led by George Swann, an enthusiastic bird-watcher with years of experience both here and overseas. He likes to keep the group small — no more than four people — and will plan itineraries to suit each group's interests. High-quality binoculars and telescopes are carried. The migratory waders arrive here from September.

KINGFISHER PARK BIRDWATCHERS LODGE

The lodge has six self-contained units and caravan/tent sites for bird-watchers at Julatten behind Port Douglas in Far North Queensland. The 5 ha (12 a) property is located in rainforest with open eucalypt forests nearby. Owners Sandra and Jeff Nicholson provide visitors with an annually updated bird-list of sightings within a half-hour drive of the property, and Lloyd Nielsen provides experienced guiding to groups or individuals.

O'REILLY'S RAINFOREST GUESTHOUSE (see page 195).

PAJINKA WILDERNESS LODGE (see page 196).

PEREGRINE BIRD TOURS

This was established by Chris Doughty 10 years ago to run bird-watching holidays in Australia and overseas. He offers a variety of tours ranging from camping safaris to look for specific and rare birds, to visits to major birding areas, staying in motels and hotels. There is virtually no corner of Australia that Chris has not visited in his quest to find rare and interesting birds.

PITTA RAINFOREST & WILDLIFE TOURS

Bill Bray, a keen bird-watcher, offers day and evening tours of the Cairns region. This part of Queensland has wet-lands, mangroves, rainforests, woodlands, dry open forest and semi-arid outback habitats, all within easy reach. You can expect to see up to 80 species on a day's outing and Bill will prepare a special program to meet specific requests and areas of interest.

GRAHAM PIZZEY

Graham Pizzey, one of Australia's best known and most widely published authorities on Australian birds, offers accommodation in his home in the Grampians, Victoria. Graham and Sue have two guest rooms and provide home-cooked meals along with expert guiding.

Bird-watching takes place on their land and the surrounding regions where some 300 bird species — more than a third of all Australian birds — are found. Tuition includes recognising the 'field marks' and calls of local birds, using your binoculars, photography, the inter-relationship of birds with flowering plants and slide shows in the evening.

SPECIALISED RIVER TOURS

Situated a little north of Cairns at Daintree village, these are for serious bird-watchers. Chris Dahlberg starts his two-hour tours early — 6 a.m. from October to March; 6.30 a.m. April to September — any later and you miss the good birds. His average sightings are 38 different species during the wet season and 49 during the dry. He also offers B&B accommodation at the Red Mill House, which has a good reference library and photographic gallery.

Photography

The tools of the outdoor photographer are light, beauty, drama, colour, landscape and wildlife. The photographer is the perfect ecotourist, arriving quietly, capturing the image on film then moving on, having no impact, leaving no damage. However, capturing that image takes time, so you need to travel with people who will spend hours to get the right shot, and who will share their knowledge.

I could find only a few companies which lead tours with the sole purpose of taking photos and talking cameras. These listed below are all excellent, allowing time to take photos and offering instruction along the way.

COATE'S WILDLIFE TOURS

Coate's 15-day tour to the Kimberley region is a photography/natural history tour with a professional photographer. Weekend tours from Perth go to the Pinnacles, the Yallingup coastline, and the Stirling Ranges during wildflower season and stay in chalets. In the evenings the leader shows slides and discusses photographic techniques. For more information see page 173.

FALCON TOURS

(See page 175).

FIRST LIGHT PHOTOGRAPHIC SAFARIS

First Light is jointly run by Stuart Grant, a photographer and experienced driver/guide and Bill Rudock, an American-based master photographer.

Its 14-day tour leaves from Kununurra in northern Western Australia in April/May and costs $2350 per person. Accommodation is in a motel at Kununurra and base camps elsewhere.

FOCUS 10

Focus 10 is owned by Andrew Thomasson, a professional travel photographer and guide. Every long weekend, Andrew runs a three-day photographic excursion based at historic Candelo, a six-hour drive south of Sydney and three hours north of Melbourne. Accommodation is in a restored bank building providing share accommodation and meals.

About $270 for the weekend, including accommodation, meals and tuition.

FRONTIER PHOTOGRAPHIC SAFARIS

Sam Lambrau is a professional photographer who leads daily nature/photography tours into the Blue Mountains, and four-wheel drive safari tours into the Outback. He will organise special tours for a group of four or more.

The safari tours average ten to 16 days, from June to November and cost from $1500 to $2300 per person. On safari you travel by four-wheel drive and sleep in tents usually working out of a base camp. You photograph Outback townships, lonely pubs, ghost towns, wetlands, deserts and wildlife. Sam provides tuition and a selection of professional cameras for everyone to try out.

IMAGERY GALLERY

Imagery gallery in Brisbane is the oldest photographic gallery in Australia. It is run by mother and son Ruby and Doug Spowart who have been leading photographic safaris for 14 years.

Transport is in a large coach and the number of people is limited to 25 to leave plenty of room for camera gear. Once on the road special lectures, video programs and demonstrations may be held and there is a tutor on hand at all times. The three-week tours are usually held from June to September and cost from about $80 a day.

TAKA II DIVE ADVENTURES

(See page 154–5).

WORLD EXPEDITIONS

This company has an eight-day tour to Lake Mungo and Mootwingee in New South Wales with photographer David Tatnall. You travel by four-wheel drive into this spectacular desert country and plenty of time is allowed for photography, especially of the magical sunsets. For more information see page 181.

ACCOMMODATION

These properties are a select few. My aim has been to find places for people who want to be close to nature but do not want to camp.

Development and the environment are generally not compatible partners, but with a bit of care and attention they can live in harmony. Australia has hundreds of properties in beautiful country settings, but I have chosen only those that are friends of the bush. These are properties set in native bush, so when you open your door you see not a cow or a sheep but the timid gaze of a wallaby or a possum. The birds you hear sing for joy and freedom — they will not end up on a dinner plate, and the soil is turned by worms and other mulching creatures, not the plough.

Bush-friendly properties blend with the environment, are proudly Australian in design, and have been built with the minimum of removal of or damage to the natural vegetation. They have raised walkways that lead you into the bush, but keep trampling feet off the vegetation and allow for the

Cradle Mountain Lodge, Tasmania

Coconut Beach Rainforest Resort, Far North Queensland

natural flow of water. They also have environmentally sustainable waste management policies and power-saving services. Their day-by-day management policies are environmentally sound; they provide their guests with information on the local environment and show them how to care for it. They have knowledgeable guides who are not just activity organisers, but know the names of the plants, the habits of the animals and the culture of the area. They have a library on the local flora, fauna and natural and cultural history, and hand out maps on local walking trails, preferably with information sheets on the plants and wildlife along the trails.

I do not approve of feeding native animals, but this is widely practised. Most places feed them only natural foods and in small amounts, so they do not become dependent on hand-outs.

The size of a property has a significant bearing on its effect on the ecosystems around it and I had to make my judgements on the current position. A large property may mean more human visitors than the environment can sustain, however, a small property may not earn enough to provide education and to install environmentally sustainable services. There are so many variables. For example, a family-owned property could start out with high ideals but might be sold to someone with different values, and some properties which are of an environmentally sustainable size now, may extend and become too big for the region.

Because room rates change so often I have grouped the charges in categories: **L** (lower range) is less than $110; **M** (middle range) is $111 to $240; and **H** (higher range) is $241 upwards. All the prices quoted are per night twin share, and I have indicated where meals are included in the price. I found most places offered special rates for children and tent and caravan sites ranged in price from $10 to $20 a night for two people. The properties are listed in alphabetical order.

Arkaroola Wildlife Sanctuary and Tourist Resort (L)

FLINDERS RANGES, SOUTH AUSTRALIA

Arkaroola is a privately owned, 61 000 ha (150 730 a) sanctuary in the northern Flinders Ranges. Its spectacular landscape features ancient granite peaks, sharp quartzite ridges, deep valleys, and creeks with inviting waterholes. Geologist Reg Sprigg bought Arkaroola in 1968 and, with his wife Griselda, set out to right all the wrongs humans had wrought upon the land. Tourism was controlled and the sheep and feral animals were eliminated from the area. Nature has been allowed to take over and after a few good wet seasons the native plants and wildlife are flourishing.

Because Arkaroola is in a remote area, a village has been built to provide accommodation and services. Accommodation ranges from air-conditioned motel rooms to camping areas and the services include a shop, garage, dining room, bar, swimming pool and laundry. Museums tell the history of mining, farming and Aboriginal occupation in the area. A hilltop astronomical observatory tells the story of the skies and an information centre has masses more information and maps on trails for four-wheel-drive vehicles and bushwalking.

On some evenings, videos and talks are given on the natural history and geology of the region. Four-wheel-drive tours (extra charge) into the rugged terrain are run by guides with a broad knowledge of the geology, botany and local natural history.

Arkaroola is busy during school holidays, especially the September break when the wildflowers are at their best. If you want solitude, try to avoid these times and book ahead if planning a September sojourn.

Located 380 km (236 m) north of Adelaide; the nearest airstrip is Leigh Creek, where staff will meet you.

Belgamba (L)

NEAR ROCKHAMPTON, QUEENSLAND

This cottage is located on 537 ha (1327 a) adjoining the Bouldercombe Gorge Reserve which has excellent bushwalks in unspoilt eucalypt forests and great views over the Gorge and Dee Valley. This is a popular walking area for individuals and clubs from Rockhampton who often stay at Belgamba cottage. Cathy and Ian Herbert are keen conservationists and have been revegetating the land to restore the natural bush after years of cattle grazing. They often lead walks and spotlighting tours or will leave you at peace and let you do your own thing. They say this is what most people who come here prefer.

The self-contained house has three bedrooms and sleeps six comfortably. It has a wood heater for winter evenings and all bedding and linen is supplied; meals can be provided. There is no telephone or television.

Located 40 km (25 m) south of Rockhampton and 15 km (9 m) from Mount Morgan.

Binna Burra Mountain Lodge (M–H)

LAMINGTON NATIONAL PARK, QUEENSLAND

There are cabin-style units with ensuite, units with shared bathrooms or multi-share rooms with shared facilities, and a camping area with furnished tents and tent sites. There is no television or radio in the room. All buildings are designed for their mountain-top location and to catch the best views.

The resort offers guided walks or you can collect a detailed map of walking trails and a packed lunch and set off on your own. Other free activities include abseiling, caving, and bus trips to some of best lookouts. There is a games room, a library and a fire. Binna Burra organises activity weeks and weekends with specialised courses in nature photography, music, spinning, pottery, watercolour painting and other creative pursuits.

Price includes all meals and activities. Located 150 km (93 m) south of Brisbane and 50 km (31 m) inland from Surfers Paradise.

Bungaree Earth Cottages (L)

BLUE MOUNTAINS, NEW SOUTH WALES

Ian and Joanne Curtis made the mud bricks used to build the cabins on site and you can see the pond where they toiled. The sandy coloured bricks have been combined with plantation timbers to make delightfully comfortable cabins with a faint fragrance of earth and bush. Soil disturbed during building was mulched and later returned so the native seeds could revegetate. This is a true hideaway — 'Bungaree' is an Aboriginal word implying a feeling of oneness with the land. There are only three cabins, each is well hidden and no more are planned.

Great use has been made of natural energy — solar panels have been used for lighting (12 volts), rain fills the water tanks, the mud bricks are good insulators against heat and cold, and the deep soil is well able to absorb all waste from septic tanks. Gas is used for cooking, hot water and refrigeration. All of the cabins are self-contained, with a kitchen, linen if required, books on local flora and fauna and log fire for chilly evenings. Two of the cabins have a double bedroom downstairs and an upstairs bunk room. The third has one bedroom and has wheelchair access. Ian and Joanne have marked walking trails on their land and give guests a self-guide leaflet which explains the plants and wildlife of the area.

Turn off the Great Western Highway at Wentworth Falls village, take a sharp right into Railway Parade and carry on until you come to the sign on your left.

Coconut Beach Rainforest Resort (M–H)

CAPE TRIBULATION, FAR NORTH QUEENSLAND

This resort is located in an environmentally sensitive area between the World Heritage listed Daintree Rainforest and the Great Barrier Reef. Most of the buildings are on the inland side of the coast road and rise up a hill densely covered in magnificent tropical rainforest. However, the main dining area — the Long House — and one swimming pool are near the beach and are visited by day trippers, especially tours from Cairns which stop here for lunch.

The resort has an excellent library of books, maps and videos of the area and gives a free evening orientation slide show and walk. Other activities which can be booked through reception include guided rainforest walks, bird-watching, horse riding, reef cruises, crocodile spotting and four-wheel-drive safaris. Or you can just laze on the long, isolated beach.

A 96-bed budget-priced Education and Adventure Lodge was opened in 1994 to cater for study groups. Education programs on the reef and rainforest are being developed and research projects are studying local problems and the environment's reaction to human contact.

Price includes breakfast. Located 150 km (93 m) north of Cairns on Cape Tribulation Road.

Cradle Mountain Lodge (L–M)

TASMANIA

This rustic lodge with its warm dining room and bars where you can sink into deep leather couches in front of huge fires is on the boundary of the famous Cradle Mountain–Lake St Clair wilderness area. Accommodation choices include camping, bunk-houses, four rooms in the main lodge and 86 self-contained log cabins with a cosy wood heater — some cabins also have a spa. No telephone, television or clock–radio disturbs your peace and quiet. The cabins are scattered through the bush so nature is literally at your doorstep — I opened my door to find a little pademelon sitting on my welcome mat. Some 2500

indigenous seedlings have recently been planted to attract more wildlife. A small store and place to buy unleaded petrol provide basic supplies for travellers.

The main reason people come to Cradle Mountain Lodge is to walk and photograph the wilderness, mountains and lakes, which start immediately across the creek beside the lodge. The world-famous Overland Track starts (or ends) here. Your first stop should be the visitors' centre and ranger station (across the bridge), which has excellent displays, general information and maps on the wilderness walks.

The lodge has knowledgeable guides who lead walks, or you can get a map and take yourself. The daily activities sheet includes a weather forecast, which is important for bushwalkers. Other activities which can be booked include four-wheel-drive trips, horse riding, flyfishing tuition, abseiling, canoeing and gold panning. Wild animals are fed fruit and vegetables outside the main lodge each evening.

Driving time is 1¼ hours south of Devonport and nearly five hours northwest of Hobart.

Daintree Eco Lodge (H)

FAR NORTH QUEENSLAND

This is a delightful place built with a true feeling for the tropical climate and the rainforest. The ground is quite steep and the 17 individual lodges are built on stilts and reached by a boardwalk so there is minimum disturbance to the rainforest vegetation. Each lodge is long and spacious with a screened balcony and glass louvred walls so you can sleep with the breezes rather than the air-conditioning. The furnishing is cane with brightly coloured upholstery and the floors and bench tops are of marble from local quarries. There is a television and telephone in all rooms. The open-plan restaurant/bar straddles the creek that runs down the valley.

The management philosophy of environmental harmony has been achieved through minimum damage to the rainforest during building and the use of non-harmful chemicals and insecticides. All replanting is of natives, although there are some exotics which were planted by the previous owner and are too well established to remove. An excellent library on local plants, animals and the rainforest is in the foyer as well as a daily bird list from a local bird-watcher.

Free interpretative tours are run daily to the nearby waterfall, which lulls you to sleep at night. Other tours which can be booked at reception include early morning bird-watching and reef cruises.

Price includes a full breakfast and return transfers to Cairns. Located 98 km (61 m) north of Cairns, just before Daintree village.

Crystal Creek Rainforest Retreat (M)

NORTHERN NEW SOUTH WALES

Six self-contained cabins placed carefully among the trees by the conservation-minded owners, provide a comfortable getaway amid birds, wildlife and subtropical rainforest.

Judy Rimmer and Ralph Kraemer treat their land as an extension of the Buminbah Nature Reserve and have had experts prepare plant and bird lists for guests. They have constructed walking tracks to the special features of the land to contain damage as much as possible.

The owners guide rainforest, bird-watching and spotlighting walks and organise special interest weeks, such as Bird Week and Rainforest Week when they bring in ornithologists, botanists and ecologists.

Located 20 minutes from Murwillumbah. Pick-up can be arranged from the Coolangatta and Murwillumbah airports and the Murwillumbah rail station.

Daintree Wilderness Lodge (M)

FAR NORTH QUEENSLAND

This is a true tropical hideaway with secluded cabins hidden in the rainforest. When Anna and Mal Graham visited the area, they fell in love with the rainforest and bought 8 ha (20 a). They have since built ten bungalows, which branch off from raised boardwalks that conceal the power and water service lines. There is no telephone, television or air-conditioning in the bungalows. Boardwalks lead to a small bar and dining room with indoor and outdoor tables and a spa.

Walking trails have been established through the rainforest and guests are given lists of plants to identify along the way.

Price includes breakfast. Located on Cape Tribulation Road, 13 km (8 m) north of the Daintree River car ferry.

Ferntree Rainforest Resort (M)

CAPE TRIBULATION, FAR NORTH QUEENSLAND

This property is very Australian, with bleached wood buildings, soft-green tin roofs and a verandah with comfortable chairs for a quiet read and an evening cocktail.

Accommodation is in villas or suites. The villas have air-conditioning, a double bed, telephone and ensuite downstairs, and a loft-style room which has two single beds and glass louvres on three sides to let the breezes flow through. The suites are located alongside the pool, but instead of making the pool a feature, the bedroom faces outwards into the rainforest and a private balcony on a higher level overlooks the pool. The high-ceilinged bar and restaurant overlook the pool, but the dining tables are placed along the boardwalk and in two open-sided huts which straddle a rainforest creek. Outdoor dining in separate areas like this has a relaxed casualness which suits the tropical climate. It is a five- to ten-minute walk to the beach and tours of the rainforest and reef can be booked through reception.

Located just off Cape Tribulation Road, 140 km (87 m) north of Cairns.

Freycinet Lodge (M)

TASMANIA

The 38 wood cabins are roomy, with deep decks, and some have a spa. Another 22 self-catering cabins suitable for families are planned. Raised boardwalks protect the vegetation and Aboriginal midden sites and carry the conduits which would otherwise have necessitated digging trenches and disturbing the natural environment. No telephone, radio or television in the rooms.

You can walk over the Hazards in a couple of hours or follow the trails around the coastline. Walking, swimming, fishing and lazing around are favourite pastimes here. The resort employs an experienced naturalist who gives free walks and four-wheel-drive tours. For early birds, she offers a 4 a.m. breakfast on Mount Amos to watch the sun rise.

Located halfway up the east coast, a 2-hour drive from Launceston or Hobart.

Heron Island (H)

QUEENSLAND

This 2-ha (5-a) tropical paradise is perfect for diving, bird-watching, turtle watching and being very lazy. It has no glitz and does not allow access to day-trippers. The 109 rooms include budget cabins with shared bathroom facilities, motel-style units, and large one-room suites. There is also a beach house on the waterfront. No telephone or television clutter the rooms but there is a radio. General facilities include a souvenir shop, dive centre, tennis court and a big chess set near the swimming pool.

Heron is a national park and rangers living here monitor the wildlife to ensure it is not being disturbed by human presence. The island is an important breeding ground for green turtles (females come ashore to lay their eggs November to March) black noddy terns and the wedge-tailed shearwater.

The resort's guides give island

walks, reef walks and nature slide shows and the dive shop takes divers and snorkellers to the outer reef.

Heron Island also manages Wilson Island, a nearby coral cay, which has accommodation for 16 people in eight stylish tents with wooden balconies and hot showers close by.

Price includes all meals and some activities. You can reach Heron Island from Gladstone by launch (2 hours) or helicopter (30 minutes).

Jemby-Rinjah Lodge (L)

BLUE MOUNTAINS, NEW SOUTH WALES

Margaret and Peter Quirk have developed Jemby-Rinjah in stages since 1985. Nine self-contained cabins with two bedrooms and a slow combustion fireplace are hidden along little trails in the bush. Three lodges have two bedrooms and a bathroom on either side, a mezzanine floor with two extra single beds, and a communal lounge opening onto a large deck. These are linked to the main lodge by raised boardwalks to protect the native vegetation.

A small library provides information on local flora and fauna and maps are available for self-guided walks.

The Quirks encourage environmental study groups and student groups to come here and work closely with the national park rangers who provide expert infor-mation and guidance. They set the example by using only timbers from renewable plantations, low-energy lights (solar power is being introduced) and environmentally

sound waste management.

Price includes breakfast for lodge guests only. Easily found near the canyon end of Evans Lookout Road.

Kingfisher Bay Resort and Village (M)

FRASER ISLAND, QUEENSLAND

When this resort opened in 1992 it introduced luxury accommodation for the first time on this World Heritage listed sand island. Environmental care has been a priority and the buildings are Australian in design with timber walls, tin roofs and deep verandahs. The resort has several restaurants and bars with outdoor areas overlooking the pool and Hervey Bay. Boardwalks connect the rooms, no building is higher than the trees and everything is coloured to blend with the environment.

The resort's rangers give guided nature walks and island tours or you can hire a four-wheel-drive vehicle and do your own thing. Activities include canoeing, sailing, fishing, tennis, bird-watching, wildlife spotlighting and whale-watching with a marine biologist from August to October.

The island is reached by fast catamaran or vehicular barge from Urangan Harbour, Hervey Bay.

O'Reilly's Rainforest Guesthouse (M–H)

LAMINGTON NATIONAL PARK, QUEENSLAND

O'Reilly's has that simple, old-world charm which is often missing in modern resorts. The guesthouse is run by second and third generations of the O'Reilly family who are proud of the little sanctuary their family has created. Forty-one units range from basic with shared bathrooms, to modern with ensuite and balconies. There is no telephone, television or radio in the rooms and all meals are hearty country fare. The main building has a bar and fireplaces for curling up by on cold mountain nights.

The favourite activities here are bushwalking, feeding the wild birds and walking over the nine suspension bridges built through the rainforest canopy. Free guided walks and drives to the best lookouts are provided or you can ask for the bird and plant lists and a picnic lunch and explore on your own. Evening activities include slide shows and talks, visits to glow-worms, spotlighting and campfire dinners.

O'Reilly's is world renowned for its variety of birds and for 17 years it has held a Bird Week in November.

Price includes all meals and activities. Two hours' drive south of Brisbane and 1½ hours west of Surfers Paradise.

Pajinka Wilderness Lodge (H)

FAR NORTH QUEENSLAND

You cannot go much further than this before you walk off the northernmost point of Cape York. Pajinka is owned by the Injinoo people, who have lived here for many generations, and while at the lodge, you will have a chance to learn about their culture and heritage. Accommodation includes camping sites and 24 cabins which have verandahs and louvre walls to let the breezes flow through. There is no telephone, television or clock.

The restaurant serves local produce when possible and there is a licensed bar. If you are lucky, you will be there during a celebration when *kup mari* (food wrapped in banana leaf) is cooked in a ground oven and the Aboriginal people tell the stories of the area in corroboree and song.

There are guided four-wheel drive and walking tours (extra charge) or you can collect self-guiding maps at reception.

Other activities include walking to the northernmost point of the continent to see where the Arafura Sea meets the Coral Sea, bird-watching, fishing, and night walks to see wildlife and plants that blossom after dark. Mountain bikes and dinghies are available for hire. Pajinka is renowned for its variety of birds and hosts a Nature Week for twitchers in January, which is the peak time for migratory birds.

Price includes all meals. Pajinka can be reached by four-wheel drive or by air to Bamaga airport, where lodge staff will meet you. If driving, you will need a permit to enter Injinoo land (telephone (070) 69 3252 for information).

Novotel Karri Valley Resort (M)

WESTERN AUSTRALIA

This delightful, all-wood resort has 36 self-contained, two- and three-bedroom chalets spaced between the trees, 32 motel units jutting out over the lake, and a camping area near the road. The cabins are self-sufficient with kitchen, barbecue, verandah and a pot-bellied stove. The units have balconies extending over the water's edge with unrestricted views of the lake and the tall trees on the far bank. The units have telephone, television and radio. The spacious restaurant and bar also juts out over the water.

The resort is surrounded by magnificent karri forests which contain some rare species of orchid and wildflowers. The lodge staff give free guided tours and horse rides (at an extra charge) which travel only on established trails. Other activities include canoeing on the lake, tennis and trout fishing (trout is an important industry in the area and the lake is stocked).

Located 367 km (228 m) south of Perth and 19 km (12 m) from Pemberton.

Seven Spirit Bay (H)

TOP END, NORTHERN TERRITORY

Seven Spirit Bay is a mere speck in the vast Aboriginal-owned wilderness of Cobourg Peninsula in the Northern Territory. The area is so remote that even getting to the resort has an element of adventure to it — by light aircraft from Darwin, then four-wheel drive. Once here you are in the lap of luxury.

There are only 24 habitats (rooms) so human impact on the region is minimal and tranquillity is assured. Each individual, hexagonal habitat has louvres on all sides to bring the outside in and let the cooling breezes flow through. Even the open-style bathrooms are separate from the rooms, so a kimono, torch and umbrella are provided. The main building has deep, shaded decks for sipping evening cocktails and gazing across the swimming pool. The meals feature freshly caught seafood and

hand-picked vegetables from the resort's garden. A small library displays shells and other items of interest and wildlife videos are provided for guests.

Daily activities are usually quite leisurely. A naturalist leads walks into the pristine country where wallabies, dingos, bandicoots, goannas, birds and a few imported animals live wild and free. The few European attempts and taming this land were unsuccessful and you will see the sad remains of their settlements. Other activities include sailing, fishing and crocodile spotting. The coastline is a marine park with golden beaches, mangroves, freshwater and paperbark swamps, reefs, sponge beds and monsoon rainforests.

The name Seven Spirit Bay is derived from the seven seasons identified by local Aboriginal people — lightning, thundering, rainmaking, greening, windstorming, fire-raging and cloudless blue — so think carefully before planning your trip. Although the temperatures change little (28–32°C (82–89°F) all year), the humidity does and the seasons are very different.

Price includes all meals and activities. Transfers from Darwin cost about $275 return.

Silky Oaks Lodge (H)

FAR NORTH QUEENSLAND

The all-wood main lodge and chalets perch on poles surrounded by tropical rainforest and overlooking the Mossman River, which weaves its way down the valley floor. Obviously it never gets cold here because the dining room, bar and lounging areas are wide open to the elements, which is very pleasant and relaxing.

The spacious chalets are individually placed among the trees and have balconies and air-conditioning, but no tlephone or television. The furnishings are rather English cottage-style, which I found a bit out of place in the tropics, however, I quickly forgot this minor irregularity when I sat on my balcony in the fading evening, feeling the warmth of the air and listening to the river rippling over the stones. There are 60 chalets, some with glimpses of the river through the trees and some near the tennis court and swimming pool.

The river is a focal point here and flows gently, forming glorious emerald pools where you can swim or paddle a canoe. The lodge has canoes, kayaks and bicycles for guests' use and reception will supply maps and plant identification sheets for the local bush walks. The activities manager offers guided walks and there is a library on local flora and fauna near the bar. Once here, of course, you are close to the Daintree rainforest and the Great Barrier Reef, and tours to both areas can be arranged from the lodge.

Price includes a tropical breakfast and some activities. Located 83 km (51 m) north of Cairns and 7 km (4 m) from Mossman.

Undara Lodge (M)

QUEENSLAND

The main reason people come here is to see the lava tubes formed 190 000 years ago during a series of volcanic eruptions. However, the sweeping savannah countryside and the quaint accommodation in old railway carriages are also an attraction.

The land has been owned by several generations of the Collins family but is now a national park. Bram Collins is the driving force behind the resort and the Savannah Guides, who take tours to the lava tubes, and has kept everything as natural as possible. He saved the old railway carriages from the scrap heap and tidied them up into comfortable rooms with a hand basin, rich panelling and old-fashioned sliding louvre windows. Toilets and bathrooms at the end of the carriages are shared and you walk along an outside platform to reach them. The bar and restaurant, also old carriages, are formed around an open square which is a great gathering place for drinks and meals. After dinner, the staff arrange spotlighting walks or light the big campfire and tell stories and sing country songs.

Several camping areas have been separated into different zones: travellers with their own caravan or tent; coach and four-wheel drive groups, and a village of permanent, furnished tents which have electric lighting. Each camping zone has its own communal kitchen, ablution block and a large campfire encircled with log seating.

Price includes all meals. The lava tube tour costs extra and does not operate from 1 October to 31 March.

Located 275 km (171 m) south-west of Cairns and 40 km (25 m) east of Mount Surprise.

Addresses

State and Territory Tourist Offices

Australian Capital Territory
ACT Tourism Commission
Visitor Information Centre
Northbourne Avenue
Dickson ACT 2602
Tel: (06) 205 0044
Fax: (06) 205 0776

New South Wales
New South Wales Travel
Centre 19 Castlereagh Street
Sydney NSW 2000
Tel: (02) 231 4444
Fax: (02) 232 6080

Northern Territory
Northern Territory Tourist
Commission Holiday Centre
67 Stuart Highway
Alice Springs NT 0871
Tel: (089) 51 8555 or
008 808 244
Fax: (089) 51 8550

Queensland
Queensland Government
Travel Centre Cnr Adelaide &
Edwards Streets Brisbane Qld
4000 Tel: (07) 221 6111;
Fax: (07) 221 0320

South Australia
SA Tourism Commission
Travel Centre 1 King William
Street Adelaide SA 5000
Tel: (08) 212 1505
Fax: (08) 303 2249

Tasmania
Department of Tourism,
Sport and Recreation —
Tasmania Central Information
Services GPO Box 399D
Hobart Tas. 7001
Tel: (002) 30 8250
Fax: (002) 30 8232

Victoria
RACV/Victorian Tourist
Information Centre
230 Collins Street
Melbourne Vic. 3000
Tel: (03) 790 3333

Western Australia
WA Tourist Centre Forrest
Place (Cnr Wellington Street)
Perth WA 6000
Tel: (09) 483 1111
Fax: (09) 481 0190

Australian Tourist Commission

The ATC operates 'Helplines'
throughout the world for
travellers requiring
information on Australia.

New Zealand
Auckland 09 302 77218
Outside Auckland
0800 65 0303

Europe
United Kingdom
081 780 2227
Germany/Luxembourg
069 274 0060
France 1 45 79 8044
Scandinavia 08 210 588

North America
USA/Canada 708 296 4900

Japan
Tokyo 03 3582 2191
Osaka 06 229 3601

Asia
Hong Kong 802 7817
Singapore 255 4555

General

Western Australian Heritage Committee
7th Floor, 184 St George's
Terrace Perth WA 6000
Tel: (09) 322 4375

Great Barrier Reef Marine Park Authority
PO Box 1379
Townsville Qld 4810
Tel: (077) 81 8811
Fax: (077) 72 6093

National Parks

Australian Nature Conservation Agency,
GPO Box 636,
Canberra, ACT 2601
Tel: (06) 250 0200;
Fax: (06) 250 0399

ACT Parks and Conservation Service,
PO Box 1119, Tuggeranong,
ACT 290
Tel: (06) 207 2333;
Fax: (06) 207 2335

National Parks and Wildlife Service,
PO Box 1967,
Hurstville, NSW 2220
Tel: (02) 585 6333;
Fax: (02) 585 6555

Conservation Commission of the Northern Territory,
Information Officer,
Smith Street Mall,
Darwin, NT 0800
Tel: (089) 89 3881;
Fax: (089) 81 7346

Department of Environment and Heritage, Naturally Queensland Information Centre, PO Box 155, Brisbane Albert Street, QLD 4002 Tel: (07) 227 8186; Fax: (07) 227 8749

Department of Environment and Natural Resources, GPO Box 1047, Adelaide, SA 5001 Tel: (08) 204 1910; Fax: (08) 226 4156

Department of Parks, Wildlife and Heritage, GPO Box 44A, Hobart, Tas. 7001 Tel: (002) 33 6625; Fax: (002) 23 8308

Department of Conservation and Natural Resources, PO Box 41, East Melbourne, Vic. 3002 Tel: (03) 412 4011; Fax: (03) 412 4151

Department of Conservation and Land Management, PO Box 104, Como, WA 6152 Tel: (09) 334 0333; Fax: (09) 334 0466

Australian Odysseys, PO Box 494, Penneshaw, Kangaroo Island, SA 5222. Tel/Fax: (0848) 31 294

Broken River Mountain Retreat, Eungella, via Mackay, Qld 4757. Tel: (079) 58 4528

Carnarvon National Park, via Rolleston, Qld 4701. Tel: (079) 84 4505

Croajingolong National Park, Department of Conservation and Natural Resources, Princes Highway, Cann River, Vic. 3890 Tel: (051) 58 6351

Eungella National Park, Dalrymple Heights, Qld 4757 Tel/Fax: (079) 58 4552

Kangaroo Island Wilderness Tours and Wedgwood Host Farm, PO Box 33, Parndana, Kangaroo Island, SA 5220. Tel: (0848) 96 043; Fax: (0848) 33 282

Kosciusko Mountain Retreat, PMB 3, Jindabyne, NSW 2627 Tel: (046) 56 2224

Ku-ring-gai Chase National Park–Garigal National Park, PO Box 134, Forestville, NSW 2087 Tel: (02) 451 8124

Mount Buffalo National Park, Department of Conservation and Natural Resources, PO Box 20, Bright, Vic. 3741 Tel: (057) 55 1577; Fax: (057) 55 1176

Oasis Lodge, Nature Australia Ltd, Central Reservations, Beechmont, Qld 4211 Tel: (079) 844 503

Port Campbell Caravan Park, Tregea Street, Port Campbell, Vic. 3269. Tel: (055) 98 6369

Royal National Park, PO Box 44, Sutherland, NSW 2232 Tel: (02) 542 0648

Up the Creek with Kate, Kate Stanton, Stokes Bay, Kangaroo Island, SA 5223 Tel: (0848) 36 251

Wilpena Pound Motel, Suite 6, 219 East Terrace, Adelaide, SA 5000 Tel: (08) 232 5454 or 1800 805 802

Wilsons Promontory National Park, Ranger-in-charge, Tidal River via Foster, Vic. 3960 Tel: (056) 80 9555

Wildlife Parks and Sanctuaries

Australian Wildlife Park Wallgrove Road, Eastern Creek, NSW 2766 Tel: (02) 675 0187

Ballarat Wildlife Park Corner Fussell and York Streets, Ballarat, Vic. 3354 Tel: (053) 33 5933

Cleland Wildlife Park Summit Road, Mount Lofty, SA Tel (08) 339 2444

Currumbin Sanctuary Gold Coast Highway, Currumbin, Qld 4221 Tel: (075) 34 1266

Eagles Heritage Raptor Wildlife Centre, Boodjidup Road, Margaret River, WA 6285 Tel: (097) 57 2960

Earth Sanctuaries Ltd Stock Road, Mylor, SA 5153 Tel: (08) 370 9422

Earth Sanctuaries' Yookamurra Sanctuary Pipeline Road, Sedan, SA Tel: (08) 370 9422 or (085) 62 5011

Fleays Fauna Centre West Burleigh Road, Burleigh Heads, Tel: (075) 76 2411

Healesville Sanctuary Badger Creek Road, Healesville, Vic. 3777 Tel: (03) 728 2000

Lone Pine Koala Sanctuary Jesmond Road, Fig Tree Pocket, Brisbane, Qld 4069 Tel: (07) 378 1366

Phillip Island Phillip Island Road, Newhaven, Vic. 3925 Tel: (059) 56 7447

Serendip 100 Windermere Road, Lara, Vic. 3212 Tel: (052) 82 1584

Territory Wildlife Park
Cox Peninsula Road,
Berry Springs, NT 0837
Tel: (089) 88 6000;
Fax: (089) 88 6210

Tidbinbilla Nature Reserve
Tidbinbilla Road,
RMB 141,
Tharwa, ACT 2620
Tel: (06) 237 5120;
Fax: (06) 237 5176

Trowunna Wildlife Park
Mole Creek, Tas. 7304
Tel: (003) 63 6162

Bushwalking

Alpine Nature Rambles,
PO Box 236, Falls Creek, Vic.
3699 Tel: (057) 58 3492

Country Walks,
PO Box 65,
Leura, NSW 2780
Tel: (047) 84 3266;
Fax: (047) 57 3982

Craclair Tours,
PO Box 516,
Devonport, Tas., 7310
Tel: (004) 24 7833;
Fax: (004) 24 9215

**Cradle Huts Pty Ltd and
Freycinet Experience Pty Ltd,**
PO Box 1879, Launceston,
Tas. 7250. Tel: (003) 31 2006
or (003) 34 4615;
Fax: (003) 31 5525

Echidna Walkabouts,
15 Crichton Avenue, Port
Melbourne, Vic. 3207.
Tel/Fax: (03) 646 8249

Exploranges,
37 Walker Street,
Somerton Park, SA 5044
Tel: (08) 294 6530

Footprints Expeditions,
15 Bentley Close, Mt
Claremont, WA 6010
Tel/Fax: (09) 385 2534

Forest Walks & Ecotours
PO Box 59, Meander, Tas.
7304 Tel/Fax: (003) 69 5150

Great Australian Walks,
81 Elliott Street,
Balmain, NSW 2041
Tel: (02) 555 7580

**Happy Walker Adventure
Tours,**
PO Box 886,
Croydon, Vic. 3136
Tel: (03) 725 2723

**Jungle Tours and Trekking
Australia,**
196 McCormack Street,
Manunda,
Cairns, Qld 4870 Tel: (070)
32 2111;
Fax: (070) 32 2333

Open Road Rentals WA,
18 Tickenham Road,
Victoria Park, WA 6100
Tel: (09) 362 3166;
Fax: (09) 470 2358

Walks on The Wildside,
PO Box 59,
Meander, Tas. 7304
Tel/Fax: (003) 69 5150

Wild Escapes,
PO Box 116,
Asquith, NSW 2077.
Tel: (02) 482 2881;
Fax: (02) 477 3114

Willis's Walkabouts,
12 Carrington Street,
Millner, NT 0810
Tel: (089) 85 2134;
Fax: (089) 85 2355

Principal Bushwalking Clubs

**Confederation of
Bushwalking Clubs of NSW
(Inc),**
GPO Box 2090,
Sydney, NSW 2001
Tel: (02) 548 1228

**Federation of Victorian
Walking Clubs Inc.,**
GPO Box 815F,
Melbourne, Vic. 3001
Tel: (03) 859 8554

**Federation of South
Australian Walking Clubs
Inc.,** State House, 1 Sturt
Street, Adelaide, SA 5000
Tel: (08) 213 0624;
Fax: (08) 211 7115

Perth Bushwalkers (Inc),
PO Box 8321, Perth Business
Centre, Perth, WA 6849
Tel: (09) 362 1614

Birdwatching

**Royal Australian
Ornithologists Union,**
21 Gladstone Street, Moonee
Ponds, Vic. 3039
Tel (03) 370 1422;
Fax: (03) 370 9194

**Bird Observers Club of
Australia,** 183 Springvale
Road, Nunawading, Vic. 3131
Tel: (03) 877 5342;
Fax: (03) 894 4048

Herman Bakker,
PO Box 252, Meningie, SA
5264 Tel: (085) 75 1206

Cassowary House,
Black Mountain Road,
Kuranda, Qld 4872
Tel: (070) 93 7318

**Chambers Rainforest
Holiday Apartments,**
PO Box 87, Yungaburra, Qld
4872 Tel/Fax: (070) 95 3754

Emu Tours,
PO Box 4, Jamberoo, NSW
2533 Tel: (042) 36 0542;
Fax: (042) 36 0176

Gipsy Point Lodge,
Gipsy Point, Vic. 3891
Tel/Fax: (051) 58 8205

Inland Bird Tours,
94 Hunter Street,
Deniliquin, NSW 2710
Tel: (058) 81 5278;
Fax: (058) 81 5295

Kimberley Birdwatching,
PO Box 220, Broome, WA
6725 Tel: (091) 92 1246

Kingfisher Park Birdwatchers
Lodge,
PO Box 3, Julatten, Qld 4871
Tel: (070) 94 1263;
Fax: (070) 94 1466

Kirrama Bird Tours,
PO Box 133, Silkwood, Qld
4856 Tel: (070) 65 5181;
Fax: (070) 65 5197

O'Reilly's Rainforest
Guesthouse,
'Green Mountains',
Lamington National Park,
via Canungra, Qld 4275
Tel: (075) 44 0644;
Fax: (075) 44 0638

Peregrine Bird Tours,
2 Brice Avenue, Mooroolbark,
Vic. 3138 Tel: (03) 727 3343;
Fax: (03) 727 1545

Pitta Rainforest & Wildlife
Tours, PO Box 5092, Cairns,
Qld 4870 Tel: (070) 31 1521;
Fax: (070) 51 8663

G.M. Pizzey,
PO Box 200, Dunkeld, Vic.
3294 Tel: (055) 77 2501

Point Stuart Wilderness
Lodge,
GPO Box 1672,
Darwin, NT 0801
Tel: (089) 78 8914;
Fax: (089) 81 3730

Specialised River Tours,
Red Mill House, Daintree
Village, Qld 4873
Tel: (070) 98 6169

Wildman River Wilderness
Lodge, GPO Box 1397,
Darwin, NT 0801
Tel: (089) 81 5144;
Fax: (089) 81 5391

Wildflowers

Footprints Expeditions (see
Bushwalking page 201)

Western Australian Tourist
Centre,
Forrest Place,
Perth, WA 6000 Tel: (09)
483 1111 or 008 812 808

Westrail Travel,
City Rail Station, Wellington
Street, Perth, WA 6000
Tel: (09) 326 2159;
Fax: (09) 326 2063

Wildflower Society of
Western Australia,
71 Oceanic Drive, Floreat,
WA 6014 Tel: (09) 383 7979

Cycling

Brake Out,
PO Box 427, Kingston, Tas.
7050 Tel: (002) 78 2966;
Fax: (022) 78 1056

Chambers Rainforest
Holiday Apartments (see
Birdwatching page 201)

Dan's Tours,
20 Shannon Drive, Bayview
Gardens, Qld 4868
Tel/Fax: (070) 54 5492

Freewheelin Cycle Tours,
314 Gilles Street, Adelaide,
SA 5000 Tel: (08) 232 6860;
Fax: (08) 232 1455

Jackies Toy Box,
c/o Kangaroo Island Central
Backpackers, 21 Murray
Street, Kingscote, SA 5223
Tel: (0848) 22 787
or (0848) 22 719 a/h;
Fax: (0848) 22 694

Morrell Adventure Travel,
PO Box 277, Rose Bay, NSW
2029 Tel: (02) 388 1200;
Fax: (02) 388 1318

Office for Recreation, Sport
and Racing Resource Centre,
11 Hindmarsh Square,
Adelaide, SA 5000
Tel: (08) 226 7373

Raging Thunder,
111 Spence Street,
Cairns, Qld 4870
Tel: (070) 51 4911;
Fax: (070) 51 4010

Remote Outback Cycle
Tours, 88 Guthrie Street,
Osborne Park, WA 6017
Tel: (09) 244 1200;
Fax: (09) 445 2284

Stirling Tours,
51 Loch Street, Claremont,
WA 6010 Tel: (09) 389 1735

Youth Hostels Association of
NSW Inc, GPO Box 5276,
Sydney, NSW 2001
Tel: (02) 261 1111;
Fax: (02) 261 1969

Cycling Clubs

Bicycle Victoria,
GPO Box 1961R, Melbourne,
Vic. 3001 Tel: (03) 328 3000;
Fax: (03)328 2288

Bicycle Institute of
Queensland, PO Box 5753,
West End, Qld 4101
Tel: (07) 899 2988

Bicycle Institute of NSW,
GPO Box 272, Sydney, NSW
2001 Tel: (02) 283 5200;
Fax: (02) 283 5246

Bicycle Tasmania,
Environment Centre,
102 Bathurst Street, Hobart,
Tas. 7000 Tel: (002) 34 5566

Bicycle Institute of South
Australia, GPO Box 792,
Adelaide, SA 5001
Tel: (08) 271 5824

Diving

Adventureland Diving,
PO Penneshaw, Kangaroo
Island, SA 5222
Tel: (0848) 31 072;
Fax: (0848) 31 002

Bicheno Dive Centre,
4 Tasman Highway, Bicheno,
Tas. 7215 Tel: (003) 75 1138

Bluewater Tours,
65 Stewart Street,
Port Welshpool, Vic. 3965
Tel: (056) 88 1585

Coraldive, Coral Bay,
via Carnarvon WA 6701
Tel/Fax: (099) 42 5940

Coral Divers,
Shop 3, 42 Stuart Highway,
Stuart Park, NT 0820
Tel/Fax: (089) 81 2686

Dive Boss Charters,
Dunsborough Bay Village
Resort, Dunn Bay Road,
Dunsborough, WA 6281
Tel: (097) 55 3397;
Fax: (097) 55 3790

Dive Centre Manly,
10 Belgrave Street,
Manly, NSW 2095
Tel: (02) 977 4355;
Fax: (02) 977 3664

Diver's Mecca,
472 Esplanade,
Hervey Bay, Qld 4655
Tel: (071) 25 1626

Fannie Bay Dive Centre,
GPO Box 246,
Darwin, NT 0801
Tel: (089) 31 3049;
Fax: (089) 81 4913

Fun Dive Frolics,
255 Stanmore Road,
Stanmore, NSW 2048
Tel: (02) 569 5588;
Fax: (02) 560 3872

**Geelong Dive and Outdoor
Centre,**
178 Moorabool Street,
Geelong, Vic. 3220
Tel: (052) 21 3342;
Fax: (052)21 4078

Heron Island, (See
Accommodation page 205)

Lady Elliot Island,
PO Box 206,
Torquay, Qld 4655
Tel/Fax: (071) 53 2485;
Tel: 1800 072 200

Marlin Coast Divers,
PO Box 50,
Palm Cove, Qld 4879
Tel: (070) 59 1144;
Fax: (070) 57 7390

Ocean Spirit Cruises,
143 Lake Street, Cairns, Qld
4870 Tel: (070) 31 2920;
Fax: (070) 31 4344

Port Douglas Dive Centre,
PO Box 105,
Port Douglas, Qld 4871
Tel: (070) 99 5327;
Fax: (070) 99 5680

Pro Dive,
PO Box 5551,
Cairns, Qld 4870
Tel: (070) 31 5255;
Fax: (070) 51 9955

Quicksilver Diving Services,
PO Box 228,
Port Douglas, Qld 4871
Tel: (070) 99 5050;
Fax (070) 99 4065

Southern Diving Centre,
Roy Terrace, Christies Beach,
Adelaide, SA 5165
Tel: (08) 382 1322

Taka II Dive Adventures,
131 Lake Street, Cairns, Qld
4870 Tel: (070) 51 8722;
Fax: (070) 31 2739

TUSA Dive,
Corner Aplin Street and The
Esplanade, Cairns, Qld 4870
Tel: (070) 31 1248;
Fax: (070) 31 5221

Coast Watching

Albany Sailing Academy,
PO Box 634,
Albany, WA 6330
Tel: (098) 44 4146;
Fax: (098) 44 4400

**Bicheno Penguin and
Adventure Tours,**
Foster Street, Bicheno, Tas.
7215 Tel: (003) 75 1333;
Fax: (003) 75 1533

Cat Balou Cruises,
PO Box 50, Eden, NSW 2551
Tel: (064) 96 2027

Coraldive, (see Diving, page
202)

Dolphin Watch Cruises,
47 Owen Street, Huskisson,
NSW 2540
Tel: (044) 41 5012;
Fax: (044) 41 6723

Hervey Bay Visitors' Centre,
63 Old Maryborough Road,
Pialba, Qld 4655
Tel: (071) 28 2603 or
24 4050; Fax: (071) 24 1556

**Lady Musgrave Barrier Reef
Cruises,**
1 Quay Street,
Bundaberg, Qld 4670
Tel: (071) 52 9011 or
1800 072 110;
Fax: (071) 52 4948

Narooma Visitors' Centre,
Princes Highway,
Narooma, NSW 2546
Tel: (044) 76 2881;
Fax: (044) 76 1690

Nullarbor Adventure Tours,
PO Box 605,
Ceduna, SA 5690
Tel: (086) 25 2447;
Fax: (086) 25 2602

Polperro Dolphin Swims,
PO Box 13,
Hampton, Vic. 3188
Tel (059) 88 8437 or
018 17 4160

Underwater World,
Hillarys Boat Harbour,
West Coast Drive,
Hillarys, WA 6025
Tel: (09) 447 7500;
Fax: (09) 447 7856

Whale Watch Safari,
45 Cunningham St,
Hervey Bay, Qld 4655
Tel: (071) 25 1522;
Fax: (071) 25 5336

Tour Operators

Amesz Tours,
PO Box 1060,
Midland, WA 6056
Tel: (09) 250 2577;
Fax: (09) 250 2634

**Australian Alps Wilderness
Tours,** PO Box 53,
Tallangatta, Vic. 3700
Tel: (060) 71 2800;
Fax: (060) 71 2838

**Australian and New Zealand
Scientific Exploration
Society,**
PO Box 174, Albert Park,
Vic. 3206 Tel: (03) 690 5455;
Fax: (03) 690 0151

**Australian Trust for
Conservation Volunteers,**
PO Box 423, Ballarat, Vic.
3353 Tel: (053) 33 1483 or
008 03 2501;
Fax: (053) 33 2290.

Australis Pty Ltd,
PO Box 386,
Canterbury, Vic. 3126
Tel: (03) 888 6081;
Fax: (03) 888 6082

Bogong Jack Adventures,
PO Box 221, Oxley, Vic. 3678
Tel: (057) 27 3382;
Fax: (057) 27 3559

Coate's Wildlife Tours,
PO Box 7517, Cloisters
Square, Perth, WA 6850
Tel: (09) 324 2552;
Fax: (09) 324 2238

**Davidson's Arnhemland
Safaris,** PO Box 41905,
Casuarina, NT 0811
Tel: (089) 27 5240;
Fax: (089) 45 0919

Denise Goodfellow,
PO Box 39373, Winnellie
NT 0821 Tel: (089) 81 8492

Desert Tracks,
PO Box 360,
Ayers Rock Resort, NT 0872
Tel: (089) 56 2144;
Fax: (089) 56 2222

Discovery Ecotours,
GPO Box 381, Darwin, NT
0801 Tel: (089) 81 1100;
Fax: (089) 81 1102

Earthwatch Australia,
Level One, 457 Elizabeth
Street, Melbourne, Vic. 3000
Tel: (03) 600 9100;
Fax: (03) 600 9066

Eco-Escapes,
10 Warri Street, Pindimar,
NSW 2324
Tel: (049) 97 0573

Ecotrek,
PO Box 4, Kangarilla, SA
5157 Tel: (08) 383 7198;
Fax: (08) 383 7377

Falcon Tours,
1 Simons Drive,
Roleystone, Perth, WA 6111
Tel/Fax: (09) 397 5125

**Gawler Ranges Wilderness
Safaris,** PO Box 11,
Wudinna, SA 5652
Tel: (086) 80 2020;
Fax: (086) 80 2001

Go Bush Safaris,
PO Box 71, Gladesville, NSW
2111 Tel: (02) 817 4660;
Fax: (02) 816 1642

**Green & Gold Adventure
Tours,** PO Box 201,
North Cairns, Qld 4870
Tel: (070) 55 9359;
Fax: (070) 31 4924

**interNATIONAL
PARKtours,** Binna Burra
Road, Beechmont, Qld 4211
Tel: (075) 33 3583;
Fax: (075) 33 3683

Jankangyina Tours, PO Box
1579, Katherine NT 0851
Tel: (089) 72 1044;
Fax: (089) 72 3989

**Landscope Expeditions,
UWA Extension,** The
University of Western
Australia, Nedlands WA 6009
Tel: (09) 380 2433;
Fax: (09) 380 1066

**Little Desert Tours and
Lodge,** 26 Brougham Street,
Nhill, Vic. 3418
Tel: (053) 91 5232

Manyallaluk Tours,
PO Box 1480, Katherine NT
0851 Tel: (089) 75 4727;
Fax: (089) 75 4724

MudMaps Pty Ltd,
PO Box 31, Campbell ACT
2601 Tel: (008) 80 3565;
Fax: (06) 257 4823

**Nangar Wilderness
Expeditions and Natural
History Field Trips,**
PO Box 1209,
East Victoria Park, WA 6101
Tel/Fax: (09) 458 9738

Odyssey Safaris Pty Ltd,
GPO Box 3012,
Darwin NT 0801
Tel: (089) 48 0091;
Fax: (089) 48 0646

Osprey Wildlife Expeditions,
PO Box 738,
Stirling, SA 5152
Tel/Fax: (08) 388 2552

**Raft 'N' Rainforest
Company,**
PO Box 1938,
Cairns, Qld 4870
Tel: (070) 51 7777;
Fax: (070) 31 4777

Savannah Guides,
57 McLeod Street,
Cairns, Qld 4870
Tel: (070) 31 7933;
Fax: (070) 31 7939

Southern Sea Ventures,
51 Fishermans Drive,
Emerald Beach, NSW 2456
Tel: (066) 56 1907;
Fax: (066) 56 2109

**Spindrift International
Guiding,**
PO Box 45,
Warburton, Vic. 3799
Tel/Fax: (059) 66 5110

Tasmanian Expeditions,
110 George Street,
Launceston, Tas. 7250
Tel: (003) 34 3477;
Fax (003) 31 7759

TraveLearn Australia,
The University of
Queensland, Qld 4072
Tel: (07) 365 7000;
Fax: (07) 365 7099

Trezise Bush Guides,
PO Box 106, Freshwater,
Cairns, Qld 4870
Tel: (070) 55 1865;
Fax: (070) 31 2016

Umorrduk Aboriginal Safaris, Australian Wilderness Expeditions,
GPO Box 1677,
Darwin, NT 0801
Tel: (089) 41 3882;
Fax: (089) 41 3881

West Coast Adventure Holidays,
PO Box 467,
Exmouth WA 6707
Tel: (099) 49 1625;
Fax: (099) 49 1972

WildQuest,
PO Box 62,
Howard Springs, NT 0835
Tel: (089) 83 1557;
Fax: (089) 83 1585

World Expeditions,
3rd Floor,
441 Kent Street, Sydney,
NSW 2000
Tel: (02) 264 3366
or 008 803 688;
Fax: (02) 261 1974

Photographic Tours

First Light Photographic Safaris,
13 Forster Road,
Mt Waverley, Vic. 3149
Tel: (03) 807 8470

Focus 10,
6 Oberon Street,
Randwick, NSW 2031
Tel/Fax: (02) 399 9964

Frontier Photographic Safaris,
36 Thomas Street,
Chippendale,
Sydney, NSW 2008
Tel: (02) 698 7661;
Fax: (02) 319 3458

Image Gallery,
Level One,
Commonwealth Bank,
89 Grey Street,
South Brisbane, QLD 4101
Tel: (07) 844 8207
Fax: (07) 846 5303

Accommodation

Arkaroola Wildlife Sanctuary and Tourist Resort
Arkaroola Travel Centre,
50 Pirie Street, Adelaide, SA
5000 Tel: (08) 212 1366;
Fax: (08) 211 7215

Belgamba
PO Box 794,
Rockhampton, Qld 4700
Tel/Fax: (079) 38 1818

Binna Burra Mountain Lodge
Beechmont, Qld 4211
Tel: (075) 33 3622 or (008)
074 260; Fax: (075) 33 3658

Bungaree Earth Cottages
PO Box 97, Wentworth Falls,
Blue Mountains, NSW 2782
Tel: (047) 57 3096

Coconut Beach Rainforest Resort
Cape Tribulation, Far North
Queensland, Qld 4870
Tel: (070) 52 1311;
Fax: (070) 51 6432

Cradle Mountain Lodge
PO Box 153,
Sheffield, Tas. 7306
Tel: (004) 92 1303;
Fax: (004) 92 1309

Daintree Eco Lodge
Daintree Road, Daintree, Qld
4873 Tel: (070) 98 6100;
Fax: (070) 98 6200

Crystal Creek Rainforest Retreat
Brookers Road, Upper Crystal
Creek, NSW 2484
Tel: (066) 79 1591;
Fax: (066) 79 1596

Daintree Wilderness Lodge
PO Box 352, Mossman, Qld
4873 Tel: (070) 98 9105;
Fax: (070) 98 9021

Ferntree Rainforest Resort
PO Box 7662,
Cairns, Qld 4870
Tel: (070) 31 7793;
Fax: (070) 51 9430

Freycinet Lodge
Freycinet National Park,
Coles Bay, Tas. 7215
Tel: (002) 57 0101;
Fax: (002) 57 0278

Heron Island
GPO Box, 5287,
Sydney, NSW 2001
Tel: (02) 13 2469;
Fax: (02) 299 2477

Jemby-Rinjah Lodge
336 Evans Lookout Road,
Blackheath, NSW 2785
Tel: (047) 87 7622;
Fax: (047) 87 6230

Kingfisher Bay Resort and Village
PMB 1, Urangan, Qld 4655
Tel: (071) 20 3333 or
(008) 072 555;
Fax: (071) 27 933

O'Reilly's Rainforest Guesthouse
'Green Mountains',
Lamington National Park,
via Canungra, Qld 4275
Tel: (075) 44 0644;
Fax: (075) 44 0638

Pajinka Wilderness Lodge
PO Box 7757, Cairns, Qld
4870 Tel: (070) 31 3988
or (008) 80 2968;
Fax: (070) 31 3966.

Novotel Karri Valley Resort
Vasse Highway,
Pemberton, WA 6260
Tel: (097) 76 2020 or
(008) 090 600;
Fax: (097) 76 2012

Seven Spirit Bay
GPO Box 4721, Darwin, NT
0801 Tel: (089) 79 0277;
Fax: (089) 79 0284.

Silky Oaks Lodge
Finlayvale Road, Mossman,
Qld 4873 Tel: (070) 98 1666;
Fax: (070) 98 1983

Undara Lodge
Mount Surprise, Qld 4871
Tel: (070) 97 1411;
Fax: (070) 97 1450

INDEX

Page numbers in *italics* indicate illustrations

NP–National Parks